MILE 1

Beyond the first step and into the heart of following Jesus

PAUL CARTER

MILE 1

Beyond the First Step and into the Heart of Following Jesus

ISBN-13: 978-1-77069-018-9

Printed in Canada.

Word Alive Press
131 Cordite Road, Winnipeg, MB R3W 1S1
www.wordalivepress.ca

WORD ALIVE PRESS
Just Write!

To Shauna Lee,

who lives out the belief that it takes two people to live one great life. Your share in this is larger than mine.

Library and Archives Canada Cataloguing in Publication

Carter, Paul, 1974-
    Mile 1 : beyond the first step and into the heart
of following Jesus / Paul Carter.

Includes bibliographical references.
ISBN 978-1-77069-018-9

    1. Christian life. I. Title. II. Title: Mile one.

BV4501.3.C393 2010   248.4   C2010-903471-6

ACKNOWLEDGEMENTS

A project of this scope owes a great deal to many people. Chief among them would be my wife, Shauna Lee, who never made me feel guilty for doing what God called me to do. Special thanks goes as well to my congregation at FBC, Orillia; their wise feedback and user input has made this a much more effective tool. I am also deeply grateful for the encouragement I received from my friends John and Michelle—you believed in this project and its potential benefit to the Bride and supported me in it from start to finish. Heartfelt thanks must also go to Rebecca Grant, my editor, who's excessive attention to detail must drive everyone else around her insane. I appreciate you and any mistakes remaining in this book must be credited to my account. Last, but important above all, thank you to my Lord and Saviour Jesus Christ. You created me, called me, chose me,

MILE 1

saved me and equipped me and by God's grace, I am what I am. May this book bring you glory and extend your fame throughout the earth.

vi

INTRODUCTION

"Every journey of a thousand miles begins with a single step." Ever heard that before? There is a sense in which that is true and a sense in which that is wildly unhelpful. As Christians we celebrate the fact that a lifetime of sin can be fully and completely covered over in the blood of Jesus Christ.

> If we confess our sins, he who is faithful and just will forgive us our sins and cleanse us from all unrighteousness. (1 John 1:9, NRSV)

> As far as the east is from the west, So far has He removed our transgressions from us. (Psalm 103:12. NRSV)

Mile 1

We use dramatic words like conversion, salvation, redemption and atonement to talk about the moment when our sins fall under the power of the cross. But when the force of those words wears off and the last organ strains of "Just As I Am" have faded into the balcony, we quickly realize that there is more to this than a single step. Beyond the moment there is a movement. Beyond the decision there is a lifestyle. Beyond the crisis there is a "Christ-walk." To use Biblical language, beyond the 'narrow gate' there is a 'narrow way'. How do we find that way and how do we walk on it? Those are the questions the church has done a poor job of answering for the newly converted. This book is for those people. This book is not about how to get saved—there are lots of those books. This book is not about step one, it's about **Mile 1**. This book is about how to move from the valley you got saved in to the elevated highway that leads to life.

> A highway shall be there, and it shall be called the Holy Way; the unclean shall not travel on it, but it shall be for God's people; no traveller, not even fools, shall go astray. (Isaiah 35:8, NRSV)

That's the road we are looking for and that is what this book is about.

The house I live in was built on a hill. Our neighbourhood is built on the highest ground in the city. Given that our city was founded at the narrows between two large lakes, being on high ground is a good thing. However, most of the jogging trails in our city follow the lakeshore. There is an incredible network of gravel jogging trails which makes this city one of the best places in the country to live. Exactly one mile from my house I can access a network of trails that allows me to run all the way to Barrie (about 38 km south) or Coldwater (26 km west). These gorgeous trails run through woods, meadows, marshes and across rivers and streams and they collectively represent my favourite place on earth. But these trails do me no good if I can't find them. Suppose I was on my driveway dressed in heavy rubber boots and a trenchcoat. Imagine that by some gift and grace of God I was immediately transformed and found myself attired in shorts, a shirt and a great pair of jogging shoes. All of my heavy baggage and hindrances had been miraculously transported to some other place, never to reappear. How wonderful, how exciting, but even still, I am not yet jogging on my favourite trail, am I? I am equipped and free but I am not yet in the right place. I need to find the trail.

For me, the first mile of my run is the hardest part of the entire journey. My cardiovascular system takes a while to turn on. My ankles sometimes creak until my tendons warm. I am unusually aware of the temperature until my body engine starts to heat—Mile 1 is tough! By the time I turn off the pavement onto the grain-sized gravel of the Lightfoot Trail, I am ready to fly. Mile 1 is tough, but Mile 1 is worth it! That's what this book intends to be: a guide to get you on the trail. The trail is good. Getting there is tough and it takes more than a first step.

I am 36-years-old so I grew up with a strange mixture of Imperial measurements and the metric system. In my brain, there are 1600 metres in a mile. That is how long it takes to reach the trail, that's how long it takes for my lungs to come alive, my muscles to loosen up and my feet to fit their shoes. **Mile 1** is organized around sixteen things you need to do as a new believer to find the Holy Way. There is a highway that leads to life. In a sense that journey does begin with a single step. Beyond that step there is **Mile 1** and beyond that, there is life and life abundant.

"Come, follow me…"

—JESUS

NOTES ON HOW TO USE THIS BOOK

This book is designed to be used in one of two ways. First of all, it can be used as a Small Group curriculum for groups of new believers or inquirers who want a tour of the first mile before making their decision. Secondly, it can be used in a one-on-one setting between a new believer and a mentor. Ideally the new believer would read the material at the start of each section on their own so that the meeting time can focus on the comprehension tasks that follow. The leaders will find the FAQ sections particularly helpful.

New believers should develop an expectation and even an appetite for correction. In our wildly over sensitive culture we are far too easily offended by well-intended feedback. Failure to receive instruction and correction means that growth happens

VERY SLOWLY or not at all. In fact, the Bible talks a lot about that, saying:

> The fear of the Lord is the beginning of knowledge; fools despise wisdom and instruction. (Proverbs 1:7, NRSV)

> The reproofs (corrections, rebukes) of discipline are the way of life. (Proverbs 6:23, NRSV)

> Poverty and disgrace are for the one who ignores instruction, but one who heeds reproof is honoured. (Proverbs 13:18, NRSV)

> Those who ignore instruction despise themselves, but those who heed admonition (rebuke, correction) gain understanding. (Proverbs 15:32, NRSV)

> Listen to advice and accept instruction, that you may gain wisdom for the future. (Proverbs 19:20, NRSV)

This is a great place to stop being like the people of the world and start being like a follower of Jesus. Followers of Jesus are humble enough to take correction and to seek instruction—that's why they are called disciples. A disciple means "a learner"—that's what you are now—A LEARNER. If you go into this thinking you know; that your guesses or instincts will be correct, you will get very little out of it and you will progress very little in your walk of faith. If however, you seek out instruction, get a mentor, invite them to correct and instruct you and make that dialogue a priority, you will grow quickly and establish yourself firmly in the faith.

In my church we encourage people to meet with their mentor every two weeks for no more than ninety minutes at a time. That helps avoid mentor burn out and still allows enough continuity for each meeting to be efficient and useful. If you only meet once every two months, a lot of meeting time is taken up with the obligatory, "So what's been going on in your life?" sorts of conversations. Keep it moving and keep focused. You will be amazed by how much new life is born in you over the nine months or so it takes to complete Mile 1.

TABLE OF CONTENTS

0-100 M
Connect in Tribe

T he Book of Acts is a very helpful section of Scripture. Everyone in it is a new believer—the church was only days, weeks and years old, so everything in it can be used as a clue for new converts in their first hundred metres. One very helpful passage is found in Acts 2. Peter had just preached a pretty kick butt sermon and three thousand people became brand new baby Christians. Look at what they did next:

> All who believed were together and had all things in common; they would sell their possessions and goods and distribute the proceeds to all, as any had need. Day by day, as they spent much time together in the temple, they broke bread at home and ate their food with glad and

generous hearts, praising God and having the goodwill of all the people. (Acts 2:44-47, NRSV)

The first thing they did when they got saved was invest deeply in the experience of community. They sold their stuff and became members of a tribe that lived according to the new things they had learned about Jesus. Christianity is not a solo sport despite some of the hollow rhetoric you hear from quasi-Christian celebrities. There is a very odd notion out there with some speakers, authors and rock stars that following Jesus is a very personal, private thing that does not require you to love, serve or submit to other people. That is easy to hear but hard to swallow. All of the images Jesus used to explain faith were community images: he washed the disciples' feet and then he said: "This is what following me is about, serving one another in humility." Well that's hard to do if you are not in a community. He compared the kingdom of God to a shepherd who went looking for the one sheep to add to his flock of ninety-nine. He called us his body and the Bible compares us to hands, feet, eyes and ears. Any way you look at it, this is a team sport. This is a shared journey.

The Book of Hebrews says:

> And let us consider how to provoke one another to love and good deeds, not neglecting to meet together, as is the habit of some, but encourag-

ing one another, and all the more as you see the
Day approaching. (Hebrews 10:24-25, NRSV)

According to this, Christians need to meet together or we
don't achieve our full potential, we fail to live at our capacity and
the whole thing falls apart. That little phrase, "to meet together"
is actually a translation of the Greek word *episunagoge*. You
probably recognise the word "synagogue" in there, which is
what our Jewish friends still call their Sabbath gatherings; it was
the word used for "church" in the first generation of Christianity. *Episunagoge* literally means "extra-church" or "over-and-
above-church" and reflects the fact that in the earliest days of
our faith, most believers were part of a Jewish synagogue. They
would meet for their main service and then gather again, early
on Sunday morning, for extra-synagogue, where they talked spe-
cifically about Jesus and his unique call on us as his followers. So
the author of Hebrews, writing to Jewish Christians, is saying,
"Don't forget or neglect to go to extra church so that you can
encourage each other and help each walk in the way. You will
need this more and more as the years go by."

Too many of us think the opposite. We think that we need
church less and less as the years go by. In fact, in some circles it
is fashionable to talk about the church like it's a bad thing: "I'm
not into church, man, I'm a Christ follower—I don't go in for
that old, institutional garbage." Where did that come from?
How can you be a Christ-follower and not do what Jesus said to
do? Jesus wouldn't buy that logic. He said:

> If you love me, you will keep my commandments. (John 14:15, NRSV)

A real Christ-follower goes to church, commits to a tribe, and runs with a team. My advice to you is to take a little bit of time to find a church you can commit to for the long haul. Visit a few churches in your town, and try and avoid going to a big fancy church that you have to drive forty-five minutes to get to. You may like it more, but you'll go less and get less involved. If you can't get to it in fifteen minutes you shouldn't go to it. Unless, of course, you live thirty-five minutes from everything!

You should also find a church that has a sense of its calling and knows what it wants to accomplish in the community. A church that doesn't know probably doesn't intend to do much of anything in its community and you don't need to get involved with that. You should also look for a church that unashamedly teaches the whole Word of God. I've heard some pretty amazing speakers in my life and there is not a single one I'd get out of bed at 7:30 a.m. on a Sunday morning to listen to. I will walk a long way through the snow without boots, however, to hear the Word of God explained to me. Prefer steak to sizzle and you will have fuel for the whole journey. Also consider demographics. Do you have young children? Go to a church with other young families. This will save you the agonising decision in later years to leave the church you have grown to love in order to support your teenager who is looking for Christian friends his own age to hang out with.

Finally, in terms of connecting in tribe, go the distance. Our society has a very "consumeristic" approach to relationships of all types and church is no exception. I cringe every time I hear a "believer" say to another: "I left such and such a church because they didn't meet my needs. I went to that other church for a year or two but then found things getting stale and now I've found my way to "church of the moment" there on the hill where I'm sure all of my selfish appetites will be catered to." Of course no one actually says that. It sure would be refreshing to hear a little honesty. The things they do say come pretty close and reveal the same heart. Church is a tribe, an extended family. You walk with them until they get it right so that you can share in the celebration party. Commit to tribe. That's the first 100 metres.

TEN GOOD REASONS TO CONNECT IN TRIBE:

1. The Bible says so. (Do you really need nine more?)
2. It's hard to serve one another if we do faith by ourselves.
3. The experience of living in community smoothes out the wrinkles and rough spots in our character.
4. A healthy tribe, full of all age groups and demographics, provides a variety of mentors and role models for you and your family members.
5. One of the primary ways we hear God's voice is through other Christian people.

6. No individual has all of the spiritual gifts—we are only fully equipped when we work as a team.
7. You are probably the answer to someone else's prayer.
8. God is efficient and there is economy in scale.
9. Where else can you find so many potential babysitters?
10. Good company cements good character.

PERSONAL STUDY AND REFLECTION:
Read 1 Corinthians 12:4-27

One of the things you will notice if you read the Bible long enough is that the Christian life is often defined as existing in the tension between two extremes or poles of reality. We are told that God exists in the tension between grace and truth, love and justice, and mercy and righteousness. If we fall headlong into one extreme and lose touch with the other end of the spectrum, God is distorted. People who think God is only grace, tend to be very permissive. People who think God is only truth, tend to think God is very harsh and angry. The path of life lies between two ditches and the Bible reflects that kind of mindset. We see that here in terms of 'body life' or 'tribe life'. The church (tribe, body or faith community) is two things that seem opposite but aren't. It is about unity and diversity. "Good church" or "healthy tribe" exists in the tension between unity and diversity.

Reread the passage listed above and then take a look at the ten statements below that focus on that space - the road between the two ditches. See if you can locate the six correct statements and circle them. The correct answers are indicated in small print on the next page.

1. People may be wired differently by God, but he intends us to work together to pursue our created purpose.
2. Spiritual gifts that are given to an individual are not really for the blessing of that individual. They are really for the common good of that person's tribe or church.
3. When looking for a tribe or church to connect to, it is important to find one where the people are just like you. If you are a young professional, for example, you should try and find a church targeted at and full of young professionals.
4. The more Biblical approach is to find a tribe or church where all age groups and demographics are present. This will allow for a diverse group of people to learn from each other and bless each other with their various giftings.
5. There are certain people in a tribe who have more important gifts or characteristics than others. These people have more value to the kingdom than others.

6. God doesn't look at things quite like we do. God measures what we do with what we are given and is primarily interested in our obedient use of whatever gifts he has given.

7. Every gift, and therefore every person having a gift, is important to a church because to be healthy and whole, every gift is needed.

8. I am perfectly equipped, all by myself, to accomplish all that the Lord desires me to do. I don't need other people to fulfil my calling, though I may choose to associate with others for fun and fellowship.

9. God created Adam and then said it was not good for a man to be alone. In the same way, God gifts us so that we can't function properly without partners and friends. God actually makes us "strategically deficient" to make us seek out community and tribe.

10. I am a one man show. Watch me and cheer!*

---

* The correct answers are: 1, 2, 4, 6, 7, and 9. 10 is wildly incorrect.

QUESTIONS AND NOTES:

CONNECT IN TRIBE
FAQ

When I was in Youth Ministry I used to say, "Youth Ministry is the fine art of answering the same fifty questions one thousand times." That was more than a little bit true. By the end of my twelve years in youth ministry I had had many earnest, tearful conversations with teenage boys about self-control, the danger of the internet and the importance of striving for purity in all things. I became an expert on internet filter programs and how to install them. Likewise, I had countless conversations with teenage girls about why it is important to respect mom and trust her counsel even though it is wildly unfair that she is judging Bobby without ever having given him a chance. I have been asked to explain how dinosaurs fit into God's Creative process so often that I feel like I may have been a dinosaur in a previous life (P.S. I don't believe in previous lives!), and I have been asked, "If God is so good how come my grandmother got cancer and died?" more times than I ever would have wanted. That is not to trivialise those questions—in fact, those are THE FAITH questions for a sixteen-year-old boy, a seventeen-year-old girl and teenagers everywhere and always. The fact that they come up often does not make them stupid or trite. It just reminds us that humanity is a somewhat common journey that many people have travelled long before our own problems became the focus of our attention. It is also a subtle reminder of the beauty of life in community. It is a wonder that God spoke and left his Word and Spirit to guide and lead us—praise the Lord!

The FAQ (frequently asked questions) section at the end of each segment attempts to gather together the most frequently asked questions by the people who have travelled through this way before you. The answers originated with many people smarter and nobler than me. Often times I can't remember where I heard them first and I've heard them so often that they can be classified as "share-ware". Where they are not quoted directly from the Bible, they represent collective community wisdom. Though hopefully, as the Apostle Paul said, when lacking a direct Scripture quote, we have the Spirit on these things too.

Let's turn our attention to the most frequently asked questions on the matter of connecting in tribe.

1. I am a part of a small group (substitute Campus Ministry, Business Fellowship Group, Youth Ministry, Women's Ministry etc.) and therefore receive an experience of community and some good Bible teaching. Do I still need to belong to a local church?

ANSWER: Yes. A church is a very unique thing. It brings together people from a variety of ages, socio-economic perspectives and ethnicities and it forces them to journey and process together. That is unlike any other form of association in human culture.

Most free associations happen around affinity and shared interest. For example, "I like cars. You like cars. That's why we are in the car club together." "I am a 30 something runner. You are a 30 something runner. That's why we are in the running club together." Small Groups at a church function the same way: "I am part of a young couple with kids and so are you. Let's form a group and grouch about our kids!" (Hee hee! I know that eventually we do get to Bible Study but COME ON!! Enough with the "my kid wakes up three times a night" stories. That's what kids do! ☺) The bottom line is, groups aren't church, they're groups. Church is beyond group. It is TRANSGROUP. It is diversity finding unity in the Holy Spirit. They used to call the church "the Third Race", meaning that it was beyond Jew or Gentile. It was a new primary identity that was deeper than ethnicity, deeper than gender, deeper than blood. It was unity in the shared experience of the Holy Spirit. That's church—accept no substitutes.

That is also why "targeted church" is to be avoided. There are a few churches out there that intentionally target people just like them. They will proudly say, "We are a church for young professionals." That is so not like Jesus! If that were the way things should be, who would found a church for mentally handicapped people? Who would found a church for poor old people with diabetes? Who would form a church for single moms? No one! Often single moms function in church with a service deficit—they need more help than they have time to return. So do the old, the sick and the handicapped. BUT the Bible says that there is strength in weakness and there is blessing in need. We BELIEVE that community is better if we include people who cannot bless us back in any way that makes sense from a human perspective. Don't try and figure it out. Just trust that God's ways are right and find a church.

2. Is membership required?

ANSWER: Yes. I used to have teenagers ask me where it says in the Bible that you couldn't make out with a girl in the back seat of a car. The answer is that the Bible doesn't explicitly say that because the context of the Bible was so different that such a statement would have had no meaning. The Bible world was a world where the 13-year-old girl and the 18-year-old boy were meeting each other for the first time ON THEIR WEDDING DAY. They would have had no opportunity to "make-out" in the back of anything, let alone a 20th century automobile. They certainly would not have "made-out" on the donkey they rode to the ceremony, as they were kept separate and well-supervised until the big day. Besides, donkeys are notoriously unkind to riders who are occupied with other thoughts and activities.

Similarly, (though you have to have been paying real close attention to this analogy to follow it) the Bible could not conceive of the casual approach to association that characterizes many "believers" today. Most of the people who got saved in the Bible became outcasts to their birth culture. Bible scholars tell us that the Apostle Paul appears to have lost his wife, his family and his money by becoming a Christian. His wife likely divorced him. See his comments on this in 1 Corinthians 7 where such things were quite common early on. His family appears to have disowned him and cut him off from the family finances. Such was life in a religious Jewish family for one who crossed over to the Christian faith. For a Roman, becoming a Christian was only slightly less dislocating. The Romans persecuted Christianity off and on for 300 years and it could be very bad for your health to become a Christian. Nero used Christians as human torches in his garden. Becoming a Christian was not a decision one came to lightly. As such, belonging to a local tribe of Christians was SUPER IMPORTANT. They would have been your only source of support and you would have been destitute without them. Imagine that you were a 45-year-old Roman woman when you became a Christian in AD 64. Your husband was kind enough to divorce you instead of having you killed (which was his legal right). Your grown son has disowned you so as not to be kicked out of his tanning guild. You are without support, food, lodging and have nowhere to go. The church is your only hope. They take you in, provide you with a place to live and with a monthly pension. Does it ever occur to you to forsake membership and simply meet periodically with your like-minded friends at Starbucks for Christian chat and $5 lattes? No it does not.

The Bible assumes that belonging will immediately follow believing. In fact, a few times belonging comes first. The Bible does not imagine, nor does it condone believing without belonging. As for the form that belonging takes, remember that Jesus said:

> I will give you the keys of the kingdom of heaven, and whatever you bind on earth will be bound in heaven, and whatever you loose on earth will be loosed in heaven. (Matthew 16:19, NRSV)

Jesus gave his followers the freedom to make certain logical rules as long as they were in keeping with the Spirit of his commandments. Every church defines membership differently. As long as your church has chosen a way of doing membership that agrees with the Spirit of Jesus' teaching, you are obligated to submit to that. The Bible also says:

> Obey your leaders and submit to them, for they are keeping watch over your souls and will give an account. Let them do this with joy and not with sighing—for that would be harmful to you. (Hebrews 13:17, NRSV)

You need to submit to the way your tribe defines membership so that you can be held accountable and so that you can be supported when support is required. In my church we do this in an organized way because we like organization. Organization is not of the devil, in fact, the Bible reminds us that God moves things from chaos to order. So all of you anarchists out there are on the wrong team. We invite people who have been among us for six months or more to go through a process. It involves an orientation meeting, a survey, an interview with two elders and possibly some follow up and homework. Then if everything is in order, we exchange mutual pledges. We pledge to provide the new member with support, love, encouragement, correction, fellowship and practical help in times of trial.. They pledge to tithe, obey the teaching of the Bible, respect the church leadership, serve in a weekly ministry and abide by our community standards for ministry and conduct. Everything is above board and clearly communicated. At the next communion service we publicly celebrate and welcome them in. They are then allowed access to all facets of church life and ministry. We write their name down on a little chart in the computer in the main office and they are officially a "member." Other churches do it far more casually. You meet with the pastor, read a pamphlet and then the next Sunday you take communion and you are in. No paper trail. The process isn't important, but having a good attitude towards the community and its leadership IS IMPORT-ANT. Everyone will bind and loose membership differently, but however it's done, it's not optional.

3. I just recently became a Christian, how long should I wait before I get baptised?

ANSWER: Biblically speaking? About 38 seconds. Let me show you:

> Then an angel of the Lord said to Philip, 'Get up and go towards the south to the road that goes down from Jerusalem to Gaza.' (This is a wilderness road.) So he got up and went. Now there was an Ethiopian eunuch, a court official of the Candace, queen of the Ethiopians, in charge of her entire treasury. He had come to Jerusalem to worship and was returning home; seated in his chariot, he was reading the prophet Isaiah. Then the Spirit said to Philip, 'Go over to this chariot and join it.' So Philip ran up to it and heard him reading the prophet Isaiah. He asked, 'Do you understand what you are reading?' He replied, 'How can I, unless someone guides me?' And he invited Philip to get in and sit beside him. Now the passage of the scripture that he was reading was this:
>
> Like a sheep he was led to the slaughter,
> and like a lamb silent before its shearer,
> so he does not open his mouth.
> In his humiliation justice was denied him.
> Who can describe his generation?
> For his life is taken away from the earth.
>
> The eunuch asked Philip, 'About whom, may I ask you, does the prophet say this, about himself or about someone else?' Then Philip began to

speak, and starting with this scripture, he proclaimed to him the good news about Jesus. As they were going along the road, they came to some water; and the eunuch said, **'Look, here is water! What is to prevent me from being baptized?'** He commanded the chariot to stop, and both of them, Philip and the eunuch, went down into the water, and Philip baptized him. When they came up out of the water, the Spirit of the Lord snatched Philip away; the eunuch saw him no more, and went on his way rejoicing. (Acts 8:26-39, NRSV)

How much time seems to have passed between his arriving at saving faith and his receiving baptism? About 38 seconds. Do you think that might be an exception rather than the rule? Take a look at Acts 16 where Luke recalls:

A certain woman named Lydia, a worshipper of God, was listening to us; she was from the city of Thyatira and a dealer in purple cloth. **The Lord opened her heart** to listen eagerly to what was said by Paul. When **she and her household were baptized**, she urged us, saying, 'If you have judged me to be faithful to the Lord, come and stay at my home.' And she prevailed upon us. (Acts 16:14-15, NRSV)

Now to be fair, the Bible doesn't say exactly how much time there was between when the Lord opened her heart and when she received baptism. If it wasn't 38 seconds it couldn't have

18

been much more than that and it was certainly within the day. Most scholars agree that in the Bible baptism was associated with belief and the decision of faith. So much so that baptism is almost spoken of as a synonym for believing faith:

> The one who believes and is baptized will be saved; but the one who does not believe will be condemned. (Mark 16:16, NRSV)

It seems pretty clear that "believe and be baptised" was almost a longer way of saying "believe" which implied "and be baptised." Otherwise you might have expected: "the one who does not believe and is not baptised" or "the one who believed but was not baptised" will be condemned. It is clear from this passage and several others that baptism was inseparable from saving faith in the New Testament. This comes out in passages like Galatians 3:26-27:

> For in Christ Jesus you are all children of God through faith. As many of you as were baptized into Christ have clothed yourselves with Christ. (NRSV)

In this passage, being in Christ through faith is presented as being synonymous with being baptized into Christ.

Why then do we treat baptism like a high school graduation in today's Christianity? Great question. Unfortunately, there is no good answer. This is one of the many (far too many) examples of how the world exercises more influence over the church than the church often does over the world. In the world we are experiencing something called "extended adolescence". Our culture has been slowly widening the dividing line between child and adult. It used to be that on your 13th birthday you were considered a man or a woman. (The Jewish bar mitzvah or bat mitzvah still reflects this). As a girl, you would expect to be married shortly, as a man you would be expected to launch out into a career and begin building a home. Most 13-year-olds today can't cross the street without holding mommy's hand and they will likely still be living at home when they are 34. The church has changed right along with the world. Years ago, if you were part of a European church tradition (Catholic, Anglican, Reformed or Lutheran), you would be expected to "own" your baptism as a 13-year-old. They called this "confirmation". Because those traditions practiced infant baptism (a practice that seemed reasonable at the time given high infant mortality rates), it was expected that by the age of thirteen a person was a fully mature adult who was able to "own" in faith their baptism and confession. In the evangelical world, the same expectation was put upon 13-year-olds. Only in this context, which did not practice infant baptism, the new adult was expected to make a personal confession of faith through baptism. But today the average age for baptism is sixteen through twenty, even though most kids embrace Christ as Lord and Saviour for the first time in Jr. High. The emphasis today seems to be on "being ready". Whatever that means.

For adult conversions our practice is even more bizarre. A person gets saved at 45-years-old and no one even mentions baptism until after some mandatory five year waiting period has been served. When did obedience start requiring a waiting period? The church has unthinkingly extended adolescence, right in step with the world and has turned a birthday party into a graduation party. It's time to get back to the Bible. If the Lord has opened your heart to believe, then you should express that immediately through public confession and baptism. You need to be introduced to your new family and you need to begin your faith journey in the practice of immediate obedience.

100-200 M
Study the Word

It ought to be self-evident that if we want to live the *Way* of God we have to read and study the *Word* of God. It ought to be self-evident but for whatever reason, it apparently isn't. The church today is arguably the most Biblically illiterate it has ever been since the generation before the Protestant Reformation. This is hard to figure out given the availability and low cost of Bibles and the freedom we have to study it, talk about it and teach about it. Of course, it doesn't really matter how many low-cost modern translations of the Bible you have sitting on your bookshelf if you don't open any of them. People offer the same set of excuses for not reading the Bible that they offer for not exercising:

- It's hard.
- I don't have time. (BTW, how much time did you spend watching T.V. and surfing the net this week? Oh yeah.)
- I don't have the necessary knowledge.
- I tried it once and it didn't take.

The church often enables this attitude rather than empowering people out of it. Some churches seem to operate as though the Bible doesn't exist. The speaker (not *preacher* mind you!) chats on inanely about some current topic of interest: finance, friendship, environmental stewardship or whatever. He throws in a few video clips and some lyrics from the Beatles and then sends us home with a list of DVDs to watch for further reflection. Other churches seem not to trust us with the Bible. They speak about it in such a way that you get the impression that a simple boob like you or me could never access the hidden truths inside. Just come back next Sunday for your next instalment. Neither of these extremes is helpful though they seem to make up an alarming percentage of church experiences in North America. Try and find a church that expects you to bring your own Bible, write in it, study it mid-week and build a growing familiarity with its contents and implications. Try and find one that offers mid-week study groups or one that offers an on-line Q&A forum. A church that pushes you deeper into God's Word is a church that has a healthy understanding of its own limitations and a healthy awe of God's power to transform.

MILE 1

Assuming you have found such a place (that was after all the first 100 metres!), let's talk about how you study the Bible for yourself.

STEP ONE:

Get a Bible you can read. Grandma's dusty covered King James Version (KJV) probably isn't going to help you. This is not a slam on the KJV—I love Shakespeare and I love the rhythm and balance of the Queen's English but the best Bible is the one you read and most of us cannot wade through 17th century English in the Bible any better than we could in Grade 12 Literature classes. There are lots of good translations out there, each emphasising one value over another. Translations like the New International Version (NIV) emphasize readability and will cheat a bit on accuracy to give you the best sense of the verse. Translations like the New American Standard (NASB) or the New Revised Standard Version (NRSV) emphasize accuracy and will include phrases that are literally there in the original languages (Hebrew and Greek) but that sometimes don't make a lot of sense in English. Avoid translations that are paraphrases like the New Living Translation or The Message. While these can be fun to read, being set out almost like novels, they are really summaries and reflect the translator's ideas as much as they do the words of Scripture. If you can read the newspaper, you can read the NIV or NASB. Worst case scenario, you might need to buy a dictionary.

STEP TWO:

Get the big picture first. The Bible is fundamentally the mind and purpose of God revealed in story. In Exodus 19, God told the Jews that he was going to make of them a kingdom of priests and that they would teach the world about him. Sometimes they did this willingly but most of the time they did it unwillingly or unwittingly. They did it through their own story. By reading the story of the Exodus (the Jews being rescued out of slavery in Egypt) we learn many things about God:

- We learn that God answers prayer.
- We learn that sometimes you have to pray for a long time before God answers—400 years in fact!
- We learn that God can be compelled to act by appealing to his compassion.
- We learn that even a dominant world power cannot stand against the intention of God.
- We learn that God likes to set people free from whatever is binding them.
- We learn that God usually works through human intermediaries. He didn't throw a rock at Pharaoh, he sent Moses.
- We learn that God is preparing the answer to our prayers long before we are aware of it.

Moses was being educated in Pharaoh's court long before he even knew he would be used to lead the Jews out of Egypt.

- We learn that God's promises are usually conditional. You can't eat all of the blessings and then ignore God. He is not fickle and doesn't like it when we play hokey-pokey. You're either in or out.

- We learn that deserts and seas are not an obstacle to the Creator of the Universe. He can bring water from a rock and bread from the sky and he can blow seas hither and yon. He can handle your obstacle.

- We learn that God is a God of covenants. He likes to clearly outline where the blessings lie and he is pretty serious about those who ignore those lines.

- We learn that God likes to surprise us with the goodness of his gifts. The Jews asked for relief from their bonds and they got a good land and an advocate against their enemies.

All of those things can be learned from one story! Get to know the story and then go back and read all of the commentary and application that makes up the rest of the Bible. Read Genesis, Exodus, Deuteronomy, Joshua, Judges, 1 Samuel, 2 Samuel, 1 Kings and 2 Kings and then fast forward to the New Testament. Read Matthew or Luke and then read John. Read Acts, Romans and keep right on reading until you hit Revelation. Read that too, but don't expect to understand it. Most veteran Christians are still trying to figure that one out. Reading the Bible this way will take you about 6 months if you read 2-4 chapters a day. At the end of it you will have a very good idea of the big picture story that makes up the core of God's Word.

STEP THREE:

Journal. You forget what you read much faster than you forget what you write. So write down the important things that you read and you will remember much more. Buy a simple journal from Staples or the Dollar Store and write down any questions you might have as you read through. Also, record basic summaries. If you are pretty disciplined, write a summary after every chapter. If you are a little bit less type-A, write a summary of every book. Use a highlighter to highlight verses you really like, verses that seem to speak to you personally and verses you don't understand but would like to. Combined with your questions, they will give you something to talk about when you meet with a spiritual mentor or friend.

STEP FOUR:

Join a group. While every believer is responsible for studying the word of God on their own, we tend to do this best with a little bit of help. This is especially true for new believers. If you did a good job with the 0-100 m part of the journey, you are now attending a church that encourages you to get into the Word and provides groups to help you with that. Contact the Pastor or the main office and ask for a list of groups that you could join that would help you study the Bible. If no list is available, go back and do 0-100m again. Seriously. When you get into your group be patient but ask lots of questions. Don't assume that everybody knows more than you do and that your questions sound silly. If you follow step two above, you will know more about the Bible within six months than 50% of the people at your new church. Don't settle for that though, press on. There are bound to be a solid core of people in that church who love God's word and study it intently. Find those people and hang out with them and ask them lots of questions.

Those four steps in no way represent an exhaustive approach to studying the Bible. Remember, this isn't "Everything You Need To Know About Being a Christian", this is Mile 1. If you do steps 1 to 4, you will be on the way and that's the point.

TEN GOOD REASONS TO STUDY THE WORD:

1. The Bible says so. (2 Timothy 2:15) Do you really need nine more?
2. It will help carve new channels in your brain that will allow you to think new thoughts.

3. The words of Scripture are powerful. You can quote them in times of temptation.
4. God is accountable to the things he has said and promised.
5. God's Word is like GPS in a world where the road signs are always being moved.
6. The Holy Spirit will use the words of Scripture to convict you of sin and purify your conscience.
7. Reading the Word is part of how we "abide in Jesus" (John 15) and unless we abide in Jesus, we are useless.
8. Reading the Word allows us to recognize the voice of God. This keeps us from being deceived by the voice of the enemy.
9. Being grounded in the Word allows us to test the Spirits. If we can't do this, we will never feel comfortable operating in the Spirit realm.
10. Reading the Word provides us a map for locating the abundant permission and blessings of God.

PERSONAL STUDY AND REFLECTION:
Read 2 Timothy 3:14-4:4

One of the challenges we are facing right now in the church is Biblical illiteracy. Not since the generation before the Reformation has the church been so ignorant of the Scriptures. It is a tragedy that in the era of low cost printing when everyone can own a copy of the Scriptures for a reasonable outlay of money— so few people are actually reading God's Word and studying it. Most Evangelicals pride themselves on being "Bible People" but the truth is we have given a lifetime of study to 17 verses that tell us what we want to hear. We love verses about grace and love but forget that a huge percentage of the Bible is about prophecy and much of that has to do with God's anger at sin. Read the Scripture listed above about the study of God's Word and then complete the comprehension task below.

There are 7 statements below that correctly reflect the text you just read. See if you can find the 5 correct statements. The answers are in a footnote on the next page.

1. Once you are saved and have passed through the narrow gate, there is a path we are to continue on in. You don't just sit down in the place you got saved and wait for Jesus.
2. All Scripture is inspired by God and useful for growth in righteousness and equipping for ministry.
3. The Old Testament is less useful and less inspired. Until Jesus, God's voice was muffled and confused.
4. God's word can bring me comfort but it sounds like it also can be used to convict me of sin and rebuke me for wrong thinking and wrong actions.

5. God's Word would never make someone feel guilty or convicted. That is the work of the enemy. God's Word makes me feel loved and accepted as I am.

6. God wants to do more than save me—he wants to change me, recruit me and deploy me in the work of the Gospel.

7. The Bible predicts that people will prefer to have preachers tickle their ears and tell them funny stories than to preach to them from the Word of God.*

---

* The correct answers are: 1, 2, 4, 6, and 7.

QUESTIONS AND NOTES:

STUDY THE WORD
FAQ

The following questions represent the most frequent concerns for new believers starting out as students of the Word.

1. How often should I be reading my Bible?

ANSWER: The answer to that question is really another question: How fast do you want to grow? The Bible indicates that we grow at the pace of our desire:

> Blessed are those who hunger and thirst for righteousness, for they will be filled. (Matthew 5:6, NRSV)

> Draw near to God, and he will draw near to you. (James 4:8, NRSV)

If you press into the Word, reading as much as you can, than you will grow much faster than if you open the Bible only ever so often. In general, I would suggest that you develop a daily habit of reading the Bible for 30 minutes or so. If you are one of those people who fall asleep reading, then read in the morning. Things you read in your sleep are rarely remembered.

2. I started reading through the 'story parts' like you said, how come there is so much violence and killing in the Old Testament?

ANSWER: If I had a dollar for every time I have been asked this question, I would have many dollars. This issue is too complicated for a paragraph long answer, but let me affirm a few things. First of all, the God of the Old Testament is the same God who revealed himself in Jesus Christ. It is wrong to say: "God was angry in the Old Testament, he is 'happy' in the New Testament." God is God and he hasn't changed. People however, act differently in different seasons and in different circumstances. For example, I am a father of four children. If you saw me playing with my baby girl you might say: "Ooooh! Isn't that cute! He's so gentle and loving." That's true, except the cute part. But I also happen to be a Judo player and if you came and watched me at Judo you might say to yourself: "That guy is dangerous and aggressive." My point is not to suggest that I am a great Judo player (unfortunately, I'm not! I lose almost as often as I win). My point is to suggest that context exerts influence on behaviour and that does not make a person inconsistent to their own character. It is appropriate for me to be gentle with my daughter and it is appropriate for me to be aggressive when I am involved in a Judo contest. Neither activity is foreign to my basic character. I am a man who loves his children and I am a man who enjoys healthy athletic competition against other men. So it is with God. There are times when it is appropriate for God to act decisively against sin and that results in death and pain.

There are times when it is appropriate for God to act in accordance with his kindness and mercy and to be patient with sinners. Both reflect aspects of God's character. The Bible reminds us of that in Romans when it says:

> Note then the kindness and the severity of God: severity towards those who have fallen, but God's kindness towards you, provided you continue in his kindness; otherwise you also will be cut off. (Romans 11:22, NRSV)

If you read enough of the Bible, you will see God acting out of both of those parts of his nature in an entirely consistent manner.

3. Is it ok to write or highlight in my Bible? Will I be struck by lightning for doing this?

ANSWER: Yes. Yes it is ok to write and highlight in your Bible; NO you will not be struck by lightning—at least not for the writing and highlighting. Whether you get hit by lightning is beyond my control and I assume no legal responsibility for my predictions. My Bible looks like it has been run over by a highlighter truck. A friend of mine recently suggested that I simply leave unhighlighted the verses I think are most helpful as that would be more illustrative. I like to make notes in the margin; I like to underline things and I LOVE TO HIGHLIGHT. My

Bible is written on banana paper, and I have not yet read the verse which claims that banana paper is holy or magical in any way. The Words of God are Holy and must be treated with tremendous respect. The paper is a tool and should be treated as such. Being a good steward of any costly item is wise, and so tossing your Bible on the floor or leaving it outside at night is unwise and may offend others who think differently. However, the main thing is developing competence in the Word. Do whatever helps you achieve a level of familiarity with your copy of the Scriptures.

4. Is the Bible really reliable? Aren't there errors and contradictions?

ANSWER: The Bible is the most scrutinized book in human history and I have yet to see a convincing case made for a single error or inconsistency. That does not mean I haven't heard the candidates; they come up again and again like urban legends and internet rumours. Every university freshman can cite a few: "Aren't the genealogies in Matthew and Luke totally different?" "Doesn't one Gospel say Jesus was crucified on a Thursday and the others say Friday?" "Aren't there numerous translation errors?" While this is not the place for a detailed answer to any of those questions, the truth is all of those questions have very reasonable answers. Keep in mind that the Bible was written 2000—3500 years ago in languages that are not spoken today. The Hebrew of the Bible is very different from the Hebrew that is spoken today by modern Jews and the Greek that is in the Bible is very different than the Greek that is spoken today. It is difficult enough to translate a newspaper article written yesterday in Paris into an exact equivalent that could be understood by an English speaking person living in Miami. Try translating a book written by people who lived 3000 years ago and spoke a language no one on the planet speaks today. Translation difficulties constitute the bulk of what are called "errors" by today's arrogant and dismissive university professors (and repeated ad nauseum by the pseudo-intellectual students who've taken 1 course in comparative religion and now consider themselves experts). As for the inconsistencies, closer studies reveal that they simply require closer study. For example, one of the classic internet examples that is touted by the quasi-informed is that the Bible disagrees with itself on what day the crucifixion happened. The basic thrust of this rumour is that John says Thursday and Mark says Friday. The truth is a large number of scholars are gathering around the conclusion that Jesus was crucified on a Thursday and that the concept of "Good Friday" was an accident of European history.

Let's walk through this one example to show how closer study often reveals the need for closer study. It seems that Jesus was likely crucified on a Thursday, a day called The Day of Preparation. Before you get all agitated, let me explain. Passover for the Jews was the climax of a festival called The Feast of Unleavened Bread. It was technically 7 days long. I say "technically" because it was preceded by something called The Day of

Preparation. The Day of Preparation had a lot of wonderful traditions associated with it. The head of the household would clean out all yeast products from the house, things like bread, crackers, etc. Yeast was a symbol of sin in the Jewish culture. After all had been cleared out, he or she would sweep out the cupboards in a final ceremony and would empty the dust into the street while praying these words: "Blessed art thou, O LORD our God, King of the Universe, who hast sanctified us with thy commandments, and hast enjoined us to remove the leaven". Now it was illegal to eat the Passover in a house that had not been properly prepared. So Jesus sends his disciples ahead to PREPARE a room for them to eat the Passover. So they go and PREPARE the upper room. Now Jewish days are reckoned from sunset to sunset. So let me put this in plain English for you. On Wednesday afternoon, the disciples locate the upper room. When night falls on Wednesday, in the Jewish mind it became Thursday as soon as the sun set. So 6:30 p.m. on what we would call Wednesday night would to them be the beginning of Thursday. Thursday is the beginning of the Day of Preparation. This was the day BEFORE Passover, or the Feast of Unleavened Bread. So look at how our story begins:

> Now BEFORE the festival of Passover… (John 13:1. NRSV)

John is very clear that all of this happens on one day. They eat the Last Supper and then they go out to the Garden of Gethsemane where Jesus prays. Judas betrays him and Jesus is taken to a trial before Annas and then Caiaphas at night, meaning the early part of the Day of Preparation. After the trial before Caiaphas, they take Jesus to Pilot in the early morning, what we would think of now as Thursday. Now look at what John says about that:

> Then they took Jesus from Caiaphas to Pilate's headquarters. It was early in the morning. They themselves did not enter the headquarters, so as to avoid ritual defilement and to be able to eat the Passover. (John 18:28, NRSV)

So no one has eaten the Passover yet—**so the Last Supper was not a Passover** then right? Pilot has Jesus beaten and scourged. Then look at what John says in chapter 19:

> Now it was the day of Preparation for the Passover; and it was about noon. He said to the Jews, 'Here is your King!' (John 19:14, NRSV)

It was The Day of Preparation—Thursday, Nisan 14 by the Jewish calendar. So why do we celebrate the cross on a Friday and think that the Last Supper was a Passover? Because of what it says in Mark 14:12 about the same events:

> **On the first day of Unleavened Bread**, when the Passover lamb is sacrificed, his disciples said to him, 'Where do you want us to go and make

the preparations for you to eat the Passover?'
(NRSV)

When the Medieval Catholic Church leaders read the Gospel of Mark and Matthew and saw this phrase they thought this all happened on the first day of Passover—FRIDAY. But in the time of Jesus, Preparation Day was seen as part of the feast in the same way that Christmas Eve is seen as part of Christmas today. Now in case you think I am trying to cover up a mistake by Mark, look at what he says right after that: "when the Passover lamb is sacrificed". Passover lambs are sacrificed on Thursday afternoon. That's right in the Bible, Exodus 12:6:

> You shall keep it until the fourteenth day of this
> month; then the whole assembled congregation
> of Israel shall slaughter it at twilight. (NRSV)

Nisan 14 is a Thursday in the Jewish calendar. The word twilight there is the Hebrew word for late afternoon. So Mark knew what time it was. That's why the New Testament writers talk about Jesus as being our Passover Lamb, because he was crucified on Thursday afternoon at the exact time that every lamb in Israel was being slaughtered for the great feast on Friday. That's why Jesus and his disciples ate bread at the Last Supper and not lamb with bitter herbs.

I share all of that to illustrate that often what appears to be a contradiction simply isn't. It is just a matter that requires more study. We have to expect this to happen. Imagine for a moment that someone 3000 years from now found a letter I had written to my wife last July. In that letter I said something to the effect of: "Honey, I'm so glad we got to spend Christmas with my family this year. I appreciate you making the sacrifice so that we could do that." Now suppose that 3000 years from now Christmas has been truncated to a single day holiday. They don't understand that in the year 2009 it was an extended season. So someone finds my daytimer page for December 25th indicating that I was in Huntsville with Shauna Lee's parents on that day. "Aha!" they shout, "There are inconsistencies in this man's letters! He must have edited them later to make himself appear more generous to his own parents." Actually, we spent December 27th with my parents and we still thought of that as Christmas. That was the day we celebrated Christmas and that is an appropriate way to talk in our culture. Whether it still makes sense 3000 years from now, I cannot predict. Most so called inconsistencies fit into that category. A little effort and patience to learn the culture in which the documents were written eventually leads to a harmonizing of seemingly contradictory texts.

200-300 M
Pray with Pray-ers

In the Bible the Apostle Paul tells a group of Christians: "Pray without ceasing!" (1 Thessalonians 5:17). He tells another group: "Pray in the Spirit at all times" (Ephesians 6:18). Christians are obviously supposed to be praying, but how do you learn to do that if you haven't been a Christian very long? The best way to do that is to meet and pray with "pray-ers", that is, people who pray! If you wanted to learn how to golf, you would likely go out for a round with a friend who knew a thing or two about golf. The same applies here. Find someone in your church (if you haven't got one yet go back and do 0-100!) who loves to pray and who is successful in prayer. Why would you want to learn to play golf from someone who shoots 120? Like-wise, why would you want to pray with someone whose prayers are never answered? Find a prayer warrior whose prayers move the hand of God and pray with them. That is the best way to learn.

Alongside of looking for a prayer partner or prayer mentor in your church, the Scriptures are full of the prayers of men and women who knew how to pray. Nobody had more power in prayer than Jesus and his disciples recognized this and asked him for a lesson in prayer. This is what he said:

> "Pray then in this way: Our Father in heaven, hallowed be your name. Your kingdom come. Your will be done, on earth as it is in heaven. Give us this day our daily bread. And forgive us our debts, as we also have forgiven our debtors. And do not bring us to the time of trial, but rescue us from the evil one. For the kingdom and the power and the glory are yours forever. Amen. (Matthew 6:9-13, NRSV)

Countless millions have learned to pray using this prayer. Memorising this prayer (in whatever translation you already know some of it) is one of the wisest things you can do in life. This prayer is not magic—repeating it over and over again will not ward off evil or bring automatic blessings into your life. It was not meant as a ritual; it was meant as an instruction. It was supposed to teach us how to pray. I used the outline of this prayer for many years as a guide for my own prayers. The truth is, the prayers of most baby Christians sound like a letter written to Santa, *"Dear Jesus, I need money for rent. I also would like a new car. Please help my aunt Sue feel better. Amen."* Praying the outline of the Lord's Prayer will take you much deeper. Let's break it down into its component parts:

A. OUR FATHER IN HEAVEN, HALLOWED BE THY NAME

Spend some time reflecting on the fact that God invites you to know him and address him as Father. Remember that his perspective is a heavenly one and admit that he may know things you don't from your position on earth. Remember that God's essential characteristic is holiness. He takes sin seriously - serious enough to send his own son to die as payment. A prayer in this line might run as follows:

Heavenly Father, what a privilege to know you as my Father. You are not an angry school teacher looking to catch me at wrong doing. You are not a disinterested creator looking at me like your pet science project. You look at me like I look at my kids. You want me to do well. You want me to live well. You want me to talk to you and to grow up to be like you. You discipline me because you care and you want me to learn right from wrong. You are holy and you can't ignore the things I do which grieve you. Thank you for holding me accountable. Teach me your ways so that I can enjoy them and promote them to others.

B. THY KINGDOM COME, THY WILL
BE DONE ON EARTH AS IT IS IN HEAVEN

Spend some time committing yourself to God's purpose and his intention for humanity. Surrender to his Lordship and authority in your own life because you can't lead others anywhere you haven't been yourself. A prayer in this line might run as follows:

Lord God, you are in control of the heavens and the earth. Life and history only make sense when I remember that you are in charge. Lord, I know that many people resist you and raise their fists and shake them at you but I commit myself to seeking your will and your purposes and your kingdom and reign on this earth. Only when the God of justice and love reigns in every heart will this planet cease to know poverty, cease to know violence and cease to know war. We've made a mess of things God and we need your reign and your ways to triumph. Lord, I know this has to start with me. Help me to yield all of my ambitions and plans to you. Work out your will in me and then work it out through me, I pray.

C. GIVE US THIS DAY OUR DAILY BREAD

Most of us don't need a lot of coaching on this one as we naturally bring our needs to God. There is nothing wrong with that. It's just not where we should start or finish. Notice that we are to pray for daily bread, i.e., the basics of life. God is not a Sears catalogue and he is often not interested in making us more materialistic. He will see to your needs, not your fantasies and not your lusts. A prayer in this line might run as follows:

Father, you know my needs better than anyone. I'm short on rent this month. Lord maybe I need to find a place I can better afford and if you want me to do that Lord, I will. In the meantime, Father, I need help. Where would I go but to you? Please bless me this month with the things that I need: food, shelter and clothing. I trust you with these things, for you are God.

D. FORGIVE US OUR TRESPASSES (SINS) AS WE FORGIVE THOSE WHO TRESPASS AGAINST US

Spend some time reflecting on the ways you have lived outside the lines of God's permission. Name those to God and admit that they were outside the line and not helpful to yourself or to the general cause of righteousness. Also review with God how people have crossed your lines. Admit to God that you are not God and that your lines are arbitrary. Extend forgiveness to those who have wronged you. A prayer in this line might run as follows:

Father, you know that I have coloured outside the lines today. You want me to be slow to speak and slow to anger and I blew it with Bob today. I got angry and said some hurtful things. I know that was wrong and I'm sorry. I also want to forgive Bob for what he said that made me so angry. I take my own dignity more seriously than I take yours God and find myself feeling so offended for wrongs

I perceive being done to me. I forgive Bob and ask you to help me be less easily offended and less inclined to anger.

E. LEAD US NOT INTO TEMPTATION, BUT DELIVER US FROM EVIL

Ask the Lord to direct your steps so that you can avoid the pitfalls and walk in peace. When we pray this sort of prayer we are admitting that God sees things we don't and sometimes our wisdom is flawed. A prayer in this line might run as follows:

Lord God, there are so many things I don't understand and so many things I do not see. Sometimes I feel like I am groping about in the dark with nothing but a match to light my way. Please guide me, Lord! Warn me in advance if any decision I am contemplating would lead me to stumble. Steer me and increase my sensitivity to your touch and to your voice. Protect me from evil, Lord. Put a hedge around those I love and guard us from the evil one.

F. FOR THINE IS THE KINGDOM, THE POWER AND THE GLORY, FOR EVER AND EVER, AMEN

This is the attitude of trust and submission to God's authority. God may answer our prayers the way we want or he may not. Either way, he is God. He may keep us safe from trial or he may allow us to go through one to strengthen our faith or to warn us about the power of some unknown sin in our lives. Either way, he is God and he is in control. Praying this sort of prayer keeps us from thinking that God is a puppet on a string. A prayer in this line might run as follows:

Lord, you are God and I am not. Sometimes I ask for things I shouldn't have. Sometimes I expect you to give me things that as a wise Father you withhold. I don't control you God and you do not owe me. Thank you for hearing me today as I have poured my heart out to you. You are in control of all of this, aren't you, Father? You see my coming in and my going out and nothing touches me except what you have approved it. You are working out your purpose in me and I thank you for that. Nothing can steal me out of your hand or away from your purpose. I will rest in that today, Father. Thank you. Amen.

Using the outline of this prayer will add depth to your prayer life and will help you get past the Santa/Jesus phase most baby Christians find themselves in. When you use it, you are praying alongside the greatest prayer warrior to ever walk the face of the earth. There is power in that. You can even use this prayer as a guide for a group prayer time with each person in the circle taking a piece of the outline. Pray with pray-ers and pray along with Jesus and you will soon find yourself in a constant state of prayer. This is where you want to be as a believer. This is when you know you have found the path.

TEN GOOD REASONS TO PRAY WITH PRAY-ERS:

1. The Bible says so. (1 Timothy 2:8) Do you really need nine more?
2. By asking a veteran believer to be your prayer mentor, he or she will likely refine, re-examine and improve their own practices. Iron sharpens iron, the Bible says.
3. There is great power in agreement in prayer. (Matthew 18:19-20)
4. Being strong in prayer allows you to participate in missions without ever leaving your knees! (Ephesians 6:19)
5. Powerful prayer invites the justice of God and moves the hand of God. (Revelation 5:8)
6. Prayer often precedes the infilling of the Spirit of God. (Acts 1:14-2:4)
7. Prayer is part of how we abide in Jesus and if we fail to abide in Jesus, we are powerless. (John 15:5)
8. When we pray with boldness we unlock the blessings of God. (1 John 3:21-22)
9. Prayer aligns our hearts with the purpose of God. (Luke 22:42)
10. Prayer can unlock healing for yourself or for others. (James 5:16)

MILE 1

PERSONAL STUDY AND REFLECTION:

One of the reasons that our faith can be so small and fragile as new believers is that we often take promises meant for someone else and claim them for ourselves. Then if the promise doesn't happen, we begin to doubt God. This happens often with some of the promises in the Bible about prayer. Let's take a look at one of those and then work our way through the comprehension task that follows. Read 1 John 3:21-24.

There are seven statements below that correctly reflect the text you just read. See if you can find the five correct statements. The answers are in a footnote at the bottom of the next page.

1. Every person can have boldness before God. You can charge right into his presence and demand to be heard.
2. The one with a clean conscience can have boldness before God and can have assurance that his/her prayers will be heard.
3. The person who is being obedient to the things God has commanded can expect God to answer their prayers.
4. Every person who prays can expect God to answer their prayers.
5. It is also necessary to know what things please God, such as unity, kindness and charity, to ensure that your prayers will be answered.

6. A person who knows God's commandments and who lives to do the will of God will ask for things in accordance with God's will and can therefore expect those things to be done.

7. A person must be a true believer to expect his/her prayers to be effective. God may answer the prayers of unbelievers but is not obligated.*

---

* The correct answers are: 2, 3, 5, 6, and 7.

QUESTIONS AND NOTES:

PRAY WITH PRAY-ERS
FAQ

The following questions represent the most frequent concerns for new believers starting out with prayer.

1. My prayer mentor and other "veteran" Christians seem to speak about prayer as a dialogue, but my prayers are definitely a monologue; I speak but God seems pretty quiet. How can I learn to hear God's voice?

ANSWER: Actually "hearing" God is one of the fundamental privileges of being a Christian. In the Old Testament, the standard daily prayer was called "The Shema" and a good Jew would have prayed it three times a day. The word "shema" means "hear". The prayer begins like this, "Hear O Israel, the Lord our God, the Lord is one." Jews reminded themselves that they were a unique people largely because God had spoken to them. Did you catch that? It wasn't that they spoke to God that made them special; it was that God spoke to them.

In the New Testament this promise continues to be at the centre of the self-concept of God's people. Jesus promised:

> I have said these things to you while I am still with you. But the Advocate, the Holy Spirit, whom the Father will send in my name, will teach you everything, and remind you of all that I have said to you. (John 14:25-26, NRSV)

Jesus wanted to reassure his disciples that just like they enjoyed his teaching while he was among them in bodily form, so too they could continue to hear his teaching by listening to the Holy Spirit which he would send to be with them always. But how do we do it?

The passage above gives us a clue: before speaking of the new voice that was coming, Jesus reminded them of the old voice they were familiar with. His point was that the teaching they knew from Jesus would be useful as an authenticator for the new voice of the Holy Spirit. If a spirit came teaching something different than what Jesus taught, then it was not of God. This implies that becoming familiar with the words of Jesus is step one in learning to hear from the Holy Spirit.

Let me make a simple analogy. When I take my daughter to the park and she starts playing, I may sit down on a bench and begin to read a newspaper. I can "hear" ten to twenty voices at any time but I am not really listening. I keep reading and passively scan those voices for any sign of trouble. However, if my daughter starts to cry, I can instantly pick that voice out of the twenty others I have been passively scanning and immediately spring into action. How can I do that? I KNOW my daughter's voice; it is carved into my heart and mind. Likewise, when you

KNOW God's voice, you will be able to hear it and pick it up out of the numerous voices that are constantly in your brain under passive scan. Whenever I am thinking about a decision, I am usually aware of a number of voices in my head. There is the voice of my mother which seems to be constantly cycling through "mom-ish" council, "Don't forget to wear clean underwear." "Did you brush your teeth?" "That's not the right way to fold those socks." "A bird in the bush is worth two in the hand." "A stitch in time saves nine." I don't even know what some of those things mean but they cycle through my brain on some sort of passive scan. Likewise, the voice of my basic physical instincts is on constant rotation "That looks tasty." "I wonder if you could eat that?" "You could beat him in a fight" "She's pretty." I have learned that it is very helpful to turn that voice down to minimum volume when making decisions. The voice of the enemy is often in my head as well. He whispers his lies and if I'm not paying attention they can pass as my own thoughts. "Take it, no one will know and they don't pay you enough here anyway." "One look won't kill you. It's not a sin to look as long as you don't touch right?" "This could really help get your name out there. People should know what you are all about. There's no harm in a little self-promotion right?" If I find that voice and grab onto it, I try to exile and silence it right away. Then there is the voice of God. It tends to be quieter than all the others and if you have not developed a very sensitive search radar you might miss it altogether. But if you have become intimately acquainted with his voice and you know the things he is inclined to say, then you can grab hold of that voice and dial it in from passive to active and turn it up to maximum value. You can ask God questions and hear the answer. You can dialogue with him and invite him into your thoughts. King David knew about this. He used to talk to God this way all the time. He said in Psalm 5:

> In the morning, O LORD, You will hear my voice; In the morning I will order my prayer to You and eagerly watch. (Psalm 5:3, NASB)

The Hebrew word translated there as "order my prayer" is *arak* and means "to lay out" or "to set out". There is no direct object provided, meaning it literally says, "In the morning I will set out or lay out before you." We assume the word prayer, or in some translations we assume "case", as in "I lay my case out." But the most literal meaning is that David is saying that in his morning prayers, he just sets himself out before the Lord. He says, "Here I am Lord! This is what I'm thinking about. This is what I need to be doing today. What do you think God?" David wanted God to speak into his inner thoughts. He said elsewhere:

> Search me, O God, and know my heart; test me and know my thoughts. (Psalm 139:23, NRSV)

To invite God into your thoughts is one of the most exciting aspects of prayer. It is also the most dangerous. The devil can disguise himself as an angel of light and he specializes in deceiving words and prophecies. That is why God speaks very quietly and very infrequently to people until they have put in the time to study the Word of God in Scripture. Only then will they be able to test his voice and trust in it. The Bible says:

> Beloved, do not believe every spirit, but test the spirits to see whether they are from God; for many false prophets have gone out into the world. (1 John 4:1, NRSV)

Only when you know the Word of God can you test a spirit to know if it is the voice of God or the deceiving whisper of the enemy. Some people find this so dangerous that they forbid it altogether but the Bible says we are not to do that:

> Do not despise prophecies. (1 Thessalonians 5:20, NKJV)

We must not let the fear of deception keep us from seeking and hearing the voice of the Lord. We were born for this; we were made for this very thing. Only when we hear God can we reclaim our role as the stewards of the earth and the sons and daughters of God on the earth. Put the work in. Study the Word. Learn the voice. Seek the voice. Heed the voice.

2. I can't seem to pray for much more than 10 minutes. After that, I get bored or just run out of things to say. What should I do?

ANSWER: I used to have the very same problem. I would start to pray and I would really want to pray for a long time but after you've told God how thankful you are for a lovely wife, healthy kids, a roof over your head and a hot meal, you move on to your basic needs. You ask for help with finances, a better attitude for your grouchy neighbour, healing over aunt Sue's wonky hip and maybe a little snow for the upcoming ski season. What is there really left to talk about? I'd find that if I tried to stretch it out too much I ended up circling around to the same material, "Dear Lord, I'm not sure if I mentioned this earlier but Aunt Sue really has a wonky hip. Last week she fell down the stairs and almost knocked herself unconscious. That can be really dangerous you know. I heard a story once about a guy who fell down and because he lived alone he had to eat his own pocket lint for two weeks before anyone even found him. Did you hear that one? Oh yeah, I guess you did. Anyway, if you could help out with that, I sure would appreciate it. Amen." Then I would look at my watch and realize that I had only prayed for 11 minutes. What worked for me was using a more organized outline. I started using the Lord's Prayer as an outline as demonstrated earlier in this section. I also started keeping a prayer journal. I would write the names of people and things I felt compelled to pray about. This gave me a lot more material to speak to the Lord about and it also broadened out my prayers from two categories (thanksgiving and asking) to six categories (those of the Lord's Prayer). Now I struggle to get done in less than 75 minutes. A little organisation and advance planning made a big difference for me.

3. My prayer mentor is big on "morning prayer" but I'm kind of a night owl. Is praying in the morning mandatory?

ANSWER: I have discovered that you are what you do. When I was in youth ministry I worked a lot of late nights and therefore came to think of myself as a night owl. I got used to going to bed at 12:00 or 1:00 a.m. and waking up at 8:30 a.m. Prayer at 5:00 a.m. didn't seem to fit into that mix. I discovered, however, that habits are not as engrained as we think. When I made the decision to begin doing prayer at 5:00 a.m. every morning it took me about two weeks to train my body not to hate it. I found that I started going to bed at 9:45 p.m. The only thing that fell out of my life was late night T.V. and the last period of hockey games. Since my team loses every game anyway, my life has not been terribly affected. The truth is that I could never go back. Like David, I want to lay myself and my day out before the Lord in the morning and have him enter into the discussion. I find I am way more productive, way more "spiritual" and way more blessed by doing it this way. It was the habit of David and it was the habit of Jesus to pray in the early morning. Of Jesus it is said:

> In the morning, while it was still very dark, he got up and went out to a deserted place, and there he prayed. (Mark 1:35, NRSV)

If Jesus did it, you should do it. That is after all, the basic idea behind being a "Christ follower"; it implies a measure of imitation. Yes, early stinks, but only for a few weeks. Then your body adjusts, your habits shift and your life gets infinitely more interesting. Late night T.V. is bad. I have no Scripture for that one, but I think I have the Spirit. Generally speaking, that is the only price to pay for early-morning prayer.

4. What does it mean to "pray in the Spirit"?

ANSWER: Wow, this one is complicated but we need to figure it out because praying in the Spirit is a command of the Bible:

> Pray in the Spirit at all times in every prayer and supplication. To that end keep alert and always persevere in supplication for all the saints. (Ephesians 6:18, NRSV)

What does the Apostle Paul mean by praying in the Spirit? Luckily, Paul used this term more than once and by comparing other uses we can begin to compile a definition. In 1 Corinthians 14:14-19 we see:

> For if I pray in a tongue, my spirit prays but my mind is unproductive. What should I do then? I will pray with the spirit, but I will pray with the mind also; I will sing praise with the spirit, but I will sing praise with the mind also. Otherwise, if you say a blessing with the spirit, how can anyone in the position of an outsider say the 'Amen' to your thanksgiving, since the outsider

does not know what you are saying? For you may give thanks well enough, but the other person is not built up. thank God that I speak in tongues more than all of you; nevertheless, in church I would rather speak five words with my mind, in order to instruct others also, than ten thousand words in a tongue. (NRSV)

Obviously, comparing verse 14 and 15 indicates that "to pray in the Spirit" is "to pray in tongues". But does it always mean that? Or is praying in tongues, the obvious reference in 1 Corinthians 14, simply one way to pray in the Spirit? For example, an orange is a fruit, but not all fruits are oranges, so praying in tongues is praying in the Spirit. But is all praying in the Spirit a matter of praying in tongues? Perhaps not. In Galatians 4 we find Paul saying:

And because you are children, God has sent the Spirit of his Son into our hearts, crying, 'Abba! Father!' (Galatians 4:6, NRSV)

Paul says that when we place saving faith in Jesus Christ, God sends the Holy Spirit (the Spirit of Jesus) into our hearts and the immediate activity is assistance in prayer to God the Father. The first job of the Holy Spirit is to re-open the communication lines between children and the Father so that life can be restored to its original intent and blessing. Paul teaches this same duty of the Spirit elsewhere saying:

> Likewise the Spirit helps us in our weakness; for
> we do not know how to pray as we ought, but
> that very Spirit intercedes with sighs too deep
> for words. And God, who searches the heart,
> knows what is the mind of the Spirit, because
> the Spirit intercedes for the saints according to
> the will of God. (Romans 8:26-27, NRSV)

So it is possible, even likely, that for Paul, all prayers offered by true believers are prayers "in the Spirit" and so to say "pray in the Spirit" is to simply say, "Pray, believer, pray!" However, it is also true to say that praying in tongues was an important part of how Paul practiced his prayer life:

> I thank God that I speak in tongues more than
> all of you. (1 Corinthians 14:18, NRSV)

It is equally true that he would heartily recommend that the same be true of all Christians:

> I would like all of you to speak in tongues. (1
> Corinthians 14:5, NRSV)

Praying in the Spirit most likely then refers to all believing prayer, an important sub-set of which is praying in tongues.

300-400 M
Welcome the Holy Spirit

The climactic promise in the Old Testament was concerning the coming gift of the Holy Spirit. Ezekiel puts it this way:

> I will sprinkle clean water upon you, and you shall be clean from all your uncleannesses, and from all your idols I will cleanse you. A new heart I will give you, and a new spirit I will put within you; and I will remove from your body the heart of stone and give you a heart of flesh. I will put my spirit within you, and make you follow my statutes and be careful to observe my ordinances. (Ezekiel 36:25-27, NRSV)

MILE 1

The people of Israel had tried and failed to live out God's word and his ways; they simply couldn't do it on their own. So God promised to come and do a work in their hearts that would clean them out and make them totally new and fit for his own indwelling Spirit. This Spirit would help them live out God's holiness and his will. That promise was fulfilled when Jesus died on the cross and provided a way for our hearts to be cleansed. Now all we must do is call out to Christ in faith and that miracle will be done in our hearts:

> If we confess our sins, he who is faithful and just will forgive us our sins and cleanse us from all unrighteousness. (1 John 1:9, NRSV)

Once our hearts are cleansed and prepared we can become a host for the Holy Spirit. Jesus promised this very thing:

> If you love me, you will keep my commandments. And I will ask the Father, and he will give you another Advocate, to be with you for ever. This is the Spirit of truth, whom the world cannot receive, because it neither sees him nor knows him. You know him, because he abides with you, and he will be in you. (John 14:15-17, NRSV)

Jesus practically repeated the promise of Ezekiel verbatim. He said that for those who were intent on obeying the will and Word of God, a helper would come (that's what the word Advocate means) and take up residence within their very hearts. This is the Holy Spirit and he will live in you. That is why in the New Testament believers, both as individuals and as a gathered church are referred to as "the temple of the Holy Spirit." The Apostle Paul said:

> Do you not know that you are God's temple and that God's Spirit dwells in you? If anyone destroys God's temple, God will destroy that person. For God's temple is holy, and you are that temple. (1 Corinthians 3:16-17, NRSV)

Here Paul is speaking to the Corinthian church as a whole (the word "you" is plural in the Greek), but it is also true to say that the individual Christian is a temple for the Spirit. Paul says later in the same letter:

> Or do you not know that your body is a temple of the Holy Spirit within you, which you have from God, and that you are not your own? For you were bought with a price; therefore glorify God in your body. (1 Corinthians 6:19-20, NRSV)

In a very real sense, the exciting promise of the Old Testament, the fact that one day the Spirit of God would live inside the human heart has been realized in both individual believers and in the church as a whole. Of course, the believer and the church are inseparable as 1 Peter 2:4-5 make clear:

> Come to him, a living stone, though rejected by mortals yet chosen and precious in God's sight, and like living stones, let yourselves be built into a spiritual house, to be a holy priesthood, to offer spiritual sacrifices acceptable to God through Jesus Christ. (NRSV)

The Apostle Peter is calling on Christians (living stones in whom the Holy Spirit dwells) to allow themselves to be built into a spiritual house (the church) in which the Spirit will dwell also. As believers we often skip this stage. We are so excited to be a living stone that we sit happily by ourselves and enjoy the warmth of our inner fire. That is why we began this journey with a discussion about connecting in tribe. It is very important that as a new believer you welcome every way the Spirit wants to work in you—both as an individual and as a member of a local church body.

But how do we do that? How do we welcome the Holy Spirit to work? We do it the same way we would do it with any human dignitary who took up residence in our home. We would learn the things that please him and do them. We would learn the things that displease him and not do them. The Bible says clearly that we have more power in the Spirit realm when we do this:

> Beloved, if our hearts do not condemn us, we have boldness before God; and we receive from him whatever we ask, **because we obey his**

commandments and do what pleases him. (1 John 3:21-22, NRSV)

Likewise, the Bible teaches clearly that we can quench or anger the Spirit:

Do not quench the Spirit. (1 Thessalonians 5:19, NRSV)

For if we wilfully persist in sin after having received the knowledge of the truth, there no longer remains a sacrifice for sins, but a fearful prospect of judgement, and a fury of fire that will consume the adversaries. Anyone who has violated the law of Moses dies without mercy 'on the testimony of two or three witnesses.' How much worse punishment do you think will be deserved by those who have spurned the Son of God, profaned the blood of the covenant by which they were sanctified, and **outraged the Spirit of grace?** (Hebrews 10:26-29, NRSV)

The Bible says as well, that if we foolishly label the work of the Holy Spirit as the work of the enemy, we are in big trouble. Jesus warned a group of Pharisees about that once. He was doing many wonderful deeds by the power of the Spirit and they accused him of doing it by the power of Satan. He replied:

Truly I tell you, people will be forgiven for their sins and whatever blasphemies they utter; but

whoever blasphemes against the Holy Spirit can
never have forgiveness, but is guilty of an eternal
sin, for they had said, 'He has an unclean spirit.'
(Mark 3:28-30, NRSV)

It always amazes me how many Christians flirt with this sin.
They seem to delight at pointing their fingers at a thing and saying, "That is of the enemy! God would never do that!" Are you
sure? Have you studied every passage in the Bible that talks
about the Holy Spirit and his effect on people? How about this
one?

> He went there, toward Naioth in Ramah; and
> the spirit of God came upon him. As he was go-
> ing, he fell into a prophetic frenzy, until he came
> to Naioth in Ramah. He too stripped off his
> clothes, and he too fell into a frenzy before
> Samuel. He lay naked all that day and all that
> night. Therefore it is said, "Is Saul also among
> the prophets?" (1 Samuel 19:23-24, NRSV)

If you saw someone at church fall under a frenzy, strip off
their clothes and utter prophecies and then lie naked across the
front of the auditorium would you rise up and say, "That is not
of God! That is of Satan!" Yet the Holy Spirit did that once. My
advice to you is to be cautious in categorizing things as being of
God or of Satan. Read the Word and you will soon realize that
the Holy Spirit is a person, has a personality and is therefore
hard to predict with 100% precision. He will never contradict

the Word but that still leaves a lot of room for caution and humility in our approach. The worst thing you can do as a new believer is give God a list of restrictions, "God you can live in my heart provided you never cause me to prophesy (especially in the nude!), provided you do not make me raise my hands when I sing, provided you never make me share my faith in public or pray in a foreign language. P.S. I also don't like to dance or clap. That is all." God made different people do all of those things in the Bible, so it's possible he may ask you to do some or all of them. We all privately hope that we won't have to prophesy naked but you never know! Two different people in the Bible had to do it! God doesn't like man-made restrictions, so don't give him any.

TEN GOOD REASONS TO
WELCOME THE HOLY SPIRIT:

1. The Bible says so. (Revelation 3:20) Do you really need 9 more?
2. We overcome mountains and obstacles "not by might, not by power, but by my Spirit says the Lord." (Zechariah 4:6)
3. The Spirit gives gifts that enable us to participate in the mission of the kingdom. (1 Corinthians 12:1-31)

4. The Spirit lives the character of God out through us, bringing forth divine love first of all. (1 Corinthians 13:1-13)

5. Jesus foretold of a day when his followers would worship in SPIRIT and in truth. (John 4:23)

6. Having the Spirit inside of us gives us assurance of salvation. (Romans 8:14-16)

7. When we flow in the Spirit it is a testimony to the world that the kingdom of God is at hand. (Joel 2:28-29, Acts 2:1-47)

8. The Holy Spirit leads us into all truth. (John 16:13)

9. The Holy Spirit helps us understand the Bible. (John 14:26)

10. The Holy Spirit gives us joy. (1 Thessalonians 1:6)

PERSONAL STUDY AND REFLECTION:

Paul told the Ephesians, "be always being filled with the Spirit" (Ephesians 5:18) and he said to Timothy, "kindle up the gift that is in you" (2 Timothy 1:6). These verses indicate that there are things we can do to enlarge our sharing in the Spirit. If we find ourselves feeling "low in the Spirit", are there some things we can do to "kindle up"? Read the following three Scriptures together before proceeding to the comprehension task that follows.

- 2 Chronicles 7:12-16
- Acts 1:6-14, 2:1-4
- Isaiah 55:6-12

Consider the 7 statements below. Five of them represent things you might do to "kindle up" the Spirit based on the passages you read above. Two are wildly unhelpful. The correct answers are in a footnote on the next page.

1. It may be helpful to enter into an intense time of prayer and fasting.
2. It may be helpful to do a thorough self-inspection and to repent of things you find in yourself that may be displeasing to the Lord.
3. It may be helpful to shave your head and make a coat of the clippings.
4. It may be helpful to enter into a time of intense fellowship with other believers.
5. It may be helpful to seek the Lord diligently and communicate through your time that God is more important to you than other things.
6. It may be helpful to shout very loud at God and try to work yourself up to a pitch of emotional ecstasy.

7. It may be helpful to dig deep into God's Word to better familiarize yourself with his requirements and character.*

---

* The correct answers are: 1, 2, 4, 5, and 7. 3 is not just wrong, it's downright creepy.

QUESTIONS AND NOTES:

WELCOME THE HOLY SPIRIT
FAQ

The following questions represent the most frequent concerns for new believers starting out in their journey with the Holy Spirit. I have shared more of these questions in this section than in any other because the Holy Spirit is doing business with the church in a new and powerful way and many Christians are experiencing things in their walk that are considered "new" and "dangerous" to some. Of course, a longer view of history reveals that just because it didn't happen to your mom or your grandma doesn't mean it's "new." Sometimes new things are old things we've forgotten about. Let's take a look at these new old questions.

1. What are the Biblical "proofs" that a person has the Holy Spirit within them?

ANSWER: Sometimes this question is asked in a reactionary way, meaning that a person has heard from a well-meaning Christian friend that there are certain "proofs" that are universal in people who have the Holy Spirit within them. Often the proof being referenced is speaking in tongues. Let's be clear: Nowhere in the Bible does it suggest that you have to speak in tongues to prove you have the Holy Spirit. Nowhere. Some people say that while the Apostle Paul does not suggest this, Luke does. Not only is that idea alarming from a Biblical perspective (what would it mean if authors in the Bible disagreed with one another on important issues like this?), it is simply not true. Luke wrote two books in the New Testament, The Gospel of Luke and The Acts of the Apostles. In the Gospel of Luke, the presence of the Holy Spirit almost always manifests in bold, inspired, even prophetic speech, though not once was that speech in tongues. Let's look at a few examples. Referring to John the Baptist, Luke records an angelic prophecy:

> Even before his birth **he will be filled with the Holy Spirit**. He will turn many of the people of Israel to the Lord their God. With the spirit and power of Elijah he will go before him, to turn the hearts of parents to their children, and the disobedient to the wisdom of the righteous, to make ready a people prepared for the Lord. (Luke 1:15-17, NRSV)

Luke records the angelic prophecy that the presence of the Holy Spirit in John would manifest itself in bold, prophetic utterances not unlike those of the prophet Elijah. He says nothing about tongues.

When Elizabeth was filled with the Holy Spirit, Luke records:

And **Elizabeth was filled with the Holy Spirit
42and exclaimed with a loud cry**, 'Blessed are
you among women, and blessed is the fruit of
your womb. 43And why has this happened to
me, that the mother of my Lord comes to me?
44For as soon as I heard the sound of your
greeting, the child in my womb leapt for joy.
45And blessed is she who believed that there
would be a fulfilment of what was spoken to her
by the Lord.' (Luke 1:41-45, NRSV)

Again, the presence of the Holy Spirit manifested itself in
bold, prophetic proclamation, likely in Aramaic and certainly
not in tongues.

When Zechariah was filled with the Holy Spirit, Luke records:

**Then his father Zechariah was filled with the
Holy Spirit and spoke this prophecy:**
Blessed be the Lord God of Israel,
for he has looked favourably on his people and
redeemed them.
He has raised up a mighty saviour for us
in the house of his servant David,
as he spoke through the mouth of his holy
prophets from of old,
that we would be saved from our enemies and
from the hand of all who hate us.
Thus he has shown the mercy promised to our
ancestors,
and has remembered his holy covenant,

the oath that he swore to our ancestor Abra-
    ham,
to grant us that we, being rescued from the
    hands of our enemies,
might serve him without fear, in holiness and
    righteousness
before him all our days.
And you, child, will be called the prophet of the
    Most High;
for you will go before the Lord to prepare his
    ways,
to give knowledge of salvation to his people
by the forgiveness of their sins.
By the tender mercy of our God,
the dawn from on high will break upon us,
to give light to those who sit in darkness and in
    the shadow of death,
to guide our feet into the way of peace.
(Luke 1:67-79, NRSV)

Again, the presence of the Holy Spirit is manifested in bold, prophetic speech, not in tongues. Sometimes people will say that tongues is "initial evidence" of the Holy Spirit, but that is clearly not the case. The initial evidence in all of these cases in Luke's Gospel was bold, prophetic speech. Perhaps things change in Luke's second book, The Acts of the Apostles? Well, Luke records the events of Pentecost where he says:

When the day of Pentecost had come, they were all together in one place. And suddenly from heaven there came a sound like the rush of a

violent wind, and it filled the entire house where
they were sitting. Divided tongues, as of fire,
appeared among them, and a tongue rested on
each of them. **All of them were filled with the
Holy Spirit and began to speak in other languages**, as the Spirit gave them ability. (Acts
2:1-4, NRSV)

In this case, their bold, prophetic speech WAS IN
TONGUES, so the presence of the Holy Spirit will manifest in
tongues. But did Luke mean to imply that this would ALWAYS
be the case? Well, two chapters later he records this:

When they had prayed, the place in which they
were gathered together was shaken; and **they
were all filled with the Holy Spirit and spoke
the word of God with boldness**. (Acts 4:31,
NRSV)

The point Luke seems to be making is that the presence of
the Holy Spirit manifests in bold, Gospel speech, inspired by the
Holy Spirit, which may or may not be given in tongues. The
common factor is the bold, Gospel speech; the rare factor is being in tongues. In reality, most Pentecostal theologians have
abandoned the teaching that tongues is a universal proof of the
Holy Spirit. They now claim that bold, prophetic, Gospel
speech is the proof of the Holy Spirit and that **may** come in the
form of speaking in tongues. To say something is universally
available (which speaking in tongues is) is different from saying

that it has to be present at conversion to prove that a person received the Holy Spirit.

Now that you have a headache, let's return to the question: what is the proof of the Holy Spirit residing in a person? We've already mentioned one, "bold, Gospel speech" or "bold, prophetic utterance"; whichever phrase strikes your fancy. Jesus said:

> And I tell you, everyone who **acknowledges me before others**, the Son of Man also will acknowledge before the angels of God, but whoever denies me before others will be denied before the angels of God. (Luke 12:8, NRSV)

The Apostle Paul added:

> No one can say, "Jesus is Lord," except by the Holy Spirit. (1 Corinthians 12:3, NIV)

Paul, Luke and Jesus all seem to agree: the first thing the Holy Spirit inspires in a person is bold Gospel testimony. If he doesn't, then he isn't there and the person isn't saved.

There are other proofs, or fruits of the Holy Spirit. The Apostle Paul said:

> The fruit of the Spirit is love, joy, peace, patience, kindness, generosity, faithfulness, gentleness, and self-control. There is no law against

such things. And those who belong to Christ Jesus have crucified the flesh with its passions and desires. (Galatians 5:22-24, NRSV)

The primary proof of the Holy Spirit, beyond bold Gospel speech, is character change and sanctification. As Paul famously put it:

> **If I speak in the tongues of mortals and of angels**, but **do not have love**, I am a noisy gong or a clanging cymbal. (1 Corinthians 13:1, NRSV)

Speaking in tongues is great, but character fruit (love) comes first. After saving confession comes character growth. Any gift added to a person who has not love is a dangerous and reckless gift that is unwisely given. God is not unwise and he always does things in the right sequence.

2. When does a person receive the Holy Spirit? At conversion or sometime later?

ANSWER: Both. There can be a lot of hurt in the church when we are not careful with our words, so let's take our time with this one. When did the disciples receive the Holy Spirit? If you ask that question to an adult Sunday School class, 9 times out of 10 the answer you will get is "at Pentecost." But is that true? Let's take a look at John 20. This story happens AFTER the resurrection but BEFORE the ascension of Jesus. Look at what it says:

> When it was evening on that day, the first day of the week, and the doors of the house where the disciples had met were locked for fear of the Jews, Jesus came and stood among them and said, 'Peace be with you.' After he said this, he showed them his hands and his side. Then the disciples rejoiced when they saw the Lord. Jesus said to them again, 'Peace be with you. As the Father has sent me, so I send you.' When he had said this, he breathed on them and said to them, '**Receive the Holy Spirit**. (John 20:19-22, NRSV)

So before Jesus left to go to heaven, he breathed on them and he said, "**receive the Holy Spirit**." So let me ask you, several days later, after Jesus was up in heaven and the disciples are waiting in Jerusalem, did they not already have the Holy Spirit within them? Of course they did. They had the Holy Spirit within them; they were waiting for POWER FROM ON HIGH TO DESCEND **UPON** THEM. They were waiting for an anointing power, and the one they received was visible, bodily, tangible and observable in its effects.

Much confusion and even hurt could be avoided in the church if we understood the difference between indwelling and empowerment. If you are a born again Christian you have the Holy Spirit inside you. Guaranteed. Don't let anyone tell you that you don't because you haven't had a tangible, bodily em-powerment experience. You cannot be a Christian unless you have the seal of the Holy Spirit, but you may still be waiting for your power from on high. You may be waiting for a subsequent anointing. But there is not just one or two, there is always one and sometimes two, three, four or more. That's why we have to keep reading the Bible when we make our theology. Those who doggedly hold that there is just one experience of the Holy Spirit and force everything they know about that into the Acts 2 story struggle to make sense of John 20, as well as Acts 4 where it says:

> When they had prayed, the place in which they were gathered together was shaken; and they were all filled with the Holy Spirit and spoke the word of God with boldness. (Acts 4:31, NRSV)

This is just two chapters after they were anointed and dumped upon in Acts 2 and now here it is again. The Holy Spirit AGAIN descends on them powerfully, visibly, tangibly and ob-servably and they are empowered for ministry. That's three Holy Spirit experiences in just a few weeks. My point is this: all ministry in the church is Holy Spirit ministry. Everything Jesus did in Luke's Gospel was done in the power of the Holy Spirit. Let me just show you a few examples:

> Jesus, full of the Holy Spirit, returned from the Jordan and was led by the Spirit in the wilder-

ness, where for forty days he was tempted by the devil. (Luke 4:1-2, NRSV)

Luke 4:14 says:

> Then Jesus, filled with the power of the Spirit, returned to Galilee, and a report about him spread through all the surrounding country. He began to teach in their synagogues. (NRSV)

Luke 5 says:

> One day, while he was teaching, Pharisees and teachers of the law were sitting nearby (they had come from every village of Galilee and Judea and from Jerusalem); and the power of the Lord was with him to heal. (NRSV)

And on and on we could go. Why does Luke emphasize this? Why doesn't he just say, "Jesus went around doing Jesus things out of the vast store of his Jesus-ness?" Because we can't do that! But we can do things through the power of the Holy Spirit because we can HAVE THAT!! We can be filled with the Holy Spirit. We can be empowered from on high. We can experience outpourings of POWER to work God's purposes. That we can do. We have to do that or we will do nothing of value at all. That is why Paul said, "Be ever being filled with the Spirit." (Ephesians 5:18)

Let me just finish by explaining this once and always tension around the baptism of the Holy Spirit. We get baptized once in the Christian journey. You don't come back every few weeks for another dunk. You get saved and commit to Jesus as Saviour and Lord; that is commemorated through public baptism. One time. So we tend to think of baptism as a once and only word. But Biblically the word simply means "washed or cleansed" and we need that multiple times throughout our lives. So is baptism a once thing or an ever always thing? Both. In that sense, it is kind of like communion. The two sacraments explain each other if we let them. How many times did Jesus die on the cross? Once. But he said to do this (take communion) often in remembrance of me. We do communion regularly so that the benefits of the cross can be applied afresh to our lives on an on-going basis through faith. A once-for-all time historical experience that is freshly and regularly applied through faith. So it is with baptism in the Holy Spirit. When you come to Christ you are baptised into the Holy Spirit. 1 Corinthians 12 makes this absolutely clear:

> For in the one Spirit we were all baptized into one body—Jews or Greeks, slaves or free. (NRSV)

The grammar makes it clear that we are baptised INTO the Spirit. Think of it like being dipped in strong white dye. You are now white. The dye took. You have been dipped in the dye; you are now of the dye. You are white as snow. But if you get dusty, as you will, you may revisit the dye as often as you wish. But regardless, under the dust, you are still of the dye. The benefits of the initial experience can be freshly applied. Here is the practical point: Jesus went back for more because we need to go back for more. The first thing was a great thing but Jesus went BACK FOR MORE. Being conceived by the Holy Spirit was wonderful but he sought out the baptism of John. The baptism of John was wonderful but he sought out the desert because he wanted to stay hungry. The desert was great but he was oft on the mountain alone in prayer, through the night because he wanted MORE!!!! Blessed are those who hunger and thirst for they will be FILLED. I want the benefits of my baptism in the Holy Spirit FRESHLY APPLIED TODAY and I make no apology for that. And it's more than just the reapplication of an old thing. The Bible calls our baptism in the Holy Spirit a pledge, a guarantee of better things to come. I want the better things of the Spirit; I want fresh gifts and more power. We need this, for without it we can do nothing. Not by might and not by power but by my Spirit says the Lord.

3. Are encounters with the power of the Holy Spirit messy and overwhelming?

ANSWER: They can be. When King Saul met the Holy Spirit on the road to Naioth it was messy:

> He went there, toward Naioth in Ramah; and the spirit of God came upon him. As he was going, he fell into a prophetic frenzy, until he came to Naioth in Ramah. He too stripped off his clothes, and he too fell into a frenzy before Samuel. He lay naked all that day and all that night. Therefore it is said, "Is Saul also among the prophets?" (1 Samuel 19:23-24, NRSV)

How would you like to be Samuel? You're at home minding your own business and all of the sudden this big, giant dancing Hebrew comes up to you and strips off all his clothes, prophesies and then lies naked across your front porch all night. That can't help your reputation with the neighbours. Naked, sprawling, frenzied prophets on your front porch do not raise the real estate value of your home.

When Daniel had a Spirit dream it messed him up as well. The Spirit shows up and Daniel says:

> My strength left me, and my complexion grew deathly pale, and I retained no strength. Then I heard the sound of his words; and when I heard the sound of his words, I fell into a trance, face to the ground. (Daniel 10:8-9, NRSV)

At least Daniel got to keep his clothes on. The Apostle John had trouble with the Spirit as well. In Revelation 1, John tells us that he was "in the Spirit" or literally "he came into the Spirit." Look at what happened to him:

When I saw him, I fell at his feet as though dead. (NRSV)

It does not say, "When I saw him, I bowed with deep respect and dignity." No this was not a controlled bow; this was a Holy Spirit face plant. This was a protein spill—"Clean up on aisle six." All I'm saying is that I want you to be well-warned: encounters with the Holy Spirit are often messy.

4. What is blasphemy against the Holy Spirit?

ANSWER: This is a complicated one so let's start with the text. In the Gospel of Mark, Jesus was going around doing some pretty incredible things in the power of the Holy Spirit. The religious people of the day weighed in with their opinions as to whether this was of God or the Deceiver. Jesus gave this warning:

> 'Truly I tell you, people will be forgiven for their sins and whatever blasphemies they utter; but whoever blasphemes against the Holy Spirit can never have forgiveness, but is guilty of an eternal sin'—for they had said, 'He has an unclean spirit.' (Mark 3:28-30. NRSV)

Now this saying is so harsh and so scary that whole books have been written on exactly what Jesus means here. I'm not going to go into all of that or try to explain the minute details of exegesis here because I think the main point is pretty clear: blasphemy against the Holy Spirit is bad. It's a big deal. It's us being the judge of God and God does not receive that well. The Father will not sit under the scrutiny of the children so just don't go there. I'm throwing this out there because this one worries me. I know me. I know that if the Holy Spirit fell on someone in my church and they danced and frenzied their way up to the front of the sanctuary, stripped off their clothes and started speaking words of prophecy before flinging themselves down to lie naked on top of the communion table for the rest of the service—I would be inclined to label that a work of the enemy. I would be weirded out by that. But what if that was just the Holy Spirit doing something he's already done before? Would we dare to condemn that as a work of the enemy? And what if he did something even stranger, something we don't have an example of already in the Bible. Would we be able to handle that? I've decided that on my journey, I'm going to be very slow to speak words of judgement on possible manifestations of the Spirit because I'm worried I don't know enough of the Spirit to spot all his activities. I recommend a similar commitment to you.

5. My church has started to flow in some new and exciting spiritual gifts. Is this the end of order and structure? Does spirituality oppose order and decency?

ANSWER: This was a common question in the early church so we are blessed to have an abundance of material on this concern. Let's take a look at 1 Corinthians 14:1-33:

> Pursue love and strive for the spiritual gifts, and especially that you may prophesy. For those who speak in a tongue do not speak to other people but to God; for nobody understands them, since they are speaking mysteries in the Spirit. On the other hand, those who prophesy speak to other people for their building up and encouragement and consolation. Those who speak in a tongue build up themselves, but those who prophesy build up the church. Now I would like all of you to speak in tongues, but even more to prophesy. One who prophesies is greater than one who speaks in tongues, unless someone interprets, so that the church may be built up.
>
> Now, brothers and sisters, if I come to you speaking in tongues, how will I benefit you unless I speak to you in some revelation or knowledge or prophecy or teaching? It is the same way with lifeless instruments that produce sound, such as the flute or the harp. If they do not give distinct notes, how will anyone know what is being played? And if the bugle gives an indistinct sound, who will get ready for battle? So with yourselves; if in a tongue you utter speech that is not intelligible, how will anyone know what is being said? For you will be speaking into the air. There are doubtless many dif-

ferent kinds of sounds in the world, and nothing is without sound. If then I do not know the meaning of a sound, I will be a foreigner to the speaker and the speaker a foreigner to me. So with yourselves; since you are eager for spiritual gifts, strive to excel in them for building up the church.

Therefore, one who speaks in a tongue should pray for the power to interpret. For if I pray in a tongue, my spirit prays but my mind is unproductive. What should I do then? I will pray with the spirit, but I will pray with the mind also; I will sing praise with the spirit, but I will sing praise with the mind also. Otherwise, if you say a blessing with the spirit, how can anyone in the position of an outsider say the 'Amen' to your thanksgiving, since the outsider does not know what you are saying? For you may give thanks well enough, but the other person is not built up. I thank God that I speak in tongues more than all of you; nevertheless, in church I would rather speak five words with my mind, in order to instruct others also, than ten thousand words in a tongue.

Brothers and sisters, do not be children in your thinking; rather, be infants in evil, but in thinking be adults. In the law it is written,
'By people of strange tongues
and by the lips of foreigners
I will speak to this people;
yet even then they will not listen to me,'

says the Lord. Tongues, then, are a sign not for believers but for unbelievers, while prophecy is not for unbelievers but for believers. If, therefore, the whole church comes together and all speak in tongues, and outsiders or unbelievers enter, will they not say that you are out of your mind? But if all prophesy, an unbeliever or outsider who enters is reproved by all and called to account by all. After the secrets of the unbeliever's heart are disclosed, that person will bow down before God and worship him, declaring, 'God is really among you.'

What should be done then, my friends? When you come together, each one has a hymn, a lesson, a revelation, a tongue, or an interpretation. Let all things be done for building up. If anyone speaks in a tongue, let there be only two or at most three, and each in turn; and let one interpret. But if there is no one to interpret, let them be silent in church and speak to themselves and to God. Let two or three prophets speak, and let the others weigh what is said. If a revelation is made to someone else sitting nearby, let the first person be silent. For you can all prophesy one by one, so that all may learn and all be encouraged. And the spirits of prophets are subject to the prophets, for God is a God not of disorder but of peace. (NRSV)

God is a God not of disorder but of peace. Now, let me just point something out, it says, "God is not a God of disorder." Correct? Correct. But then it goes on to say, "God is a God of peace." It does not say, "God is a God of ORDER." People love to say that, "God is a God of order!" Of course, they mean their order. But either way, the Bible doesn't say that. It doesn't say that God wants everything done in a rigid order. It says God does not favour or author chaos; he rather desires peace. Those who are sure that God LOVES ORDER are usually the least peaceful people in a church. Food for thought.

My point however, is simply this: spiritual gifts are NOT the death of order. They're not. People fear that and will say to me, "Pastor, if you open the door for people to speak in tongues, you will never get through a sermon! They'll be shouting out and interrupting you every 5 seconds." Or they will say, "Pastor, if you let people think God is talking to them, they will never bother to read their Bibles." Or "If you let people get healed in the church, they won't want to come for anything else! Who wants to serve and sacrifice when you can have happy healing time all service long!" These are groundless concerns. Now that is not to say they don't happen. I think we've all been to churches where the lack of leadership permitted a descent into chaos, but whose fault is that? Is it the Holy Spirit's fault or the fault of the leaders? If you lose leadership in your church and you have gifts, then you will also have chaos. If you have water flowing through your river system but you lose your banks, what do you have? A mud bath. But it doesn't have to be that way and if it is that way, it is not the fault of the Spirit.

The Apostle Paul, speaking by the Spirit, lays down some guidelines. Tongues should not be given a public platform unless there is someone who can provide a useful interpretation. So what's the problem? We have lots of people who speak in tongues at my church but we don't do "open-mike, tongue-time" in service. No problem. But in private prayer, if they are edified by that, is there harm to us in that? No. Is it a threat to our order? No. And if while we are worshipping and singing to the Lord, those with the gift of tongues wish to cry out in tongues, is that a problem? No. It does not disrupt the teaching nor does it require public interpretation because it is no more public than if they were praying quietly in English or saying "Hallelujah" or "Maranantha". By the way, those ecstatic outbursts are never criticized. But you know what I've discovered? No one knows what those words mean either; they may as well be in tongues! We've just gotten used to them and so it doesn't bother us.

But what about prophesy? Won't it create chaos in the service? Well, if we abide by the principal of confirmation that Paul advocates (similar to the one John advocated for in his churches. See I John 4:1.), then how could it? Suppose a person has a word of prophesy during the service. Do they stand up and interrupt the sermon? No. They haven't received confirmation. So they come to the pastor or an Elder after the service and they share their word. If it aligns with Scripture and is confirmed by someone else, then it could be shared the following Sunday. We could even put it down in the bulletin as part of the order of service if we wanted. This has happened in my church several times. I have carefully shared confirmed visions that other people have had from the pulpit and it in no way threatened the order of our worship time. Gifts are not the death of order.

6. What is the primary purpose for the Holy Spirit?

ANSWER: Great question! Names are often a clue to "call" in the Bible and so it is here. The fact that the Spirit of God is so often called "the Holy Spirit" gives us a good indicator of his primary activity: making us holy. There is some beautiful, descriptive, forward looking imagery of the church in Revelation 19:

> To her it has been granted to be clothed with fine linen, bright and pure. (NRSV)

When the Spirit's work is done, the church is going to be pure. She is going to be wearing white and she is going to stand blameless before her Lord. Jesus said this was the work of the Spirit from the beginning, promising:

> If you love me, you will keep my commandments. (John 14:15, NRSV)

Jesus saw a church where love and holiness were part and parcel, where relationship resulted in righteousness, praise the Lord, rather than a church where love was an excuse for selfishness and relationship an excuse for sinful indulgence. The Spirit wants to make us righteous, the Spirit wants to make us HOLY—so how does he do that?

First of all he does it by convicting us of sin. Let's quickly visit Galatians 5:16-25:

> **Live by the Spirit**, I say, and do not gratify the desires of the flesh. For what the flesh desires is opposed to the Spirit, and what the Spirit desires is opposed to the flesh; for these are opposed to each other, to prevent you from doing what you want. But if you are led by the Spirit, you are not subject to the law. Now the works of the flesh are obvious: fornication, impurity, licentiousness, idolatry, sorcery, enmities, strife, jealousy, anger, quarrels, dissensions, factions, envy, drunkenness, carousing, and things like these. I am warning you, as I warned you before: those who do such things will not inherit the kingdom of God. **By contrast, the fruit of the Spirit** is love, joy, peace, patience, kindness, generosity, faithfulness, gentleness, and self-control. There is no law against such things. And those who belong to Christ Jesus have crucified the flesh with its passions and desires. If we live by the Spirit, let us also be guided by the Spirit. (NRSV)

Very plainly the Apostle makes clear that the purpose of the Holy Spirit is to lead us away from sin and into holiness. He causes us to abhor the works of the flesh and to desire the fruit of the Spirit. If we walk in step with him, it is like being on the moving sidewalk at the airport; we make rapid progress away from the things that lead to death and into the things that make for life. The Spirit works internally to prompt and guide on this journey.

Secondly, he confronts us with rebellion. When we resist the leading of the Holy Spirit, he whispers, "Come over here child! Away from lust, away from anger, away from strife." If we answer and say, "No! I like lust. I am addicted to anger and I am always in strife," then the Holy Spirit becomes confrontational. In both the Old and New Testaments, God uses prophets to confront and rebuke people of stubborn persistence in sin. In the Old Testament, David tried to cover up his adultery with Bathsheeba but God sent the prophet Nathan to point his finger at David and say "You are the man!" David had resisted the conviction of the Holy Spirit but when he was confronted with his rebellion, David said to Nathan:

> I have sinned against the Lord. (2 Samuel 12:13, NRSV)

Prophecy works the same in the New Testament. In 1 Corinthians 14, Paul says that prophesy is primarily a gift for believers, laying bear the sins of all and that when unbelievers enter in by accident, they may get a dose of this confrontation as well:

> But if all prophesy, an unbeliever or outsider who enters is reproved by all and called to ac-

count by all. After the secrets of the unbeliever's heart are disclosed, that person will bow down before God and worship him, declaring, 'God is really among you.' (NRSV)

What great fun church will be when you can't even walk in the front door without your sins being laid bare! How opposed that is to the contemporary non-sense of seeker-friendly church. God is not interested in lowering the bar on holiness such that everybody and their brother can come in and not feel convicted. That is a lie of the enemy. God is concerned with a holy people and he would rather have 10 holy people than 1000 wicked and rebellious people, regardless of what you may have heard. God will make us holy and my advice is to respond to the conviction of the Holy Spirit in the quiet place so that you do not need to be rebuked in the public place. The Holy Spirit will move you towards holiness and it can be quiet and private or it can be noisy and public. It all depends on how quickly you respond.

Thirdly, he cleanses us from our idols—the things we love more than him. We see that promised in Ezekiel 36, looking forward to the great gift of the Holy Spirit:

> I will sprinkle clean water upon you, and you shall be clean from all your uncleannesses, and **from all your idols I will cleanse you**. A new heart I will give you, and a new spirit I will put within you; and I will remove from your body the heart of stone and give you a heart of flesh. I will put my spirit within you, and make you fol-

low my statutes and be careful to observe my ordinances. (NRSV)

The Holy Spirit is going to move through the church with a scrub brush of steel wool and he is going to remove any traces of idolatry from his bride. She will wear white on that day. There is a neat symbolic picture of that in Revelation 14. This is the vision of the full witness, the purified church giving powerful testimony to Christ during the time of tribulation. They are described as follows:

> It is these who have not defiled themselves with women, for they are virgins; these follow the Lamb wherever he goes. They have been redeemed from humankind as first fruits for God and the Lamb, and in their mouth no lie was found; they are blameless. (NRSV)

Now this is symbolic language, the Bible is not saying that in the last days the church will be full of virgins who refuse marriage. The images in Revelation are all leading up to the marriage of Jesus to his BRIDE, the church. We know this is symbolic language because it is the only place in the Bible where men are called virgins. "Virgin" is a term in the Bible that describes women, not men, so we have the double description: "not having lain with a woman" to describe men and "virgins" to describe women. Both are used here to talk about the BRIDE of Christ which is composed of men and women who are

COMPLETELY FAITHFUL IN THEIR DEVOTION to Christ, their husband. There is no hint even of idolatry or betrayal. They are faithful and they are true. This is a picture of the church cleansed of her idols.

Over the course of my ministry life, I have become convinced that the number one idol in the church today is money. If we do not surrender that "lover" voluntarily, it will be taken from us forcibly. I think that is what God is doing with our present economic crisis. He will shake us and break us free from its clutches and we will be pure as virgins before him before it is through. Our God is a jealous God and his Spirit is in charge of safeguarding our affections.

400-500 M
Become a Worshipper

The best reason I've ever been given for becoming a worshipper was written long before I was born. It was written long before people began wondering what was more heavenly, the sound of the organ or the sound of the guitar. It was written almost as if such things had nothing to do with the reason we worship. It said this:

> *"Worship is the submission of all our nature to God. It is the quickening of conscience by his holiness; the nourishment of mind with his truth; the purifying of the imagination by his beauty; the opening of the heart to his love; the surrender of will to his purpose - and all of this gathered up in adoration, the most selfless emotion of which our*

nature is capable and therefore the chief remedy of that self-centeredness which is our original sin and the source of all actual sin." (William Temple)

We worship God, William Temple says, because by nature we are inclined to worship ourselves. We are inclined to think ourselves wiser than we are, more righteous than we are, more powerful than we are and more deserving of praise than we are. When we turn our attention to the God of the Universe and his magnificent qualities, we are given something of a reality check. Against his holiness, our good deeds seem less impressive, our wisdom seems flawed and our power seems rather laughable. When we get to that place, God is ready to work in us. The Bible says:

> God opposes the proud, but gives grace to the humble. (James 4:6, NRSV)

God is opposed to anything or any person who tries to elevate themselves above their created station. This does not mean that God doesn't want us to grow as people, nor does it mean he doesn't want us to try and educate ourselves so that we can move forward in the world. It means that he wants us to understand that we are creatures and he is the creator. Original sin was not sex. I don't know who started that rumour but they should be tarred and feathered. Original sin was wanting to be God. The story is in Genesis 3:

Now the serpent was more crafty than any other wild animal that the Lord God had made. He said to the woman, 'Did God say, "You shall not eat from any tree in the garden"?' The woman said to the serpent, 'We may eat of the fruit of the trees in the garden; but God said, "You shall not eat of the fruit of the tree that is in the middle of the garden, nor shall you touch it, or you shall die." 'But the serpent said to the woman, 'You will not die; for God knows that when you eat of it your eyes will be opened, and **you will be like God, knowing good and evil**.' So when the woman saw that the tree was good for food, and that it was a delight to the eyes, and that the tree was to be desired to make one wise, she took of its fruit and ate; and she also gave some to her husband, who was with her, and he ate. (NRSV)

The first temptation is the same as every temptation! The Devil whispers into our prideful ears, "Why should God make all of the rules? You are a smart person. You are a strong and independent thinker. Let's reason this out and come to some sort of compromise." This is the lie that precedes every sinful act. This is what happens when creatures think they are creators.

That is why worship is so important. Worship is the reversal of original sin and indeed, all sin. Worship is when a creature raises his or her hands and says, "You are God! You make the rules! You are Holy and your character is the standard for my behaviour! You are the definition of what is good and what is noble and what is beautiful and I call you worthy of all praise and adoration!" Worship puts us back in our place and God back in his.

When Christians forget what worship is they generally begin to argue about style. You will notice that none of what we've said so far about worship has touched on music. Music has been used for as long as God's people can remember to help us lift praises to God but it is a tool - a means, not an end in itself. When Christians forget what worship is and why we do it, they begin to argue about music. "I love the organ! I am so thankful that God created the organ on the 7th day! I am so thankful that Jesus played the organ and that the Apostle Paul wrote all of his letters by its faithful light." When Christians say such things, they have forgotten the whole purpose of worship. Or when younger Christians say, "I'm going to leave this church because they don't know how to worship. I went to the church down the street and they rocked the house! There were lights and lasers and a smoke machine and everything! It was awesome!" They likewise reveal a strange confusion about worship. There is nothing wrong, or inherently right about organs, nor is there anything wrong or inherently right about guitars (lasers I think are somehow wrong—but don't quote me on that); either can be used to assist believers in lifting their hearts in praise to the Lord.

As a new believer try and avoid getting caught up in arguments about things that have very little to do with why we worship. If you go to a church that argues incessantly about music styles, find another church. Seriously. Those people obviously know very little about worship. A number of styles of music can be helpful in facilitating expressions of worship. Find a church that has picked one (or even a blend of a few) and has moved on to other issues. As for you as a worshipper, remember that worship is not a music recital or a concert. Buy an iPOD if you wish to listen to your favourite music. Worship is about lifting your heart, your voice, your hands and anything else you care to lift to God in praise. It is an offering of yourself to God's purpose and a surrender of your throne to his Lordship. When you do that, God visits your heart and does business inside of you and you are changed.

> Now the Lord is the Spirit, and where the Spirit of the Lord is, there is freedom. And all of us, with unveiled faces, seeing the glory of the Lord as though reflected in a mirror, are being transformed into the same image from one degree of glory to another; for this comes from the Lord, the Spirit. (2 Corinthians 3:17-18, NRSV)

Worship is about a face-to-face reality experience of God. It requires an atmosphere of freedom and humility and profits from a lack of pettiness and distraction. Alongside of the Word of God, it is the most powerful force of transformation in the universe.

Ten Good Reasons To Become a Worshipper:

1. The Bible says so (Psalm 29:2). Do you really need nine more?
2. Worship cures you of selfishness.
3. Worship re-establishes the correct order of the universe.
4. Worship undoes the path of sin in your life.
5. Worship reminds you that God is big and he can handle your problems.
6. Worship is embarrassing, especially if you are not a good singer or struggle to clap on beat. That's good because God opposes the proud and gives grace to the humble.
7. Worship tends to beat the dignity right out of us. That leaves us free to be happy and full of joy again. (See David in 2 Samuel 6:14-23)
8. Proud people who are sure they know everything are generally bad learners. Worship fixes that and makes sermon time much more profitable.
9. Worship pleases the Lord. That kind of cinches it right there, doesn't it?
10. Worship prepares us for the eternal kingdom (heaven) because it gets us comfortable with the idea of God being God and us being excited about that.

Mile 1

Personal Study and Reflection:

The Apostle John told a story once about a worship experience he had. He was in the Spirit on the Lord's Day and he had a face-to-face reality encounter with God. Read about it in Revelation 1:10-20 and then consider the comprehension task below.

Take a look at the seven statements below. Five of them reflect the enduring truth of John's worship experience and two of them are completely ridiculous. See if you can sort them out. The answers are in a footnote on the following page.

1. Jesus (one like a Son of Man) is alive and well and he is present among his people.
2. Jesus sees all of what we do and say and his holiness demands that he evaluate our behaviour and how well we are representing him.
3. The word of God which is sharper than any two-edged sword is a tool that Jesus uses to purify the thoughts, actions and attitudes of his children.
4. This vision reminds us that trances and visions are unreliable—only preaching and hymns are useful.
5. God is in control of the present and the future. The outcome of human history is not in doubt and the things we experience in the present have been decided by the Lord.

6. God has assigned spiritual beings to assist us as churches in the work he has given us. Take heart, you are not alone in this.
7. This vision proves that old men who spend long periods of time in prison should not lead worship in your church.*

---

* The correct answers are: 1, 2, 3, 5, and 6. 7 is not true—John was in prison when he had this experience and the Apostle Paul spent a fair bit of his life in prison, too.

QUESTIONS AND NOTES:

BECOME A WORSHIPPER
FAQ

The following questions represent the most frequent concerns for new believers starting out in their journey as worshippers.

1. There is a person at my church that really distracts me during worship. She weeps, dances and makes weird noises. Am I right for cherishing bitterness towards this woman and wishing she would just shut up and go away?

ANSWER: No. The truth is that when broken people who have been overwhelmed by the restoring grace of God worship, it is often a little messy. Get over it. Really, really get over it because your response to that could have serious consequences. In the Christian journey, extravagant worship has always been cause for offense. John 12 relates a story of extravagant worship that offended the early disciples of Jesus:

> Six days before the Passover Jesus came to Bethany, the home of Lazarus, whom he had raised from the dead. There they gave a dinner for him. Martha served, and Lazarus was one of those at the table with him. Mary took a pound of costly perfume made of pure nard, anointed

Jesus' feet, and wiped them with her hair. The
house was filled with the fragrance of the perfume. But Judas Iscariot, one of his disciples
(the one who was about to betray him), said,
'Why was this perfume not sold for three hundred denarii and the money given to the poor?'
(He said this not because he cared about the
poor, but because he was a thief; he kept the
common purse and used to steal what was put
into it.) Jesus said, 'Leave her alone. She bought
it so that she might keep it for the day of my
burial. You always have the poor with you, but
you do not always have me.' (John 12:1-8,
NRSV)

This story has some obvious similarities to the story that is
in Luke (Luke 7:36-51)—so much so that some liberal scholars
suggest it might be the same story just remembered differently
by John. But there is no reason to think that at all. There are way
too many differences for it to be the same story. The only reason
you might be tempted to think it is the same story is if you think
that the idea of broken people worshipping Jesus in extravagant
ways is so crazy, so exceptional that it could only have happened
once—a long time ago in a galaxy far, far away. But the Bible
mentions it not once, but as a matter of course because we are to
understand it as normative, not exceptional.

In this story the woman is Mary, as in Mary and Martha, sisters of Lazarus, the fellow that Jesus raised from the dead.
Unlike in the story of the prostitute in Luke, Mary is not wor-

shipping this way because of her many sins, but rather because she has seen the goodness of God. Mary was a little more self-controlled than the prostitute in Luke 7. She wasn't weeping or disrupting the conversation, but it was still extravagant and irritating to some of the less impacted who were there with her. But Mary didn't care about them; she was overcome with the goodness of the Lord. Jesus had raised her brother from the dead! No amount of worship could reflect the joy and gratitude that she felt. The Bible tells us that the perfume she used to worship was worth 300 denarii which in today's terms is about $30 000. Now this was in the days before RRSPs or 401Ks. People invested money in gold or precious commodities such as costly oils and perfumes. This was probably her retirement fund and she just dumped it on the feet of Jesus as an act of worship and gratitude. It was extravagant, it was large, it was flamboyant, but in Mary's eyes it was altogether inadequate. When God does good things, humble people start to celebrate in costly and extravagant ways.

What is interesting is that every time this type of worship is recorded in the Bible, good, upright people like you and me were really ticked off. Look at the reaction of Judas to this act of worship:

> But Judas Iscariot, one of his disciples (the one who was about to betray him), said, 'Why was this perfume not sold for three hundred denarii and the money given to the poor?' (NRSV)

He was angry! Now, John tells us that he was angry mostly because he liked to steal from the money bag and it would have been fun to have $30 000 in the money bag. But even still, it sounds so righteous to be angry at waste! How many nasty, sinful complaints have been hidden behind the mask of stewardship in the church over the years? "Oh, I'm so angry at that because it's just bad stewardship!" No it isn't. You just don't want to give God his due. God isn't short of money; you just don't want to lavish it on his purposes. But let's not be too hard on Judas. Matthew tells us that all of the disciples were a little offended:

> But when the disciples saw it, they were angry and said, 'Why this waste? For this ointment could have been sold for a large sum, and the money given to the poor.' (Matthew 36:8-9, NRSV)

The truth is ALL of them were annoyed—they all thought that this was too showy, too costly and altogether inappropriate. Jesus disagreed with them, as he often did. He rebuked them and told them to leave her alone. Some Christian worshippers need to hear that again (and again and again). "Leave her alone," Jesus says. "She's got it right. You've got it wrong." How did we ever get to the place where we feel it our duty to tone down the worship of the forgiven or the grateful? How did that become such an important religious duty? Leave them alone. Consider your own hearts, friends. It appears that 11 of the disciples received this rebuke from Jesus and accepted his teaching on the matter. Peter had Mark preserve this teaching in his Gospel. John records it and so does Matthew. They obviously got the message, though they were initially offended. Judas did not receive the teaching and in fact Matthew presents the story as the tipping point in Judas' life where he opened up a stronghold that the devil used to bring about his ultimate destruction.

What's the point? The point is that extravagant worship has ALWAYS been a cause of offense and how you deal with that REALLY MATTERS. If you receive the rebuke of Jesus and move past it, there will be blessings for you. If you refuse to let it go, it will open a stronghold in your life that the enemy will use to destroy you. Blessed are you who take no offense on account of my words, says the Lord.

2. It seems really hard for the church to hit the right note in worship! I've been to churches that were well-ordered but they were dead as posts. I've also been to churches that invited the Holy Spirit but the place was a gong show. Is there a happy medium? Is there a space between chaos and routine?

ANSWER: Great question! (And one I've been asked MANY times!) Let's go slowly and consult the Scriptures so that we deal with this one accurately and fairly. In Isaiah 29:13-14 it says:

The Lord said:

Because these people draw near with their mouths and honour me with their lips, while **their hearts are far from me**, and their worship of me is **a human commandment learned by rote**; so I will again do amazing things with this people, shocking and amazing. The wisdom of their wise shall perish, and the discernment of the discerning shall be hidden. (NRSV)

God hates heart-less routine. How do we know that? Maybe you are thinking, "This doesn't really sound so bad. If God doesn't like the worship, he shows up and does amazing things—that sounds kind of fun." You're thinking of the wrong kind of amazing. The Hebrew word here doesn't mean "fun"amazing. God isn't doing a magic show here. This word is *paw-law* and means "shockingly difficult and hard." It means marvellously nasty. This is the kind of amazing like when God used the Assyrians to wipe out all of northern Israel. That was amazing. People stood back from that and said, "Wow! God takes sin SERIOUSLY! God is SEVERE in his punishments." This is the kind of amazing like when God used the Babylonians to completely destroy Jerusalem and blot out the temple because the worship of the Jews had become obnoxious and offensive to God. People had been saying: 'We can worship however we like. God is obligated to us." They thought God was like a husband who was obligated to his wife so they could spit in his dinner and disrespect him in public. God AMAZED them with the severity of his response. This is not good amazing, do you understand this? This is the amazing that teaches you something you did not know about what sins REALLY bother the Lord.

When I was 10-years-old I spent the summer at my grandparents' farm. It was kind of a family tradition—all of the grandchildren spent their tenth summer with Grandma and Grandpa on the farm. We had a blast. We would feed the cows, take care of the chickens, hunt foxes and do all the things your mother would never let you do if she were anywhere within driving distance. The set up was pretty typical: Grandpa was the fun and Grandma was the love. Grandpa gave us pellet guns and bull whips and did all sorts of borderline illegal things that we found amusing. Grandma baked pies, applied bandages and gave kisses when we got homesick. All in all it was just about the best summer of my life. Anyway, one day I discovered a side of my grandmother that I did not know existed. I was having lunch with my two cousins, Gary and Graham. You see my grandparents lived on a farm that was on the property of my aunt and uncle. So my grandmother's daughter, my aunt, had a house on the same property and grandma was making us lunch in Aunt Mary's kitchen and Aunt Mary was there also. My cousin Gary was a few years older than me and seemed very cool. He was almost a teenager—I think he was 12-years-old at the time. Gary's mom, Aunt Mary, began giving Gary some instructions, clean your room, put away your toys or something like that. Gary did what a lot of 12-year-old boys might do: he backtalked to his mom. It started off pretty tame, I suppose, but somewhere along the way he crossed a line and became down right cheeky. I don't remember what he said, but all I remember was Grandma walked up and WHACK! Slapped him across the face. The eyes of everyone in the room went very wide and every sound in that house CEASED. BIRDS REFUSED TO SING AT THAT PRECISE MOMENT. And as long as I live, I will never forget the words that came out of her mouth; she said, "Gary Reid, you may talk to your mother like that but you will NOT talk to my daughter like that so help me God." I learned something in that moment: don't mess with Grandma. I had never in my life seen this side of my grandmother and I had sinned many times before. I had stolen cookies that I was told not to eat, usually with my grandfather's help. I had tracked mud across her kitchen floor. Heck, my brother once shot Grandpa in the bum with his pellet gun and I never once recall her getting angry at any of us. Every other time we sinned, she seemed to just smile and bake us a pie; but I learned that day that grandma did not tolerate rebellion and sauce talk to her children. Believe you me, I filed that away for future reference. I believe the exact thought that went through my brain in that moment was, "Note to self: if being saucy to mother, make sure Grandma is a long way away."

Do you understand that the intensity of the response reveals the significance of the sin? I learned that day that sauce talk was a high sin—a very high sin. Higher than stealing cookies, higher than tracking mud through the house and higher even than shooting grandpa in the backside. Now to be honest, her ranking of sin surprised me—I had not known about it, but I figured out that it was information I needed to have. So it is here. Most of us are surprised that God cares so much about the quality of our worship. Shouldn't he get more upset by murder or theft? Murder and theft are big deals, I should think, wouldn't you? The Bible reminds us frequently:

> For my thoughts are not your thoughts, nor are your ways my ways, says the Lord. For as the heavens are higher than the earth, so are my ways higher than your ways and my thoughts than your thoughts. (Isaiah 55:8-9, NRSV)

God doesn't think like us and he doesn't measure like us and we need to reckon with that. If I were God, I suppose that I would make murder the biggest sin or kidnapping or theft or maybe adultery. I don't know, but the Bible says that disrespect for worship is at the top of God's list. Look at this story in Numbers 15:

> When the Israelites were in the wilderness, they found a man gathering sticks on the sabbath day. Those who found him gathering sticks brought him to Moses, Aaron, and to the whole congregation. They put him in custody, because it was not clear what should be done to him. Then the Lord said to Moses, "The man shall be put to death; all the congregation shall stone him outside the camp." The whole congregation brought him outside the camp and stoned

him to death, just as the Lord had commanded
Moses. (NRSV)

Does that story surprise you? It surprised them too. I mean
what's the big deal? So the guy was gathering sticks when he was
supposed to be at worship service, so what? Maybe he wasn't
feeling good that day and so he stayed home and then he got
cold or hungry and he needed a fire. Is it really that big a deal?
They're not sure and don't know what to do so they put him in
custody and they seek the Lord. They know that God is pretty
serious about worship but in their minds, this guy should get a
warning—maybe next week he could come to church twice.
God says, "Kill the man. All of you. The whole congregation is
going to participate because this man has chosen not to be part
of the worshipping congregation, therefore he will die by its
hand." Ok, now that's amazing. Do you think some people's
jaws dropped at that verdict? I bet church attendance was very
high the next weekend. God takes the quality of our worship
seriously and those of us who doubt that will be AMAZED by
the severity of his punishment.

Now, he doesn't just want us there, he wants us to be
PASSIONATELY PRESENT. The charge in Isaiah is not that
they failed to worship—they had read this story in Numbers
and they at least had the sense to attend worship, but look:

Their worship of me is a human commandment
learned by rote. (Isaiah 29:13, NRSV)

There was no PASSION! It was heart-less routine. Have you ever seen that? I went to a Portuguese Catholic Church once in Toronto and sat through a service that seemed to me like heart-less routine. The priest mumbled through the liturgy and read his brief message off of cue cards. The people slumped in their seats and talked under their breath the whole time. The only time in the whole service that the congregation showed any life was just before the Scripture readings. In the liturgy, there were three readings. I think an Old Testament one from the Gospels and then one from the letters of Paul. Before each reading the priest would say, "Now may our minds be blessed by the Father, Son and Holy Spirit, likewise our lips by the Father, Son and Holy Spirit, likewise our hearts by the Father, Son and Holy Spirit." Each time he said "Father, Son and Holy Spirit" the congregation would stand up and make the sign of the cross over their heads, mouths and hearts but it had evolved into a bit of a competition and this was all happening in Portuguese so to me it was very shocking. All of these borderline comatose people would all of the sudden jump up and make the sign of the cross and then sit back down and fall asleep. It looked to me like a mass exorcism! I asked the priest afterwards and he explained that the men of the congregation are very competitive and it is considered a great honour to be the fastest one at making the sign of the cross. My goodness! If your worship is so boring and routine that you have to invent little games to keep yourself awake and engaged, its time to spice things up! God HATES heart-less routine.

But it's also true that the church is diminished by structure-less chaos. Paul's letter to the Corinthians (1 Corinthians) makes that point. He said in the first chapter:

> I give thanks to my God always for you because of the grace of God that has been given you in Christ Jesus, for in every way you have been enriched in him, in speech and knowledge of every kind—just as the testimony of Christ has been strengthened among you—so that you are not lacking in any spiritual gift as you wait for the revealing of our Lord Jesus Christ. (NRSV)

That's an amazing statement—good amazing. This is the only church in the New Testament that we are told had EVERY spiritual gift in abundance. Would you like to go to that church? I would. Would you like to go to a church where the gift of healing was present in abundance? You would if you had a sick child. Would you like to go to a church where the gift of prophecy existed in abundance? Sure you would. God was THERE! Amen! However, they struggled with leadership and they had some morality challenges and things occasionally got chaotic when they worshipped. They were gifted but messy. So Paul includes a chapter on how to be SPIRITUAL without being chaotic. There is a lot of useful material in this letter, particularly in chapter 14. There Paul reveals his main point in verses 22-33:

> Tongues, then, are a sign not for believers but for unbelievers, while prophecy is not for unbe-

lievers but for believers. If, therefore, the whole church comes together and all speak in tongues, and outsiders or unbelievers enter, will they not say that you are out of your mind? But if all prophesy, an unbeliever or outsider who enters is reproved by all and called to account by all. After the secrets of the unbeliever's heart are disclosed, that person will bow down before God and worship him, declaring, "God is really among you."(NRSV)

What should be done then, my friends? When you come together, each one has a hymn, a lesson, a revelation, a tongue, or an interpretation. **Let all things be done for building up**. If anyone speaks in a tongue, let there be only two or at most three, and each in turn; and let one interpret. But if there is no one to interpret, let them be silent in church and speak to themselves and to God. Let two or three prophets speak, and let the others weigh what is said. If a revelation is made to someone else sitting nearby, let the first person be silent. For you can all prophesy one by one, so that all may learn and all be encouraged. And the spirits of prophets are subject to the prophets, for **God is a God not of disorder but of peace**. (NRSV)

Are you seeing this? Paul is saying that if you give free reign to all your spirituality without any thought for structure or order, people are going to think that you are stark-raving mad.

However, if you harness all of this spiritual vigour and use it in some sort of order and structure, the church will be built up and people will come to Jesus. It's a good service when Christians are built up and unbelievers come to Jesus—and by the way, you can do BOTH in the same church and even in the same service.

The point Paul is trying to make is that there is a middle road between chaos and routine and he provides some very helpful hints for finding it.

The first thing he says is, "Do not forbid gifts of the Spirit." Look at verse 39:

> So, my friends, be eager to prophesy, and **do not forbid speaking in tongues**. (NRSV)

It bewilders me to no end that some churches blatantly defy this verse and do in fact forbid speaking in tongues. Now, I know all of the reasons, the real ones and the paper-thin pretend ones and I'm not buying any of it. The cessationist phenomena of the 20th century has thankfully been largely relegated to the scrap heap to which I say: FINALLY! That was the most ridiculous and academically transparent nonsense the church has ever seen or rejected. It was all a smoke screen anyway. The real reason we outlawed tongues had nothing to do with theology and everything to do with dignity. Tongues is embarrassing. It makes us look silly to outsiders and it lends itself to abuse. For whatever reason, tongues seems often to be a gift given to silly people with more enthusiasm than common sense and they seem to be ever so excited to use the gift and ever so ignorant of the basic rules provided by Scripture for its practice. The Bible says, "Don't feature tongues in your worship service unless it is interpreted" and yet every silly person given a microphone feels the need to babble in tongues for several minutes without interpretation. It annoys us and disrupts our services and so we OUTLAW IT. But let me tell you something, I have seen the gift of preaching abused more often in the church than the gift of tongues. I have seen preachers stand up in the authority of the pulpit and preach nothing but their own ignorant opinions rather than the word of God and the church has been terribly wounded by that. Terribly. I guarantee you that abuse of the gift of tongues does nothing compared to the damage done by abuse of the gift of preaching. Yet I have never heard a church forbid the gift or practice of preaching. We are NEVER invited to edit the gifts of the Spirit—NEVER! Do we need to teach people the rules about each gift? Of course. Do we need to be patient with the enthusiastic "newbies" who have more energy than wisdom? Of course we do. But we must NEVER forbid the practice of any spiritual gift in the church. Every gift was important or God wouldn't have given it—period.

The second helpful guideline Paul provides is that prophecy must submit to leadership. This point is made in verse 29:

> Let two or three prophets speak, and let the others weigh what is said. (NRSV)

The words of prophets are by nature vague and dark, and therefore, they have to be approved and vetted by established leaders. This is right out of the Old Testament:

> And he said, "Hear my words: When there are prophets among you, I the Lord make myself known to them in visions; I speak to them in dreams. Not so with my servant Moses; he is entrusted with all my house. With him I speak face to face—clearly, **not in riddles**; and he beholds the form of the Lord. Why then were you not afraid to speak against my servant Moses?" (Numbers 12:6-8, NRSV)

The Old Testament says that prophets receive pieces of the puzzle but don't see the whole picture—they hear from God in riddles or dark sayings. Therefore, prophets need to be humble and they need to be under the authority of anointed leaders because leaders see the big picture. Moses was entrusted with ALL God's house. God didn't speak to Moses in pieces; Moses had the eagle's eye view of things and so the word of the prophet had to submit to the oversight of the leader. By the way, in the New Testament, do you know what the most common word for the leader of a church was? *Episcopos* which means OVER SEER. The one with the big picture view. Now how do we know that this principle passes over from OT to NT? Well, it's right here in 1 Corinthians 14—look at verses 37-38:

Anyone who claims to be a prophet, or to have spiritual powers, must acknowledge that what I am writing to you is a command of the Lord. Anyone who does not recognise this is not to be recognised. (NRSV)

Paul says, "Anyone who thinks he or she is a prophet or that they have any spiritual gift whatsoever, better recognize that I, as the overseer, have the authority to set down some ground rules. And if you don't recognize that, then your gifts aren't from the Holy Spirit and you will not be recognized in this church." Gifts must submit to leadership. But you will hear people say from time to time, "My pastor didn't recognize my gift, but he isn't the Lord of my life. Jesus is, so I'm going to keep on shouting out in tongues during the service or giving prophetic words to people that haven't been tested. His leadership will not be the death of my giftedness." Wrong answer. His leadership may very well be the death of your giftedness. How did it turn out for Miriam, the prophetess, when she rebelled against Moses' leadership?

When the cloud went away from over the tent, Miriam had become leprous, as white as snow. And Aaron turned towards Miriam and saw that she was leprous. Then Aaron said to Moses, "Oh, my lord, do not punish us for a sin that we have so foolishly committed. Do not let her be like one stillborn, whose flesh is half consumed when it comes out of its mother's womb." And

Moses cried to the Lord, "O God, please heal her." But the Lord said to Moses, "If her father had but spit in her face, would she not bear her shame for seven days? Let her be shut out of the camp for seven days, and after that she may be brought in again." So Miriam was shut out of the camp for seven days; and the people did not set out on the march until Miriam had been brought in again. (Numbers 12:10-15. NRSV)

God healed Miriam the Prophetess immediately in response to Moses' prayer but he still demanded that she spend seven days outside of the camp in public repentance. Miriam was the number three leader in all of Israel, the most powerful prophet outside of Moses. But when she refused to submit her gift to his authority, God punished her and would not recognize her until she repented publicly for seven days. Here in the NT, Paul says if you won't submit your gift to leadership then you will not be recognized and allowed to participate. We stay out of the chaos ditch when we submit gifts to leadership.

In all of Paul's churches he reminded them of this middle road because the ditch on either side is deadly. To the church in Thessalonica, he said more succinctly:

Do not despise the words of prophets, but test everything. (NRSV)

That's good counsel. Advice like that will keep us out of the worship ditches and on that elusive way between chaos and routine.

500-600 M
Learn to Serve

How you view the kingdom of God will determine how you act while you live there. If you think of the kingdom of God as being like a lifeboat, you will struggle to understand why service is important. In a lifeboat it is important to sit still and listen to instructions and try not to make waves. In a lifeboat, only the uniformed officers should touch the equipment and use the oars. As a passenger, it is best if you just sit there, feeling lucky that you are in the boat and not "going to hell in a handbasket" like the rest of the world. If on the other hand, you think of the kingdom of God as being like a waiting room, where those with a ticket wait for the return of Jesus while the outside world again goes to hell in a handbasket, you will think that reading a good book and regularly checking the departure wall are the most appropriate things for you to do. Many Christians think that the Christian life is all about reading the Bible and anxiously checking the newspaper for signs that the rapture is about to occur. These Christians likewise will struggle to understand the necessity of service. If you think of your salvation as being like a safety harness (another common misperception), you will think the wisest thing to do is carry on with your business in the world and when the clock strikes twelve you will be yanked up to glory while—you guessed it—the world goes to hell in a handbasket. Once again, you will struggle to understand the importance of service.

But the Bible does not teach that the kingdom of God is a lifeboat, or a waiting room or a safety harness. It teaches that the kingdom of God is an alternative community that will one day be the only community. It is a world birthed within a world and we are supposed to be servants in and ambassadors of this alternative community. Jesus said it this way:

> 'You are the light of the world. **A city built on a hill** cannot be hidden. No one after lighting a lamp puts it under the bushel basket, but on the lampstand, and it gives light to all in the house. In the same way, let your light shine before others, so that they may see your good works and give glory to your Father in heaven. (Matthew 5:14-16, NRSV)

The kingdom of God is a city on a hill. It is within sight of the world; they look up at it and see that it is something different. It is near and accessible but it is clearly a world apart. It is a place with different values, where rich and poor, slave and free, male and female, Jew and Greek all sit around the same table and enjoy one another as brothers and sisters. It is a place with a different set of priorities where making money is less important than serving one another, where people are preferred over profit and where justice and mercy find common ground.

That sounds all well and good but who will build such a city? The answer is: you. I know you'd like the answer to be "Jesus" or "God" or really anyone but "you" but the answer unfortunately is you. Yes, Jesus did say that he was going away to make a place for us. That place will be truly marvellous and that perfect city will descend from heaven to earth at the end of time (Revelation 21:1-5). But Jesus told us to build a copy of that city here on earth to inspire faith and hope in a dying world. We are to take what we've learned about justice and love and, in the power of the Holy Spirit, we are to build a city—an alternative community that manifests those things before the eyes of the world. The city is supposed to be like an embassy of a coming kingdom. The Bible says it this way:

> But our citizenship is in heaven, and it is from there that we are expecting a Saviour, the Lord Jesus Christ. (Philippians 3:20, NRSV)

So then you are no longer strangers and aliens, but you are citizens with the saints and also **members of the household of God** (Ephesians 2:19, NRSV)

So we are ambassadors for Christ, since God is
making his appeal through us (2 Corinthians
5:20, NRSV)

We are citizens of a kingdom that is not yet fully present on
this earth but it is coming! We build an advance embassy here
based on all of the values and principles of that coming kingdom
and we serve as ambassadors of that kingdom to our surrounding world. That means, each and every one of us has two jobs:
we are civil servants and we are ambassadors at large.

Let's get one thing straight off the bat, because much confusion results if we are not clear on this first matter. Where does a
civil servant work? In his or her city. The Bible is absolutely
clear that your primary service is to be within the household of
God—within the church. The church is the embassy; the
household of God is our new primary association. That is why
James said:

> What good is it, my brothers and sisters, if you
> say you have faith but do not have works? Can
> faith save you? If a brother or sister is naked and
> lacks daily food, and one of you says to them,
> 'Go in peace; keep warm and eat your fill', and
> yet you do not supply their bodily needs, what is
> the good of that? (James 2:14-16, NRSV)

James is saying that it doesn't do you any good to say you
are a believer if you are not willing to make this embassy no-
ticeably better than the surrounding world. What good is that? If

poor people are just as poor inside our kingdom as they are inside the world's kingdom, why would people want to join us? James is saying that for the church to be effective, we need to serve our brothers and sisters. There is no question that he is talking about serving within the church. Jesus told us who our brothers and sisters were:

> A crowd was sitting around him; and they said to him, 'Your mother and your brothers and sisters are outside, asking for you.' And he replied, 'Who are my mother and my brothers?' And looking at those who sat around him, he said, 'Here are my mother and my brothers! Whoever does the will of God is my brother and sister and mother.' (Mark 3:32-35, NRSV)

When the members of a church band together to create an alternative community, amazing things happen! When widows are invited for lunch, when single moms are cared for and when children are raised corporately, the outside community notices! When the sick are visited, when the elderly are valued and cared for, when people lose their jobs but their mortgages are covered, when the rich live within their means in order to give to others, the outside world notices! If you are a new believer you have a job to do within your church. There are no free rides. Everyone can help, everyone can serve. The Bible says that the Holy Spirit gives every believer a service gift—an ability that will help you serve. Notice again where these gifts are to be deployed:

So with yourselves; since you are eager for spiritual gifts, strive to excel in them **for building up the church**. (1 Corinthians 14:12, NRSV)

When the church is a city on a hill, we will not need to have membership drives or hand out tracks door to door, I can promise you that. Jesus, just before he died, provided the disciples with an illustration of what sort of activity would make their mission prosper.

> Jesus, knowing that the Father had given all things into his hands, and that he had come from God and was going to God, got up from the table, took off his outer robe, and tied a towel around himself. Then he poured water into a basin and began to wash the disciples' feet and to wipe them with the towel that was tied around him. He came to Simon Peter, who said to him, 'Lord, are you going to wash my feet?' Jesus answered, 'You do not know now what I am doing, but later you will understand.' Peter said to him, 'You will never wash my feet.' Jesus answered, 'Unless I wash you, you have no share with me.' Simon Peter said to him, 'Lord, not my feet only but also my hands and my head!' Jesus said to him, 'One who has bathed does not need to wash, except for the feet, but is entirely clean. And you are clean, though not all of you.' For he knew who was to betray him; for this reason he said, 'Not all of you are clean.' After he had washed their feet, had put on his robe,

and had returned to the table, he said to them, 'Do you know what I have done to you? You call me Teacher and Lord—and you are right, for that is what I am. So if I, your Lord and Teacher, have washed your feet, you also ought to wash one another's feet. For I have set you an example, that you also should do as I have done to you. Very truly, I tell you, servants are not greater than their master, nor are messengers greater than the one who sent them. If you know these things, you are blessed if you do them. (John 13:3-17, NRSV)

Jesus told them to serve each other—not to run off and wash the feet of every poor person in town—he told them to serve **each other**. When the church is a place where even the rich and famous among us humble themselves to serve each other, the world will be knocking on our gates trying to get in. If you are a new believer, you need to be a part of that. You need to humble yourself and commit to a weekly act of service that blesses other people in your church. Coaching your kid's soccer team is great, but it doesn't count as Christian service. It is not in the church and it is not selfless—it benefits your kid. I'm not saying you shouldn't do it. I've coached soccer in the community for seven years and will keep doing it. But that's a different good thing. This is about building an alternative community that is different but near, wonderful yet strange, heavenly yet right here on earth. That is the call of the kingdom, and that is your call to serve.

Ten Good Reasons You Should Learn to Serve:

1. The Bible says so. (John 13:3-17) Do you really need nine more?
2. It will humble you, which is great news! God opposes the proud but gives grace to the humble.
3. It will build up your church and allow it to have a more effective witness in its community.
4. You may be the answer to a prayer that has been on someone's heart for years.
5. It takes a tribe to raise a child. You may be the role model, youth leader, Sunday School teacher or camp counsellor that changes a child's life forever!
6. The Bible says that people who don't take care of their elderly parents are worse than unbelievers. (1 Timothy 5:8) If we create an alternative community where our elderly are well-cared for, we will distinguish ourselves from the world!
7. It will make the church a refuge and a place of mercy.
8. It will allow the 20% of people at most churches who do all of the work to have a break and go on vacation for a week!
9. It will help you discover your spiritual gift.
10. You build the deepest friendships with the people you serve alongside of. One rarely hears a serving

person say, "I just don't feel connected at my church." Servers connect.

PERSONAL STUDY AND REFLECTION:

There is a very interesting story in the Acts of the Apostles about the church when it was growing like a weed. The story is found in Acts 6:1-7. Read that text now, then consider the comprehension task that follows.

Some of the language in that story is a bit foreign to us. What are "Hellenists" and why are they so hungry? Perhaps a little bit of background would be useful. Because of the preaching that went on in chapter 2-3, many new people had been added to the church. Some of them were Greek speaking Jews (Hellenists) and others were Hebrew or Aramaic speaking Jews. In Judaism, there was a bit of class prejudice against Jews that spoke Greek. This tried to carry over into the church before the Apostles put a stop to it. There are seven statements below that attempt to summarize the main teachings from the passage you just read. Five of them are correct and helpful and two are just plain ridiculous. See if you can sort them out. The correct answers are in a footnote on the next page.

1. The Apostles worked very hard to make sure that the church became a place where petty bigotry was not permitted. All people were to be treated equally.

2. The Apostles were wise enough to understand that the church was going to need a variety of servants. Some to labour in study, preaching and prayer, and others to wait on tables. No one person can do it all.
3. The Apostles were lazy and stuck up. They wanted to read books and pray all day rather than do any real work.
4. The church grew because it cared for its people in a way that the rest of the world didn't do. Widows were cared for and children too. This caused even some of the priests of Judaism to convert.
5. The church grew because it baited people with free food. People will say anything for free food.
6. Right from the start, the church has been about more than the message of salvation—it has been about building a just society where the poor are treated with dignity.
7. A growing church will usually be characterized by wise leadership, diversified service and a generous spirit.*

---

* The correct answers are: 1, 2, 4, 6, and 7.

QUESTIONS AND NOTES:

LEARN TO SERVE
FAQ

The following questions represent the most frequent concerns for new believers starting out in their journey as servants.

1. I want to serve, but I don't know what my calling is. What should I do about that?

ANSWER: The truth is, to answer that question you have to edit it. It's a bad question. I've been asked it many times but it's not a mature question. If my daughter asked me, "Daddy, when can I visit the man in the moon?", I would have some teaching to do on theology, cosmology, not to mention physics, before I could even approach that question. We would have to work through those things and then decide if her question was, "How can I travel to the moon?" or "Is there a man who lives in the moon who may be eager to make my acquaintance?" (Right now you are thinking how glad you are that you are not my daughter! ☺) The point is, a mature believer, which you are naturally interested in becoming, has a less individualistic approach to this issue. The mature believer understands that you are first and foremost called to Jesus, not to an activity. Secondly, you are called to become part of his body, the church:

> **Come to him**, a living stone, though rejected by mortals yet chosen and precious in God's sight, and like living stones, **let yourselves be built into a spiritual house**, to be a holy priesthood, to offer spiritual sacrifices acceptable to God through Jesus Christ. (1 Peter 2:4-5, NRSV)

Peter reminds us that we are all called first and foremost to Jesus, and secondarily, we are called to allow ourselves to be built into "a spiritual house" as "living stones" and become something bigger than ourselves. The real, mature question then is, "Where do I best fit within the people of God?"

The Apostle Paul reminded his people to think this way, saying:

> For **we** are what he has made **us**, created in Christ Jesus for good works, which God prepared beforehand to be **our** way of life. (Ephesians 2:10, NRSV)

We know that once we are connected to the body (the church), some differentiation is only natural—we won't all be good at the same sorts of activity. That's why it says in Romans 12:

> For as in one body we have many members, and not all the members have the same function, so we, who are many, are one body in Christ, and individually we are members one of another.

We have gifts that differ according to the grace
given to us… (Romans 12:4, NRSV)

If we are IN the body, then we are going to have a unique
function that relates to the overall purpose of the body. We are
going to have certain gifts, certain graces that will be given to us
and applied to us as paint to a stone. So how do we find that
out? How do we live faithful to our particular design? Let me
just give a few helpful guidelines:

First of all, do what you are. That flows so naturally out of
Ephesians 2:10, doesn't it? We are what he has made us, created
in Christ Jesus to do. Do what you are. Now, the trick here is, if
you do not know who you are in Christ, because you are not
properly connected to him in spiritual intimacy, this can be a
very devastating process. You will look into yourself and say,
"I'm not sure I'm much of anything. I don't really like how God
made me. I'm full of holes and full of cracks. My stone stinks." If
you are saying those things, then you are not ready for this step,
you need to go back to the beginning. You need to crawl up into
your Father's lap and say, "Daddy, who did you make me? Why
am I me? What is it that you love about me?" When you know
those things, come back here and do what you are.

Secondly, you need to "pass the ligament test." It always
amazes me when people come up and say that they feel
CALLED to do such and such a thing. We felt CALLED to leave
the church and start a splinter church. Really? You felt called to
knock down a wall in God's house and build a pile of rubble on

his kitchen floor? You felt CALLED to do that? That is the text-book definition of blasphemy, my friends. That is exactly what is meant by the third commandment which says, "Do not take the Lord's Name in vain." You take the LORD's Name in vain when you recruit God to your sinful ideas and plans. "God told me to go on Crusade and kill the Muslims," or a modern version, "God told me to invade Iraq to protect the flow of cheap oil," "God told me to leave my wife" or "God told me to split the church." That is dangerous talk and it fails the ligament test: **Who you are as an individual has to be related back in a healthy way to who we are as a tribe.** God is not going to call you to do something that hurts us. Using the ligament test in a positive way, look at what God is doing in your tribe and ask, "What is my role in that?" That is a great way to discover your particular call.

Thirdly, talk to the other stones. If you are wondering about the sense of design that you see emerging within yourself, talk to the other stones in your wall. If you think God is calling you to something, ask around and see if that is emerging in other people or ask how they react to that. Have you ever played those sliding puzzle games? We use to drive to Florida when I was a kid (before Gameboy and DS) so I used to have a couple of puzzle boards. You have to slide pieces up and over so that eventually you could get all of the pieces to align into an obvious design. Do you remember these? Well, you knew you still had work to do if the design on piece A was completely out of alignment with the design on piece B and piece C. You knew you had it figured out when all the pieces were in alignment with their neighbours. So it is with us. The first stone you should bounce your sense of call off is the stone right beside you—your spouse or your best Christian friend. Talk it over. He or she knows you and will know whether this is of God or of you; whether this is the prophetic prompting of the Lord or just bad pizza. Then bounce it wider. Hit the stones in your small group, your squash buddies, the people you serve with and the people God appointed as leaders over you. Check it out with the people who are following you too. Check it out with your kids or the people who serve under you in your ministry. Talk to the stones and your design will become clear.

2. I don't think I have a spiritual gift. Can I still serve?

ANSWER: I will often have people tell me that they don't have a spiritual gift, what they really mean is that they are not gifted at preaching, evangelism, teaching or worship leading, i.e., "the glory gifts". This mindset reflects some immature theology. The Bible says:

> Now there are varieties of gifts, but the same Spirit; and there are varieties of services, but the same Lord; and there are varieties of activities, but it is the same God who activates all of them in everyone. **To each is given the manifestation of the Spirit for the common good.** To

one is given through the Spirit the utterance of wisdom, and to another the utterance of knowledge according to the same Spirit, to another faith by the same Spirit, to another gifts of healing by the one Spirit, to another the working of miracles, to another prophecy, to another the discernment of spirits, to another various kinds of tongues, to another the interpretation of tongues. All these are activated by one and the same Spirit, who allots to each one individually just as the Spirit chooses.

For just as the body is one and has many members, and all the members of the body, though many, are one body, so it is with Christ. For in the one Spirit we were all baptized into one body—Jews or Greeks, slaves or free—and we were all made to drink of one Spirit.

Indeed, the body does not consist of one member but of many. If the foot were to say, 'Because I am not a hand, I do not belong to the body', that would not make it any less a part of the body. And if the ear were to say, 'Because I am not an eye, I do not belong to the body', that would not make it any less a part of the body. If the whole body were an eye, where would the hearing be? If the whole body were hearing, where would the sense of smell be? But as it is, **God arranged the members in the body, each one of them, as he chose**. If all were a single member, where would the body be? As it is, there are many members, yet one body. The eye cannot say to the hand, 'I have no need of you', nor again the head to the feet, 'I have no need of you.' **On the contrary, the members of the body that seem to be weaker are indispensable**, and those members of the body that we think less honourable we clothe with greater honour, and our less respectable members are treated with greater respect; whereas our more respectable members do not need this. But God has so arranged the body, giving the greater honour to the inferior member, that there may be no dissension within the body, but the members may have the same care for one another. If one member suffers, all suffer together with it; if one member is honoured, all rejoice together with it. (1 Corinthians 12:4-26, NRSV)

This passage was given by the Apostle Paul so that the church would not be uninformed about spiritual gifts. (1 Corinthians 12:1) It tells us three very important things. First of all, it suggests that each person is given a spiritual gift for the common good. This means that every believer should have a spiritual gift that is of use for the building up of their church. Secondly, it suggests that the church will operate within a dynamic tension of unity and diversity. We should not have "hand churches" or "eye churches" or "foot churches"; we should have "body" churches where a wide diversity of spiritual gifts are present. Third, it implies that the normal, human way of valuing things will not help us when it comes to evaluating spiritual gifts. If we asked NBC to come and evaluate who matters in church, I'm sure they would say, "The Lead Pastor is most important, fol-

lowed by the Worship Pastor and then the Children's Pastor."
But we don't really care about NBC's opinion do we? And we
need to be careful to be less influenced by the way they would
think. The Bible says that our human instincts will lead us astray
in assessing the value of the gifts so we need to have spiritual
understanding here. Spiritual understanding leads us to con-
clude that everything God puts in a body has an important role
and must be present for proper functioning.

A helpful analogy would be the case of the human appendix.
Back in the 1970's, it was routine for doctors to remove the appendix (and the tonsils) during any stomach surgery as it was
considered "evolutionary junk." The human body no longer required it and so it was best to remove it. Recently, however, scientists have discovered that the appendix, not to mention the
tonsils, have an important role to play in terms of the human
immune system and they should not be removed unless they are
not functioning correctly. Our human instincts (not to mention
human arrogance) can lead us to undervalue something that
actually plays a very necessary role. So it is with people and their
gifts. You have an important gift that your church needs in order
to function properly. Whether people always understand that or
not does not really matter. God does not make mistakes when
he designs a body.

3. *I don't have the gift of evangelism, do I still have to share my faith? Likewise, I do not have the gift of giving, do I still have to tithe?*

ANSWER: The best definition of a spiritual gift I've ever heard is this: a spiritual gift is a talent God gives you to use and an area of ministry God promises to bless in your life. Logically then, there are areas of ministry where one will excel, by the grace of God, beyond another, but that says nothing about whether such ministries are optional or required. Sometimes God will choose to use your plodding faithfulness and other times he will use your gifted brilliance. Either way, you must be obedient. All believers are called to share their faith, not just those that are particularly used in evangelism. The Great Commission is given to all disciples:

> Go therefore and make disciples of all nations, baptizing them in the name of the Father and of the Son and of the Holy Spirit, and teaching them to obey everything that I have commanded you. And remember, I am with you always, to the end of the age.' (Matthew 28:19-20, NRSV)

The Apostle Peter likewise told all of his sheep:

> Always be ready to make your defence to anyone who demands from you an account of the hope that is in you; yet do it with gentleness and reverence. (1 Peter 3:15-16, NRSV)

The same principle could be applied to tithing, teaching or showing compassion. These are all things that every Christian is commanded to do, but some believers will see a divine overlap that is manifested in supernatural fruit and effectiveness. Obedient faithfulness is just as important as empowered fruitfulness.

600-700 M
Grow in Giving

I f it has been a while since you did the material covering the 500-600 metre stretch of the road, go back and review the Personal Study and Reflection portion. The story there about the explosive growth of the church is an interesting one. Not only does it reflect the importance of wise leadership, a variety of service types and the attractiveness of justice and equality, it also implies that the church had access to a lot of money. Think about it; how did a bunch of simple people come to possess the capacity to feed widows and orphans from all walks of life? Jesus' disciples were not wealthy men. Other than Matthew and perhaps John, it does not appear that the disciples were rich or important, so how did they come to manage such resources? That story is in Acts 4:

Now the whole group of those who believed were of one heart and soul, and no one claimed private ownership of any possessions, but everything they owned was held in common. With great power the apostles gave their testimony to the resurrection of the Lord Jesus, and great grace was upon them all. There was not a needy person among them, for as many as owned lands or houses sold them and brought the proceeds of what was sold. They laid it at the apostles' feet, and it was distributed to each as any had need. There was a Levite, a native of Cyprus, Joseph, to whom the apostles gave the name Barnabas (which means 'son of encouragement'). He sold a field that belonged to him, then brought the money, and laid it at the apostles' feet. (NRSV)

It is amazing how far the resources can go when everybody contributes generously! People sold their things in order to contribute. The generosity of the early church was legendary. For the first fifty years of Christian history, the majority of Christians were Jews. They were Jewish people who believed that Jesus was the Son of God and Messiah. These Jews continued to pay their Jewish taxes. There were three tithes in Judaism, two that were collected each year (one for the temple and one for the priesthood) and a third that was collected every other year for the poor. Jesus did not advocate pulling out of the Jewish taxation system once a person became a believer. There is an important story in Matthew that states this very thing:

> When they reached Capernaum, the collectors
> of the temple tax came to Peter and said, 'Does
> your teacher not pay the temple tax?' He said,
> 'Yes, he does.' And when he came home, Jesus
> spoke of it first, asking, 'What do you think,
> Simon? From whom do kings of the earth take
> toll or tribute? From their children or from oth-
> ers?' When Peter said, 'From others', Jesus said
> to him, 'Then the children are free. However, so
> that we do not give offence to them, go to the
> lake and cast a hook; take the first fish that
> comes up; and when you open its mouth, you
> will find a coin; take that and give it to them for
> you and me.' (Matthew 17:24-27, NRSV)

Jesus was saying to Peter that taxes go from citizen to king
and that as the real king of the world Jesus did not need to pay
the tax, he should rather be receiving it, **nevertheless**, he paid
for himself and for Peter. So Jewish Christians paid their Jewish
dues and they also had to pay the Romans. The Romans im-
posed taxes on all subject people, usually at a rate of about 25%.
Historians estimate that between the Jewish taxes and the Roman taxes, a first century Jew had to pay over 55% of their income in taxes. That is why the early Christians had to sell their
homes and possessions in order to give to the church, yet they
did it gladly.

There is much silly argument in the church today about how
much Christians should give to the church. Anytime the point of
the conversation is establishing a minimum standard you know

you are having a stupid argument. Christians should not be asking: 'How little can I give before it's a sin?' They should be asking: 'How much can I give before I starve to death?' Some Christians claim that the tithe does not apply in the New Testament era. They claim it was part of the law that expired when the Holy Spirit took up residence in the human heart. That's hard to figure out since Jesus said:

> 'Do not think that I have come to abolish the
> law or the prophets; I have come not to abolish
> but to fulfil. For truly I tell you, until heaven and
> earth pass away, not one letter, not one stroke of
> a letter, will pass from the law until all is accom-
> plished. (Matthew 5:17-18, NRSV)

It is also odd because the tithe precedes the law—it began long before Moses gave the law. Abraham tithed and so did Jacob and that was many generations before Moses gave the law. It is true that the ceremonial law passed away when the body of Christ replaced the temple but it was surpassed, not abolished. The author of the Letter to the Hebrews makes the point that whatever was due the temple and whatever was due the Jewish priesthood is now even more so due to Christ—the new temple and the superior priesthood. (Hebrews 7) So the Jews paid about 25-30% of their income (their tithes) to the temple and the priesthood, does that mean that Christians should give 25-30% of their income to Jesus and the church? The truth is, it is a bit complicated. The first century Jews gave to a temple and a priesthood that did many things that are now done by governments. Are we to not give to the government in order to support our churches? No. The Bible says:

> Pay to all what is due to them—taxes to whom taxes are due, revenue to whom revenue is due, respect to whom respect is due, honour to whom honour is due. (Romans 13:7, NRSV)

So we have to pay our taxes but we also have to pay taxes into the alternative community that we are building. How does it all work? This is a situation where you should submit to the teaching and standard of your church leadership. In our church we expect all of our members to give above 10% of their gross income to the church. We refer to this as 'the historic minimum'. People are free to give more if they are able and many do. People are free to also support outside charities also, like the Heart and Stroke Foundation, The Cancer Society or the Gideons. But that cannot be deducted from the 10% they give to the church. Notice that in the story we read about the gifts of the early church, they were laid 'at the Apostles' feet'. This means the people trusted the church leadership to distribute the money as they saw fit. They didn't pick and choose projects and seek to lead through their givings. In the book of Malachi it says:

> Bring the full **tithe into the storehouse**, so that there may be **food in my house** (Malachi 3:10, NRSV)

The church is the household of God (Ephesians 2:19) and we all like living stones are being built into a spiritual house (1 Peter 2:4-5) and that house has a lot of work to do and a lot of mouths to feed and so it must be resourced.

As to the specific requirements, your church may have slightly different standards, find out what they are and submit to them. Jesus gave the church authority to bind and loose (Matthew 16:19) which means the authority to apply the principals of the Word to new situations. Our present situation is different than the early church but the difference is much in our favour! They paid 25-30% to the Jews, 25% to the Romans and still gave generously to the church, many even selling their homes to do so! It should be much easier for us today to give to the Lord with liberality and cheerfulness.

TEN GOOD REASONS YOU SHOULD GROW IN GIVING:

1. The Bible says so. (Malachi 3:10) Do you really need nine more?
2. It will wean you off your dependence on "stuff."
3. It will make you a more active participant in your church. People pay attention more when it is their money being spent.
4. It will teach you to trust leadership. That "lay it at the Apostles' feet" part is the hardest thing of all!

5. It will allow the church to feed the poor, the physical and spiritual bread of life.
6. Since giving is an essential characteristic of God, it is actually an act of imitation and worship.
7. Giving reminds us that we actually don't own anything. We just use some resources that are entrusted to us for a season.
8. Giving reminds us that people are more important than things.
9. Giving will confuse our neighbours and create witnessing conversations.
10. Giving is the most counter-cultural act possible at this present time. How better to become salt and light?

PERSONAL STUDY AND REFLECTION:

The Bible talks a lot about money. We sometimes act as though talking about money is dirty or "unspiritual" but that is not the case. Read the three passages about money listed below and then consider the comprehension task that follows.

- Malachi 3:7-12
- Matthew 19:16-30
- 1 Timothy 5:17-18

Consider the seven statements below. Five of them correctly summarise the teaching in the above passages—two do not. See if you can sort them out. The correct answers are in a footnote on the next page.

1. Sometimes God uses money as a test of our faith. If we really believe the promises of the Bible we would give our stuff away and live full out for Jesus!

2. When we rob God of the money he should be receiving for the kingdom, we rob ourselves of the blessings of the kingdom.

3. God allows us to test him on the matter of faithful giving. He invites us to give generously and obediently and to see if we find him untrustworthy.

4. Pastors and elders should not receive a salary—they should work for a living like everyone else.

5. Leaders in the church should be paid appropriately—there is nothing wrong with receiving your living from the kingdom.

6. You have to give away all of your possessions to be saved.

7. Refusal to part with your beloved possessions when asked by the Lord to do so reveals that you are not saved.[*]

---

[*] The correct answers are 1, 2, 3, 5, and 7.

QUESTIONS AND NOTES:

FAQ

The following questions represent the most frequent concerns for new believers starting out in their journey as givers.

1. I give about 5% of my income to my church and then another 5% to other Christian charities. That counts as tithing right?

SHORT ANSWER: No. This was covered in the material above but I am asked it so frequently that it should be covered in some detail. The concept of tithing is part of the covenant of promise, it precedes the giving of the Law to Moses and as such has some very ancient roots and base meanings. While we do not have time to go into all of the Old Testament background, it is fair to say that the tithe was a pledge of faith, indicating belief in the coming kingdom. You wouldn't pay taxes into a kingdom you didn't believe would ever be realised would you? The Bible says that this is part of what made Abraham so remarkable:

> For he looked forward to the city that has foundations, whose architect and builder is God. (Hebrews 11:10, NRSV)

Tithing is also a gesture of worship and trust in the God who provides. It is a way of saying: 'I need this but I want to recognise it as from God and I want to communicate my basic trust in God to replace it and meet my needs'. Lastly it is a symbol of submission to authority. Jesus made this point (in the New Testament by the way) when dealing with a question about whether he paid the temple tithe.

> When they reached Capernaum, the collectors of the temple tax came to Peter and said, 'Does your teacher not pay the temple tax?' He said, 'Yes, he does.' And when he came home, Jesus spoke of it first, asking, 'What do you think, Simon? From whom do kings of the earth take toll or tribute? From their children or from others?' When Peter said, 'From others', Jesus said to him, 'Then the children are free. However, so that we do not give offence to them, go to the lake and cast a hook; take the first fish that comes up; and when you open its mouth, you will find a coin; take that and give it to them for you and me.' (Matthew 17:24-27, NRSV)

Taxes are given by subjects to leaders as symbol of submission and obedience to their authority. Ultimately this authority comes from God who establishes structure and leadership for his own purposes:

> Let every person be subject to the governing authorities; for there is no authority except from God, and those authorities that exist have been instituted by God. Therefore whoever resists

authority resists what God has appointed, and those who resist will incur judgement. For rulers are not a terror to good conduct, but to bad. Do you wish to have no fear of the authority? Then do what is good, and you will receive its approval; for it is God's servant for your good. But if you do what is wrong, you should be afraid, for the authority does not bear the sword in vain! It is the servant of God to execute wrath on the wrongdoer. Therefore one must be subject, not only because of wrath but also because of conscience. For the same reason you also pay taxes, for the authorities are God's servants, busy with this very thing. Pay to all what is due to them—taxes to whom taxes are due, revenue to whom revenue is due, respect to whom respect is due, honour to whom honour is due. (Romans 13:1-7, NRSV)

This basic mindset is reflected in the way giving is described in the New Testament:

Now the whole group of those who believed were of one heart and soul, and no one claimed private ownership of any possessions, but everything they owned was held in common. With great power the apostles gave their testimony to the resurrection of the Lord Jesus, and great grace was upon them all. There was not a needy person among them, for as many as owned lands or houses sold them and brought the proceeds of what was sold. **They laid it at the**

161

apostles' feet, and it was distributed to each as any had need. There was a Levite, a native of Cyprus, Joseph, to whom the apostles gave the name Barnabas (which means 'son of encouragement'). He sold a field that belonged to him, then brought the money, and **laid it at the apostles' feet**. (Acts 4:32-37, NRSV)

This "laying it at the Apostles' feet" was a gesture of submission to authority. They recognised that the leadership of the church was given an authority by God and that the surrendering of tithes to them was an act and token of submission. They had to then trust the leaders to make good decisions with that money which the following chapter reveals that they did. They used the funds to begin a large scale food outreach that met the needs of many poor in Jerusalem.

The point is, when we "split our tithes" between a variety of Christian charities that strike our fancy we are acting in arrogance. We are saying, whether we mean to our not, "I'm not sure I trust the leaders of my church to make good decisions. I think I can manage this money for the kingdom more effectively then they can." In this time of culture money becomes a club we use to beat our leaders into taking action we agree with. A pastor in our town was recently fired by his board because some core givers began giving directly to missions as a protest against his leadership. This happens all the time and is an abomination and a great blemish on the bride of Christ. I often tell people that they are free to scrutinise our budget, they are free to speak into it, they are free to critique our faithfulness as leaders to it, but if they can't vote for it and if they can't tithe into it, than they in good conscience should seek another church whose priorities they support. Tithing is worship, it is trust and it is submission. If you change how its done, the spiritual communication is garbled and lost.

2. I thought the Biblical principle for tithing was 'give as the Lord lays on your heart'? That's what it says on my offering envelope. What gives?

ANSWER: This common confusion comes from a passage in the Bible dealing with what scholars call "The Jerusalem Collection." The text is from 1 Corinthians 9:1-15:

> Now it is not necessary for me to write you about the ministry to the saints, for I know your eagerness, which is the subject of my boasting about you to the people of Macedonia, saying that Achaia has been ready since last year; and your zeal has stirred up most of them. But I am sending the brothers in order that our boasting about you may not prove to have been empty in this case, so that you may be ready, as I said you would be; otherwise, if some Macedonians come with me and find that you are not ready, we would be humiliated—to say nothing of you—in this undertaking. So I thought it neces-

sary to urge the brothers to go on ahead to you, and arrange in advance for this **bountiful gift that you have promised**, so that it may be ready as **a voluntary gift** and not as an extortion. The point is this: the one who sows sparingly will also reap sparingly, and the one who sows bountifully will also reap bountifully. **Each of you must give as you have made up your mind, not reluctantly or under compulsion, for God loves a cheerful giver.** And God is able to provide you with every blessing in abundance, so that by always having enough of everything, you may share abundantly in every good work. As it is written,

"He scatters abroad, he gives to the poor; his righteousness endures forever." He who supplies seed to the sower and bread for food will supply and multiply your seed for sowing and increase the harvest of your righteousness. You will be enriched in every way for your great generosity, which will produce thanksgiving to God through us; for the rendering of this ministry not only supplies the needs of the saints but also overflows with many thanksgivings to God. Through the testing of this ministry you glorify God by your obedience to the confession of the gospel of Christ and by the generosity of your sharing with them and with all others, while they long for you and pray for you because of the surpassing grace of God that he has given you. Thanks be to God for his indescribable gift! (NRSV)

Historians and Biblical scholars talk a lot about "The Jerusalem Collection." Paul did most of his church planting work out in the wider Roman world among Greek- speaking Jews and their Gentile friends and neighbours. As a result of this, some of the more orthodox Jewish Christians, who spoke Hebrew or Aramaic and who lived in the Promised Land, looked at these Christians as a kind of "half-breed." These Gentile believers still struggled with sexuality, diet, language, etc. In modern day terms, this is how suburbanite Christians feel about inner city converts. They swear in their baptismal testimonies, they take a break from worship to smoke a cigarette and they seem to go through an awful lot of boyfriends before they finally get married. You know what I'm saying? So Paul comes up with this idea of a love offering. These new and raw converts may have been developmentally weak but they were materially wealthy and there was a famine in Jerusalem. So Paul gets the idea that if all of these Gentile half-breeds would make a generous offering to the Jewish Christians in Jerusalem, it might go a long way towards settling the waters and building bridges between the two groups. Now, the Corinthians had originally been very enthusiastic about the project, but then Paul got angry with some of them about their sexual practices (see 1 Corinthians 5) and there was a brief falling out. They felt that Paul was too harsh, not very gracious and they hadn't expected that he would be so serious about sin. He started practising church discipline and everyone just about had a heart attack. Once they realized that this was part of the deal in becoming a Christian, they reconciled with Paul and now the Apostle reminds them about their pledge to the Jerusalem Collection. Does that make sense? This collection was not a tithe, it did not go to their local church, nor did it go to the temple in Jerusalem. It was a free-will offering, a gift that was given freely, though quite strategically.

Failure to understand the context of this teaching in Scripture has led to all sorts of confusion. I hear people say from time to time, "I give as the Lord prospers." Meaning, if I have a good month, I give; if I have a bad month, I don't. The trick to sorting this out is to understand the difference between a tithe and a free will offering.

First of all, in the Bible, a tithe is likened to tribute (a tax), whereas offerings are likened to gifts. Again, the passage in Matthew 17 helps us here:

> When they reached Capernaum, the collectors of the temple tax came to Peter and said, "Does your teacher not pay the temple tax?" He said, "Yes, he does." And when he came home, Jesus spoke of it first, asking, "What do you think, Simon? From whom do kings of the earth take toll or tribute? From their children or from others?" When Peter said, "From others," Jesus said to him, "Then the children are free. However, so that we do not give offense to them, go to the sea and cast a hook; take the first fish that comes up; and when you open its mouth, you will find a coin; take that and give it to them for you and me." (Matthew 17:24-27, NRSV)

In this story, the temple tax or as the Jews called it, "The Second Tithe," was compared by Jesus to a King collecting tribute (tax) from his subjects. Tribute is not a gift. Taxes are not a gift. You do not pen a little note on your tax submission saying, "Dear Mr. Revenue Canada, please enjoy this little gift from mom and I. If you are a good boy, you will get another gift like this next year." Tribute is required. Revenue Canada does not send you a thank you note for your tax submission. It is not a gift. But offerings are a gift. Look at 2 Corinthians 9:5:

> So I thought it necessary to urge the brothers to go on ahead to you, and arrange in advance for this bountiful **gift** that you have promised, so that it may be ready as **a voluntary gift** and not as an extortion. (NRSV)

Offerings are not mandatory. You don't have to give them. They are gifts. They are voluntary. Tithes are tribute; they are expressions of allegiance and they are obligatory. Now tithes are obligatory in a unique sense in the kingdom of God because citizenship is voluntary. You don't have to be a citizen in the kingdom of God. You are free to live your entire life as a king unto yourself and most do. But if you want to have Jesus as your Lord and King then he is DUE tribute. You don't get a thank you note from Jesus for doing what you are supposed to do. Jesus himself said that:

> Do you thank the slave for doing what was
> commanded? So you also, when you have done
> all that you were ordered to do, say, "We are
> worthless slaves; we have done only what we
> ought to have done!' " (Luke 17:9-10, NRSV)

There is so much in the Bible that surprises us, isn't there? When was the last time you heard a sermon preached on that verse! Anyway, the point is simply this: tithes are mandatory for citizens of the kingdom, offerings are not. They are given, or not given, at the discretion of the giver.

Secondly, it is important to notice that tithes are released while offerings are targeted. The Bible speaks about the hand-off of these monetary payments in an entirely different language. Look at the language of hand-off for tithes that we've seen now a few times:

> There was not a needy person among them, for
> as many as owned lands or houses sold them
> and brought the proceeds of what was sold.
> **They laid it at the apostles' feet, and it was
> distributed** to each as any had need. There was
> a Levite... Barnabas... He sold a field that be-
> longed to him, then brought the money, and
> **laid it at the apostles' feet**. (Acts 4:34-37,
> NRSV)

Notice again that phrase:

They laid it at the apostles' feet, and it was distributed… (NRSV)

Twice we see that—"they laid it at the apostles' feet." Tithes are released. Offerings are spoken of in an entirely different way. We've already seen how Paul spoke of the Corinthians handing their gift over voluntarily and not under extortion. When he mentions the Jerusalem Collection in his letter to the Romans, he speaks of it in a similar way:

> For Macedonia and Achaia **have been pleased to share** their resources with the poor among the saints at Jerusalem. **They were pleased to do this**, and indeed they owe it to them; for if the Gentiles have come to share in their spiritual blessings, they ought also to be of service to them in material things. (Romans 15:26-28, NRSV)

They gave this offering because they wanted to. It made sense to them. It appealed to their understanding that salvation has come to them through the Jews. Therefore, it was an opportunity to bless Jewish Christians made sense and struck their fancy. This is a totally different spirit than the one applied to tithes. The verses we looked at in regard to tithing did not appear to be much interested in our fancies and inclinations. Collect this and that, take here and there and apply it such and such. Tithes and offerings are different. Tithes are obligatory and released; they indicate submission to the Lordship of Jesus as the

High Priest and King of Righteousness. Offerings are voluntary and targeted, and may reflect our own interests and passions.

3. *I'd like to be a "how much more" kind of person. After I tithe, I would like to sow generously into kingdom projects that will bless the Lord. How best should I do that?*

ANSWER: The first principle flows out of the material we've just discussed: keep tithes and offerings separate. Playing chess is wonderful, playing checkers is wonderful, sitting down at a game board when one person thinks we're playing chess and another checkers is quite tortuous. We need to keep these things separate. The church has been trying to help people with this for a long time. We even developed a proverbial saying for it, "Don't rob Peter to pay Paul." Peter was the head of the church; he was the first Bishop of Rome. He was the one to whom tithes were due. Paul was a missionary and a church planter. Do not rob Peter to pay Paul. Do not rob the church to pay the missionary. Regardless of how long we've been teaching on it, many Christians still do it. If they get mad at Peter, they write Paul a big cheque. "I don't support my church's decision to do such and such, so I'm sending my tithe to that missionary fellow who seems much nicer than Peter." Missionaries always seem nicer than Peter. Do you know why? **Because missionaries live far away**. You can't do it. You can only make an OFFERING AFTER YOU HAVE TITHED. Now of course, you can still write cheques and send them wherever you like but you have ceased to be a citizen and you are now a benefactor. What do we call someone who from another country who writes a cheque to a museum or a hospital? A benefactor. You and I pay for hospitals and museums out of our TAXES. After you and I pay taxes, we can still donate to the hospital, correct? But we are not required to. We would then be citizen donors. The goal is to be citizen donors in the kingdom, but there are many people who are foreign benefactors. Do not rob Peter to pay Paul—keep your tithes and your offerings separate.

Secondly, keep God's priorities in mind. A careful study of the Scriptures reveals that tithes were to be spent on three things: the priestly ministry, the house of God and the poor. These things were understood as the priorities of God and therefore the priorities for the use of God's money. It is interesting to note that those who gave offerings in the early church took note of these priorities. Scholars are unanimous that the Jerusalem Collection had two priorities:

- To care for the poor Jewish Christians in Jerusalem.
- To build bridges between the Jewish and Gentile wings of the church.

What concerns lay behind the offering? A concern for the poor and a concern for the church. So if you want God to bless your offering, give according to his priorities. Practically speaking, I think that means a donation to World Vision, Feed The

Children or a church planter in India is more likely to be blessed than a donation to the local museum or fire hall. Both are fine but one reflects the heart of God more than the other.

It is also important to select high-yield investments. Look at what Paul says to the Philippians:

> You Philippians indeed know that in the early days of the gospel, when I left Macedonia, no church shared with me in the matter of giving and receiving, except you alone. For even when I was in Thessalonica, you sent me help for my needs more than once. Not that I seek the gift, but **I seek the profit** that accumulates to your account. (Philippians 4:15-17, NRSV)

Paul says, "I didn't need your money—I was more than happy to do this work in poverty and scarcity, but I was very eager for the dramatic increase in fruit that your gift enabled. This increase is now reckoned to your account." Paul is speaking like a businessman here. He is saying that at his initial level of operating, he was generating a profit but it was a small scale operation. Paul was the founder and principal share-holder. To take it to the next level, he required an infusion of cash which the Philippians provided. As the owner/operator, Paul didn't mind the old system—how many small businessmen do you know who don't mind being small businessmen? Lots! Payroll is hard, HR is hard, administration is hard and all of that comes along with the move from small business to bigger business. While Paul was not eager for the extra hassles, he was eager for the extra fruit. With this infusion of cash, the operation went large scale and production was multiplied. The multiplied profit, he says, is applied to their account. Paul congratulates them for making a shrewd investment.

Now some of us bleeding heart Canadian Christians struggle with this. Shouldn't we just give without any concern for performance? Isn't that a worldly form of measurement? Do you invest in a stock without considering its return? Where did we get the idea that to be a Christian meant becoming stupid and lazy in our thinking? Jesus told a story once about a fairly ruthless and shrewd business manager and then said this:

> "And his master praised the unrighteous manager because he had acted shrewdly; for the sons of this age are more shrewd in relation to their own kind than the sons of light. (Luke 16:18, NRSV)

Jesus says, "Why can you not be more like this shrewd and cunning businessman? His morality was questionable, yes. Do not imitate that, but do imitate his wisdom and his shrewdness." Another verse we don't preach on that often. Jesus wants us to be SHREWD in our investments. Paul considered his church planting mission to be a very shrewd investment and he commended them on seizing that opportunity.

When you write your offering cheques think carefully about the yield of the particular opportunity. Be wise, be shrewd. Say "no" to some low-yield opportunities—you don't have to give money to everyone who knocks on your door. Save up for a good investment in a high-yield opportunity.

It is also wise to invest generously (and cheerfully) in a few things rather than spreading your seed too thinly. Make large investments in people and projects you believe in. Paul says to the Corinthians:

> He who sows bountifully will also reap bountifully. (2 Corinthians 9:6, NRSV)

In plain English, he says, "You'll get way better returns on this investment if you buy in BIG." Boy, I wish we took this principle seriously. So much kingdom energy is wasted by missionaries travelling around talking to every penny stockholder on the planet earth. They come home and have to speak to the Sewing Circle or the Mission's Committee at seventy-four different churches, all of whom send them $100 per month. It takes them an entire year to see every body and a month to write thank-you notes. Why churches would rather support 10 missionaries for $2000 per year rather than one for $20 000 per year, I can never figure out. If it's a high-yield opportunity, go in large. If its not, say no thank you. Sow generously into the things you believe in.

Sow cheerfully as well because, after all, you are accumulating profit. Paul says that in no uncertain terms:

I seek for the **profit which increases to your account**. (Philippians 4:17, NRSV)

Their investment in Paul's international church planting mission created INCREASE in THEIR ACCOUNT, not Paul's. Whatever increase in production can be traced to their investment is credited to THEIR ACCOUNT. So be cheerful about this because you are accumulating benefit. Don't treat your missionaries or whoever you are investing in like servants, they are account managers making increase for you.

You may also find that you will have to trust God for the seed to sow. Some of you may have skipped this section because you think this is a message for the high rollers. "Only the well-off can give over 10% of their income to the church and then still have money left over to give to missions or to other charities." Not so. First of all, this is all percentage based so it is just as hard for the rich to give 10% of their much as it is for you to give 10% of your little. Second of all, Paul tells us, trust God for the seed. He says,

> He who supplies seed to the sower and bread for food **will supply and multiply your seed** for sowing and increase the harvest of your righteousness. (2 Corinthians 9:10, NRSV)

God wants everyone to be able to play this fun game, whether you have little or much. So sit down, consider your opportunities and pray over their potential yield. When you find one you feel led to invest in, that you believe will yield a return for the kingdom, put your hand into your seed bag and ask the Lord to provide. Try it! Pick a mission project or an organization like Feed The Children or a foreign church planter or something, pray over it and then ask God to provide you with $100 a month to sow into that person or project. God will provide it - **if** you are already tithing and if you have chosen a project that reflects his kingdom priorities. Try it. Test the Lord on this and then give testimony to others.

It is also very important to honour what commitments you make. Paul was eager for the Corinthian church to honour the commitment they had previously made to this project. God doesn't like it when we say we'll invest in something and then we don't. That's why Paul says:

> But I am sending the brothers in order that our boasting about you may not prove to have been empty in this case, so that you may be ready, as I said you would be; otherwise, if some Macedonians come with me and find that you are not ready, we would be humiliated—to say nothing of you—in this undertaking. (NRSV)

Paul says, "I'm going to send some associates on ahead of me to remind you of your commitment and to help get you organized so that you can fulfil it because you would be greatly ashamed if you were not able to follow through on your commitment." There is wisdom in that, isn't there? Sometimes in the church we may need to coach people so that they can make reasonable commitments and follow through on them. Paul offered that help in his day and we may need to do it also in ours. Follow-through is important.

Lastly, expect a return. I already showed you the verse where Jesus criticises some very nice Christian people for being less shrewd and cunning than their pagan peers. Returns MATTER. Some churches operate as though they've never even heard of the word "return." They support the same missionaries year after year after year after year, simply because they are related to so and so. That's not very shrewd. Ask for reports. Demand an accounting of fruit. If there is no fruit, or not sufficient fruit, take your investment elsewhere. Is this a Christian thing to do? It's a Jesus thing to do. Jesus said:

> You ought to have invested my money with the bankers, and on my return I would have received what was my own **with interest**. So take the talent from him, and give it to the one with the ten talents. For to all those who have, more will be given, and they will have an abundance; but from those who have nothing, even what they have will be taken away. (Matthew 25:27-29, NRSV)

Jesus said that! Someone ought to write a book called: "All Of The Verses We Never Knew Were In The Bible." Jesus said that if you didn't generate a return, then what was invested in you would be taken away and given to a higher yielding person. That is why we did a Missions Audit a few years ago in our church, because we should EXPECT A RETURN on the projects and people we invest in. If we don't see it, we should invest elsewhere. Likewise in your personal offerings, if you don't see a return, invest somewhere else.

700-800 M
Submit to Authority

A ssuming that you are going to a good church, regularly reading and studying the Bible and beginning to open a dialogue with God through prayer (0-300 m), you've probably begun to notice that Christianity is wildly different from the rest of contemporary culture. You can miss this fact entirely if you go to a church that doesn't teach the Bible or encourage you to do so. You can miss this if you talk to other people about God rather than talking to God himself. But if you are actually interacting with the TRUTH of God, you will be noticing that Christianity puts you at odds with the modern world. The Bible warns that this will be the case:

"If the world hates you, be aware that it hated me before it hated you. If you belonged to the world, the world would love you as its own. Because you do not belong to the world, but I have chosen you out of the world—therefore the world hates you. (John 15:18-19, NRSV)

Following Jesus pretty much guarantees that we will be out of step with the world. When Christians work hard to make Christianity seem just like the world they are missing the point entirely. The Bible says:

Do not love the world or the things in the world. The love of the Father is not in those who love the world; (1 John 2:15, NRSV)

Do you not know that friendship with the world is enmity with God? Therefore whoever wishes to be a friend of the world becomes an enemy of God. (James 4:4, NRSV)

Christianity is counter cultural, as we already discussed, and that means that it is pretty much opposed to everything that passes for wisdom in this present world. Nowhere is that more apparent than when we begin to talk about authority. Our world glorifies the rebel. Anyone who has ever thumbed his nose at the police, caught a politician in a mistake or "bucked the system" is lifted up as a hero in our world. "Stick it to the man" is the cry of our times. But Christianity takes a different view:

Let every person be subject to the governing authorities; for there is no authority except from God, and those authorities that exist have been instituted by God. Therefore whoever resists authority resists what God has appointed, and those who resist will incur judgement. For rulers are not a terror to good conduct, but to bad. Do you wish to have no fear of the authority? Then do what is good, and you will receive its approval; for it is God's servant for your good. But if you do what is wrong, you should be afraid, for the authority does not bear the sword in vain! It is the servant of God to execute wrath on the wrongdoer. Therefore one must be subject, not only because of wrath but also because of conscience. For the same reason you also pay taxes, for the authorities are God's servants, busy with this very thing. Pay to all what is due them—taxes to whom taxes are due, revenue to whom revenue is due, respect to whom respect is due, honour to whom honour is due. (Romans 13:1-7, NRSV)

Christianity teaches that civil government has been ordained by God to maintain basic order. Police officers who round up crooks, judges who lay down penalties for wrong doing and senators that make laws and write legislation are doing God's will and are to be respected. If you resist a police officer, lie to a judge, cheat on your taxes or slander a legislator, the Bible says that God will punish you because his authority stands behind theirs. If you are a new Christian, get into the habit of obeying the law and respecting authority.

This also applies within the church. The Bible says:

> Obey your leaders and submit to them, for they are keeping watch over your souls and will give an account. Let them do this with joy and not with sighing—for that would be harmful to you. (Hebrews 13:17, NRSV)

Once again, God makes it very clear that his authority stands behind the authority of the earthly leaders he has established—here church leaders who watch over your souls—and that if we resist them or harass them we will answer to the Lord.

I realize that this sounds crazy since our entire culture is based upon rebellion and excessive individualism. By the way, how is that working out? The world's culture is built upon the foundation of original sin (you remember this one from Become A Worshipper—400-500 m) which was essentially rebellion against God's authority. The serpent tempted the man and the woman saying essentially, "Why let God make all the rules? Eat from this tree and you will be able to decide right from wrong for yourself!" If the world's culture is founded on rebellion, Christian culture is founded upon submission. Listen to the words of what historians believe is the earliest known Christian hymn:

Let the same mind be in you that was in Christ
    Jesus,
who, though he was in the form of God,
did not regard equality with God
as something to be exploited,
but emptied himself,
taking the form of a slave,
being born in human likeness.
And being found in human form,
he humbled himself
and became obedient to the point of death—
even death on a cross.
Therefore God also highly exalted him
and gave him the name
that is above every name,
so that at the name of Jesus
every knee should bend,
in heaven and on earth and under the earth,
and every tongue should confess
that Jesus Christ is Lord,
to the glory of God the Father.
(Philippians 2:5-11, NRSV)

Jesus undid the curse of rebellion by humbling himself.
Original sin was arrogant rebellion: man reaching up to grasp
something that was not for him. Salvation came when the Son of
God humbled himself and came down to a position lower than
his and demonstrated obedience to the will of God. That is the
starting place for all true Christianity: humble submission.

If you are a new believer you should go to your pastor and
express a desire to come under authority. Ask for a mentor to be

placed over you. Welcome feedback from the pastor or elders on your decision-making and attitude. We don't do this as a form of self-punishment; we do it because it is actually the fastest way to grow. The Bible says:

> Whoever heeds instruction is on the path to life,
> but one who rejects a rebuke goes astray. (Proverbs 10:17, NRSV)

I admit that this is likely the hardest thing we've hit so far—our world simply does not prepare us for this. This is the drop-out point for a lot of new believers. Get past it! Do not allow past negative experiences with leaders to give you an excuse. People will often say, "I had a bad experience with a teacher/police officer/pastor/judge once and now I think all leaders are on a big power trip." We've all had bad experiences—we live in a fallen world. That is not an excuse for resisting God's will. This is part of how we live the Christian life and it is not negotiable. The church cannot function if everyone is a god unto themselves. Pastors and elders will make mistakes and should apologize and make amends when they do. But more often than not, the decisions made are in the interests of the overall group and in the interests of the progress of the mission. Learn to submit and you will grow faster and your church will be more effective in its calling.

TEN GOOD REASONS YOU SHOULD SUBMIT TO AUTHORITY:

1. The Bible says so. (Romans 13:1-7, Hebrews 13:17) Do you really need nine more?
2. You will grow faster.
3. You will avoid repeating all of the mistakes that everyone who has travelled this road before you made.
4. Your church will not be slowed down by silly conflicts and squabbles.
5. Your church will be able to attract a higher calibre of leader if the people in it are more fun to lead. There is an old saying, "People get the leadership they deserve."
6. It will help undo the rebelliousness that is at the root of many other sins.
7. It will help you understand and appreciate Jesus better. (Philippians 2:5-11)
8. The government will have less reason to take an interest in you. (Which is a good thing! See 1 Thessalonians 4:11-12)
9. We will already face persecution just by following Jesus. We ought not to add to that persecution for being obnoxious and rebellious. (See Romans 13:4)
10. It will humble you and that is good. God opposes the proud but gives grace to the humble.

MILE 1

PERSONAL STUDY AND REFLECTION:

Most Christians struggle with authority but the truth is, without it the church falls into decay and uselessness faster than you can imagine. The Bible is full of stories where leaders had to take authority to help people grow in holiness and to help a church preserve or grow its influence. We may as well dive right into one of the toughest of those stories so that there are no surprises later on. Read 1 Corinthians 5:1-13 and then consider the comprehension task that follows.

There are seven statements below. Five of them represent a decent summary of the passage you just read and two of them are dead wrong. See if you can sort them out. The correct answers are in a footnote below.

1. The Apostle Paul exercised authority over this man because the fellow was a newer believer and did not understand the moral implications of his bad behaviour.

2. The Apostle Paul exercised authority over this man because Paul did not understand grace. We're all sinners you know. Paul should have relaxed and mellowed out.

3. The church sometimes has to exercise its corporate authority over individual believers. Believers who refuse to submit to that can even be forced to leave.

186

4. Real Christians would never ask someone to leave the church—that kind of defeats the whole purpose, doesn't it?

5. There is a big difference between how we treat believers and unbelievers. We do NOT judge unbelievers, but we DO judge believers.

6. We have leaders in the church to protect the overall holiness of the church.

7. We have leaders in the church to make sure that believers keep on growing and don't get stalled over any particular hang up.[*]

---

[*] The correct answers are: 1, 3, 5, 6, and 7. Surprised?

QUESTIONS AND NOTES:

_____

_____

_____

_____

_____

_____

_____

_____

_____

_____

_____

_____

_____

_____

_____

_____

_____

_____

_____

_____

_____

_____

_____

SUBMIT TO AUTHORITY
FAQ

The following questions represent the most frequent concerns for new believers starting out in their journey as submitters.

1. Isn't leadership just a part of the fallen world that is passing away before the progress of the eternal kingdom? I mean, as a Christian, I've put that behind me haven't I?

ANSWER: Let me show you something about God that you may not know. There is an interesting story in the Bible recorded in Genesis 18:16-19; it is the story of Sodom and Gomorrah. These were ancient cities that were wiped off the map in some sort of firestorm or meteor shower or something and they have always stood as symbols of divine judgement. Anyway, when God decided that something needed to be done about these wicked cities, he paid a call on Abraham. Let's read that:

> Then the men set out from there, and they looked towards Sodom; and Abraham went with them to set them on their way. The Lord said, 'Shall I hide from Abraham what I am about to do, seeing that Abraham shall become a great and mighty nation, and all the nations of

the earth shall be blessed in him? No, for I have chosen him, that he may charge his children and his household after him to keep the way of the Lord by doing righteousness and justice; so that the Lord may bring about for Abraham what he has promised him. (NRSV)

Right from the beginning God made a decision that he was going to bring justice and righteousness to the earth **through human mediation** and partnership. You know how the story goes. God asks Abraham to make the case on behalf of the cities. Abraham bargains with God and says, "If there are fifty righteous people in the city LORD, I think we should spare it." "Alright," says the LORD, "for fifty righteous people, I'll spare it." "Well, if we are going to spare it for fifty, how about for forty-five?" Abraham says. "Alright, you make a good point," says the LORD, "for forty-five we'll spare it." Abraham tries again and he says, "LORD forgive my boldness, but if we are going to spare it for forty-five, why not spare it for ten, after all the destruction of a city is an awful thing." "Well," says "Lord," for the sake of ten we will not destroy it." The story goes on to say that they couldn't find ten. The point is that for some crazy reason the pursuit of justice and righteousness was carried out in partnership with human wisdom and human agency which is wild and unexpected.

Now we fast-forward to Jesus. We think that Jesus was this radical departure from the Old Testament—he didn't like all that religion non-sense, but rather started something different.

Really? Let's see if that holds true here. Turn to Matthew 16:18-19:

> And I tell you, you are Peter, and on this rock I will build my church, and the gates of Hades will not prevail against it. I will give you the keys of the kingdom of heaven, and whatever you bind on earth will be bound in heaven, and whatever you loose on earth will be loosed in heaven. (NRSV)

Jesus says that we are going to "bind and loose." That is a Rabbinical term for making decisions and rules. Jesus is saying that we are going to make rules and decisions down here on earth and heaven will take note of them and write them down and they will be just as binding as if Jesus said them himself. Oh my goodness, that ought to scare you—it scares me! That means that what we decide matters and that leadership matters, even in a church over which Christ is head.

Now we turn to the middle to find the end. Turn to Isaiah 32. This is a prophecy of the ULTIMATE FUTURE—the kingdom of God. This is what Isaiah saw when God gave him a glimpse of eternity. He said:

> See, a king will reign in righteousness, (NRSV)

Now in Hebrew this really says, "See King will reign in righteousness." There is no article - no "a" or "the" and that is a

191

way of emphasizing that this is THE KING, the one who needs no introduction. We all know who this is because this is chapter 32 and Isaiah has been telling us stories about this king for a long time. We know that he'll be born of a virgin and be called Immanuel which means God with us. Later, we'll learn that he's going to die on a tree and make us righteous. But for now, we're told that one day, in the kingdom of God in the ultimate future, THE KING will reign in righteousness. That's a good thing. Now look what he says next:

> And princes will rule with justice.
> Each will be like a hiding-place from the wind,
> a covert from the tempest,
> like streams of water in a dry place,
> like the shade of a great rock in a weary land…
> the ears of those who have hearing will listen.
> The minds of the rash will have good judgement,
> and the tongues of stammerers will speak readily
>   and distinctly.
> A fool will no longer be called noble,
> nor a villain be said to be honourable.
> For fools speak folly,
> and their minds plot iniquity:
> to practise ungodliness,
> to utter error concerning the Lord,
> to leave the craving of the hungry unsatisfied,
> and to deprive the thirsty of drink…
> But those who are noble plan noble things,
> and by noble things they stand.
> (NRSV)

Not only will we have a righteous king but we will have righteous leaders. The word that is translated as "princes" is the Hebrew word sarim, which means "rulers." Now wait a second, in a world over which Christ is truly King, what need have we of human leaders? Why do we need human princes when Christ is Lord of all? Because that is who God is. He is a Trinity, he is ever relating even as he is ever reconciling. **He partners by nature.** He is God the Father who created us, God the Son who redeemed us and God the Spirit who sustains us—this is the God who partners even when doing things by himself! Now he adds to that sons and daughters and he says he will work through us as well.

Isn't that amazing? From beginning to middle to end, God works through human agency and authority. Does that blow your mind? I sometimes think of human authority as a temporary evil: something we need now because we are messed up but once Jesus returns, it will be just me and the LORD, relating one to one, mono e mono. But that's not who God is. There will always be human agency, on earth AND IN HEAVEN AND IN THE ETERNAL KINGDOM. It's already started. The Apostle John saw a vision of heaven and look at what he sees:

> After this I looked, and there in heaven a door stood open! And the first voice, which I had heard speaking to me like a trumpet, said, 'Come up here, and I will show you what must take place after this.' At once I was in the spirit, and there in heaven stood a throne, with one

seated on the throne! And the one seated there looks like jasper and cornelian, and around the throne is a rainbow that looks like an emerald. **Around the throne are twenty-four thrones, and seated on the thrones are twenty-four elders,** dressed in white robes, with golden crowns on their heads. (Revelation 4:1-4, NRSV)

Everything was fine until verse 4! Most Christians long for a heaven with Jesus on the throne but most of them will be very upset to discover that even in heaven they will have to deal with the elders! The truth is, if you can't handle human authority, you won't like heaven very much. My advice is to get over it and get on with it.

2. But what if I've had a bad experience—a really bad experience with leadership? Does this still apply to me?

ANSWER: Actually, that is part of what makes the Romans 13 passage so interesting. Look at Romans 13:1:

Let every person be subject to the governing authorities; for **there is no authority except from God,** and **those authorities that exist have been instituted by God**. (NRSV)

That's a fairly shocking statement, even more so when we consider the situation in which it was written and the person who is writing it. What makes this statement so amazing is that by this time in his ministry Paul has already born abuse at the hands of both Jewish and Roman sources of authority. Scholarship is fairly united in the claim that the Apostle wrote this letter in AD 57. When he wrote 2 Corinthians in AD 56, a year before he says this:

> Five times I have received from the Jews the forty lashes minus one. Three times I was beaten with rods. Once I received a stoning. (2 Corinthians 11:24-25 NRSV)

The first one there is a Jewish punishment. Paul who started out as Saul came from a prominent Jewish background. He studied under Gamaliel in Jerusalem which is like the Hebrew Harvard. He was the Synagogue Golden Boy, and as a returning scholar and fledgling rabbi, he would have been invited to read the Torah on the Sabbath and to expound its meaning. When he began to read the Holy words of Moses in the Pentateuch or Isaiah the prophet and claim that these Scriptures foretold of a Messiah named Jesus, there would have been shouts of rage. When he said that in this Jesus Christ, the Son of God, there is no longer Jew nor Greek, slave nor free, male nor female, there would have been shouts of indignation. The Jewish authorities were granted sweeping powers by the Romans in the regulation of their own populace and the Jews saw scourging as the correction of a brother. It could be administered to a Jew who was in danger of falling into heresy or to one who polluted himself by eating with a Gentile—something Paul resolved to do as an expression of fellowship. Whatever Paul's specific infraction, he received thirty-nine lashes as a form of correction. Watched by the same congregation that had once cheered his acceptance into Hebrew Harvard, he would have been bent and bound between two stone pillars. The hazzan, who had probably taught him to read as a boy, would have torn off Paul's robe until his torso was laid bare. The hazzan would pick up a whip formed by a four pronged strap of calf hide and donkey hide, long enough to reach the navel from behind. He stood on a stone and with all his might brought the whip down over Paul's shoulder to curl around and cut his chest. Thirteen lashes were counted, while a reader intoned curses from the Torah. "If thou wilt not observe to do all the words of this Law that are written in this book, that thou mayest fear this glorious and wonderful name, the LORD thy God, then the LORD will make thy plagues wonderful." After the thirteenth lash, the whipping was transferred from the chest target to the back—thirteen strokes across one shoulder and thirteen across the next. The synagogue elders could stop the beating if the guilty party passed out or lost control of his bowels but Paul proudly says that he bore the full punishment.

Paul suffered similar abuse from the Romans. In Antioch Pisidia, the Apostle Paul was beaten with rods—the standard Roman punishment for civic disobedience. Again the proceedings were public. He would have been pulled across the waist-high whipping pillar. His clothes were again torn off and naked he was bent over the pillar and tied. The lictor drew birch rods from a pouch and inflicted punishment. Church history reports that the Apostle Paul walked with a limp and many scholars have traced that limp to this savage beating of his legs and back. Men died under the Roman rod—Paul was beaten but not broken.

This is the man who says just a few months later:

> Let every person be subject to the governing authorities; for **there is no authority except from God**, and **those authorities that exist have been instituted by God**. (Romans 13:1, NRSV)

3. Ok, I get it. I'm supposed to obey my leaders, and the laws and authorities I exist under both political and spiritual, but what if the two are in conflict? Is there ever a time when I may have to disobey one to obey the other?

ANSWER: Yes, I think that does happen. I think there are times when our yes to God is a no to the world. Peter and John understood this in Acts 4:19-20 when they said to the Jewish courts:

> But Peter and John answered them, 'Whether it is right in God's sight to listen to you rather than to God, you must judge; for we cannot

keep from speaking about what we have seen and heard.' (NRSV)

Peter and John had to step out from the protection of law into that place where the law bites back. That still happens today. I know pastors who don't allow their messages to be recorded because technically, according to the laws of this land, if you preach on passages like Romans 1:26-27 which speaks about homosexuality, you could be in violation of hate speech laws. If you preach on 1 Timothy 2, you could be charged with sexual harassment. There will be times when to speak the whole design of God, we will step outside of the boundaries and protections of the law and civic authority but those times are few and far between. Most of the time in this country, the laws and the government are a great ally in protecting our freedom to worship, learn, serve and minister in peace. But situations do exist and they may become more prevalent in the future when to be faithful to the LORD's command we will find ourselves at odds with Caesar.

4. What should my attitude be if I find myself under forms of leadership than are not God blessed?

ANSWER: Sometimes people will say that if the Apostle Paul had written Romans 13 ten years later he might have softened his stance a little. Within ten years of reading his letter the Roman church would know severe persecution under an evil emperor. Christians would be crucified, leaders would be beheaded and whole families slaughtered for the amusement of pagan crowds. But we've already seen that Paul's attitude and convictions did not waver under persecution and indeed the testimony of God's word on this principle is consistent throughout. 1 Samuel 24:2-11 says:

> When Saul returned from following the Philistines, he was told, 'David is in the wilderness of En-gedi.' Then Saul took three thousand chosen men out of all Israel, and went to look for David and his men in the direction of the Rocks of the Wild Goats. He came to the sheepfolds beside the road, where there was a cave; and Saul went in to relieve himself. Now David and his men were sitting in the innermost parts of the cave. The men of David said to him, 'Here is the day of which the Lord said to you, "I will give your enemy into your hand, and you shall do to him as it seems good to you." Then David went and stealthily cut off a corner of Saul's cloak. Afterwards David was stricken to the heart because he had cut off a corner of Saul's cloak. He said to his men, 'The Lord forbid that I should do this thing to my lord, the Lord's anointed, to raise my hand against him; for he is the Lord's anointed.' So David scolded his men severely and did not permit them to attack Saul. Then Saul got up and left the cave, and went on his way.

Afterwards David also rose up and went out of the cave and called after Saul, 'My lord the king!' When Saul looked behind him, David bowed with his face to the ground, and did obeisance. David said to Saul, 'Why do you listen to the words of those who say, "David seeks to do you harm"? This very day your eyes have seen how the Lord gave you into my hand in the cave; and some urged me to kill you, but I spared you. I said, "I will not raise my hand against my lord; for he is the Lord's anointed." See, my father, see the corner of your cloak in my hand; for by the fact that I cut off the corner of your cloak, and did not kill you, you may know for certain that there is no wrong or treason in my hands. I have not sinned against you, though you are hunting me to take my life. (NRSV)

Oh what a great story! God had made Saul king but Saul was flawed. He was unworthy and made many mistakes so God appointed a successor who had a heart after him. David was pure and full of faith and he would walk in God's ways but Saul was still there. This God ordained, but a very imperfect leader was still on the throne. He grew jealous of David and sought his life and David hid from him to avoid confrontation. Then Saul went into a cave to relieve himself and David could have taken matters into his own hands and removed this leader who was no longer blessed by God—but he didn't. This King may be fallen, he may be wrong, his day may be drawing to a close but David knew it is not for him to rail against the things set in place by the hand of God.

What an attitude! In the face of fallen leadership, about to be eclipsed by sacred leadership, David exercises patience and faith. God will deal with Saul. God put him on the throne and God can remove him if that is his will. As for me, I will trust and obey. Can you see why God loved David so much?

New believers, let this be your model when dealing with flawed and fallen authority. Like David, we are expecting better things to come shortly. Like David, we must be patient, humble and full of faith. God will do what is God's to do. He is God and we are not. David even manages to speak tenderly of this fallen, abusive, violent and rejected leader in his life. He calls him father. He protected him from the harsh words others would speak and he rebuked those around him who would speak evil of Saul. What if as sons of Jesus, the son of David, we could do the same? What if we spoke tenderly and respectfully of our flawed leaders? Recognizing even the worst of them as people God has put in place for his purposes? What if we protected them from the harsh words of others? What if we left the judgement of leaders to the Lord God Almighty? That's a big ask, isn't it? This is a strange kingdom you have entered and by God's grace, we do the impossible.

800-900 M
Practice Self-Evaluation

C.S. Lewis (a famous Christian author and former Professor at Oxford University) wrote a book that is a favourite with many new believers called <u>The Screwtape Letters</u>. The book centres around the dialogue between a rookie demon and his more experienced mentor. The mentor demon gives his protégé a great deal of useful advice about how to distract and seduce his human charges away from the true faith, but perhaps the most important piece of counsel he gives is this: keep them busy. When a man or woman is constantly running from one activity to the next—even if those activities are "church related"—there will be no time to think, no time to wonder, no time to praise and no time to repent. Ignatius Loyola required that Christians living by his rule engage in a daily regimen of self-evaluation. At the end of each day, before retiring to sleep, his followers were required to go through the events, thoughts and actions of the day with a fine-tooth comb and evaluate all against the standard of Christ, asking the Holy Spirit to guide and convict. The Psalmist records a similar passion:

> Search me, O God, and know my heart; test me and
>   know my thoughts.
> See if there is any wicked way in me, and lead me in
>   the way everlasting.
> (Psalm 139:23-24, NRSV)

The more we learn the words of Scripture (100-200 m), the more effective this survey will be. The Apostle James says:

> Therefore rid yourselves of all sordidness and rank growth of wickedness, and welcome with meekness the implanted word that has the power to save your souls. But be doers of the word, and not merely hearers who deceive themselves. For if any are hearers of the word and not doers, they are like those who look at themselves in a mirror; for they look at themselves and, on going away, immediately forget what they were like. But those who look into the perfect law, the law of liberty, and persevere, being not hearers who forget but doers who act— they will be blessed in their doing. (James 1:21-25, NRSV)

The practice of self-evaluation is not complicated - but it is difficult and more than a little painful. Every night before you go to bed, you should review in prayer the events of the day. If you need to use your DayTimer or Blackberry to recall exactly what you did and with whom you met, then do so. Pray and ask the Holy Spirit to reveal to you any incorrect motive, thought or action and then begin to move through events as you recall them. Ask yourself questions like, "When I met with Linda to discuss the Thompson account, was I unnecessarily abrupt or rude? Did I offer her any words of praise or was I uniformly harsh in my comments?" "When I chose my outfit for the day, was I aiming for "professional" or "eye-catching?" "When I went out for lunch with Bob, did I pocket the receipt intending to file it as a business expense even though we never talked about business?" "When the pretty waitress took our order, was I polite or flirtatious?" "When I told that funny story at the gym that made Jo laugh, was it 100% true or did it involve more than a little macho exaggeration?" "When I did the bedtime routine with the kids was I engaged and listening to their chatter or was I in a hurry to catch the opening face-off of the game on T.V.?" "When my wife/husband asked me about what time I'd be home tomorrow night, was I irritable or honest and forthcoming?" By asking these sorts of questions as you comb through the day, you will catch yourself in numerous compromises and downright sins. Don't be afraid of the word "sin"—it means "the ways we miss the mark." Jesus established a mark - a standard of behaviour, and all of us who are his followers are engaged in pursuing that mark by the grace of the Holy Spirit. The Apostle Paul says it this way:

> And all of us, with unveiled faces, seeing the glory of the Lord as though reflected in a mirror, are being transformed into the same image from one degree of glory to another; for this comes from the Lord, the Spirit. (2 Corinthians 3:18, NRSV)

Paul says that when we behold Christ as the standard and fix our eyes on that standard, the Spirit works with us to effect inner transformation or character change! But if you don't regard Christ as the standard and you don't measure yourself against that standard (as James says, "like in a mirror"), then you are unlikely to change.

This daily discipline is what separates the perpetually failing from the perpetually growing. We all know people who seem to look more or less the same now as they did ten years ago when they took Christ as Lord and Saviour. We also all know people who have changed dramatically—some over as little as one year. More often then not, this practice is the difference. Sitting in church week after week, listening to sermons is great. That will give you the content you need, but if you don't apply that content at the personal level through intense, personal scrutiny, it will not work like it is supposed to. Use whatever knowledge you have now of the Scriptures, aided by the Holy Spirit and begin this exercise and you will be amazed at what you discover about yourself that does not align with the teachings of the Word and the example of Jesus. Take those things to the cross and confess them as sin—use the word SIN. The reason the world hates the word "sin" is because, in their pride, they reject the idea that they are doing anything wrong. God opposes the proud but gives grace to the humble. Tell God that you have found some stuff that does not align with his Word of Holiness and does not square with the example of His Son. Label it: SIN. Repent of it and leave it at the cross. Ask the Holy Spirit to help you embrace new attitudes, behaviours and practices in the days and weeks to come. Do this as a daily ritual and you will grow at an amazing rate!

TEN GOOD REASONS YOU SHOULD PRACTICE SELF-EVALUATION:

1. The Bible says so. (James 1:21-25) Do you really need nine more?
2. If you don't catch your flaws, the people you live with in Christian community will and that can be embarrassing.
3. It will multiply your growth rate exponentially.
4. Sin leads to death, so whatever you catch and correct will result in less death/pain/loss in your life and more life/blessing and gain.

5. It will humble you, which is good because God opposes the proud but gives grace to the humble.
6. It will make you appreciate grace. People who think they are perfect often treat their salvation carelessly.
7. It will take up all the time you once spent pointing out the flaws in others. This will make you more popular at parties. ☺
8. God the Father loves to renovate so this is something you can do together!
9. You will be able to plot out growth and celebrate the places where God is at work in your life.
10. When you are aware of your weak spots (whether pride or lust or greed), you will be able to put up fences in your life to keep you from harm. If you notice that for one hundred and seventy-two days in a row you have caught yourself watching T.V. that is not honouring to God or your wife/husband, you might decide to… cut the cable!

PERSONAL STUDY AND REFLECTION:

This is one of the most rewarding practices in all of the Christian life—but also one that takes a little bit of getting used to! It takes a little bit of humility, a little bit of discipline and a whole lot of honesty—not things we are naturally born with! Read the three Scriptures below and then consider the comprehension task that follows.

- 1 Timothy 4:16
- Psalm 139:1-24
- James 1:19-25

Consider the seven statements below. Five of them summarize the benefits of practising self-evaluation and two of them are wildly unhelpful. See if you can sort them out. The correct answers are in a footnote on the following page.

1. By evaluating carefully the things we believe and the things we say and teach to others against the truth of Scripture, we will avoid spending years and years trapped in small or false ideas. We will also avoid passing those errors on to our kids or friends.
2. Self-evaluation is dangerous, you might even say narcissistic. It will only make you more self-centred and self-obsessed.
3. Self-evaluation is an act of supreme humility when it is done right. When you intentionally hold yourself accountable to the Bible, you admit that God is the standard of right and wrong, and you are not.
4. Self-evaluation against the Word of God will help us root out the errors, attitudes and habits that have robbed us of joy and success in the past.

5. Self-evaluation is like weeding. It isn't enough to plant good flowers, you have to also find the bad ones and rip them out.
6. Self-evaluation keeps us daily aware and thankful for the grace of God.
7. Self-evaluation should produce a constant feeling of hopelessness and inadequacy within us.*

---

* The correct answers are: 1, 3, 4, 5, and 6.

QUESTIONS AND NOTES:

Practice Self-Evaluation
FAQ

The following questions represent the most frequent concerns for new believers starting out in their journey as self-evaluators.

1. Isn't all of this self-evaluation and self-criticism a form of narcissism and self-negation? Isn't the Bible "pro-self?"

ANSWER: As you might have inferred from the wording, this question is commonly asked by University students taking first year philosophy classes. Actually, the Bible is not "pro-self", it is "pro-Jesus." The Apostle Paul says:

> I have been crucified with Christ; and it is no longer I who live, but it is Christ who lives in me. And the life I now live in the flesh I live by faith in the Son of God, who loved me and gave himself for me. (Galatians 2:19-20, NRSV)

That is the very definition of self-negation—Paul crucified himself, that is VERY NEGATING! Elsewhere, the Apostle says:

> I die every day! (1 Corinthians 15:31, NRSV)

Every day Paul woke up and decided to die to himself, his ambitions, his fleshly desires and his agenda and decided to live for Christ. This has always been what Christianity is all about. Jesus said:

> If any want to become my followers, **let them deny themselves** and take up their cross and follow me. For those who want to save their life will lose it, and those who lose their life for my sake, and for the sake of the gospel, will save it. (Mark 8:34-35, NRSV)

In the Bible, the goal is to put to death the desires of the lower man, the strictly animal-being and to allow Christ, the breath of God, to bring something new to life within. Paul describes watching this process in his converts this way:

> My little children, for whom I am again in the pain of childbirth until Christ is formed in you. (Galatians 4:19, NRSV)

The particular Greek word used in this verse refers to the embryo growing inside a mother's womb. Paul is saying that he is watching Christ being formed inside of a person and hoping that Christ grows and grows until he is fully formed inside of them. This process is what self-reflection is all about. It is about noticing where YOU are still in charge; where YOUR instincts, YOUR lusts and YOUR hang-ups are still calling the shots. You submit those things to Christ and ask for the Spirit of Christ to be fully formed in the void that is left by the death of those things.

2. It's great to say that I should use the character of Jesus as a standard against which to evaluate my own character and conduct, but what does that really mean? Is there any sort of objective criteria laid down in the Bible that is based on the character of Jesus but specified in a way that can be imitated?

ANSWER: Actually, there is. In several of the Apostle Paul's letters there is an obvious shift from the theological to the ethical. Paul's style was often to teach a piece of content that they needed to know and then carefully demonstrate how this new teaching would need to be worked out in practical living. No where is this more clean than in the Letter to the Romans. For eleven chapters Paul teaches the basics of Christian theology and then he immediately switches gears and says:

> I appeal to you therefore, brothers and sisters, by the mercies of God, to present your bodies as a living sacrifice, holy and acceptable to God, which is your spiritual worship. Do not be conformed to this world, but be transformed by the renewing of your minds, so that you may discern what is the will of God—what is good and acceptable and perfect. (Romans 12:1-2, NRSV)

So if all of what we've just said about the mercy of God in Jesus is true, then the correct ethical response is found in Romans. From Romans 12:1- 15:13 we have the largest continuous body of ethical teaching in the Bible. (Ethical means how we live practically in light of what we know to be true.) It is possible to see twelve basic character markers that Paul organizes this material around. They would be as follows:

i.   Transformed mind. (Romans 12:2)
ii.   Humility. (Romans 12:3)
iii. Commitment to group. (Romans 12:4-8)
iv.   Genuine love. (Romans 12:9-10, 13:8-10)
v.   Discernment and witness. (Romans 12:9-10, 17, 13:11-12)
vi.   Showing honour. (Romans 12:10b, 13:1-2, 13:7)
vii. Serving with zeal. (Romans 12:11)
viii. Living with hope and joy. (Romans 12:12)
ix.   Persisting in prayer. (Romans 12:12)
x.   Mercy and compassion. (Romans 12:13, 12:20-21)
xi.   Gracious and forgiving. (Romans 12:14, 12:17, 14:19)
xii. Authentic and true. (Romans 13:12-14)

It's not hard to see that all of these characteristics were distinctive of the life of Christ and Paul has used them to instruct his own converts on how to live. He tells his followers to "clothe yourselves with the Lord Jesus Christ." (Romans 13:14, NIV) That means they are to put on his character, play his role and act out his life in their life. To know whose life you are living, you have to practise some self-evaluation.

900-1000 M
Confess Your Sins

Through your discipline of self-evaluation (800-900m), you have likely become aware of some habits, attitudes or behaviours you have harboured that have caused injury to other people. The Bible says:

> Therefore **confess your sins to one another**, and pray for one another, so that you may be healed. (James 5:16, NRSV)

As a new believer, you confessed your sins to God and called upon his mercy as part of your conversion experience. This likely required you to develop some humility which will now come in very handy because it is not only to the Lord that we are required to confess. The Scriptures are clear that we must deal in similar humility with the people whom we have wronged.

> So when you are offering your gift at the altar, if you remember that your brother or sister has something against you, leave your gift there before the altar and go; first be reconciled to your brother or sister, and then come and offer your gift. (Matthew 5:23-24, NRSV)

The Scriptures teach that if you have wronged a brother or sister and refuse to confess that, it can interrupt your worship and even keep you from getting healed. Confession is an important part of growth, but how much confession is required and how do we go about it?

The first question we should consider is the matter of to whom confession is made. All sins are against God, first and foremost, and therefore all sins should be confessed to God as we become convinced and aware of them. When the prophet Nathan confronted King David about his adultery with Bathsheeba, David said:

> I have sinned against the Lord. (2 Samuel 12:13, NRSV)

Even though his sin had victimized Bathsheeba and her husband Urriah, David understood that first and foremost, all sin is against God. So every sin that we are convicted of by the Holy Spirit should be confessed to God. But what of sins that victimize others? According to the teaching of Matthew 5:23-34 (cited above), when we are convicted of wrong doing against another, we need to make it an urgent priority to confess and seek restoration. There are some sins that appear to have no obvious human victim, but those sins are few in number. If you have sinned against another person, perhaps by over-charging on a job, perhaps by gossiping about them behind their back, perhaps by snapping at them in frustration, then you need to confess and seek restoration of the relationship. I've had to do this many times and it is never pleasant or easy.

A short while ago my wife and I were travelling and we got stuck in O'Hare airport in Chicago. A snowstorm in Green Bay had fouled up the entire chain of departures and our flight was in danger of being cancelled. We had been moved from gate to gate and we were tired, grumpy and worried that our newborn baby who we left at home with Grandma would run out of formula and starve to death while we read paperback novels and chewed our fingernails in frustration. We had to decide whether to try and switch flights or whether to hope that our connection would eventually come through in time for us to get home. We sat down in a little Tex Mex restaurant to try and gather our thoughts. The waitress came by and asked us what we would like to order. "We'll just need a minute to think things through." I said, rather politely. About twenty-eight seconds later, she came back, "Have you decided yet?', she asked. "We'll need a few more minutes," I replied, in a way that just barely qualified as polite. About forty-three seconds later, she came back and asked, "Have you decided yet?" This time I did not meet the standard for politeness. "If you don't mind we just need two minutes of privacy so that we can figure out our travel plans. If you give us that, then I'm sure we'll be able to concentrate on the menu and order some food." Immediately, I knew that I had crossed the line. As my mother was fond of saying, "It's not what you say it's how you say it." A few minutes later, I went up to the waitress and apologized for my rudeness. She accepted and I had peace in my conscience. I've learned not to let even small sins go unconfessed. I prefer peace in the Holy Spirit to false impressions of perfection.

I recommend keeping very short accounts with people. If you lie, confess it. If you gossip, apologize. If you cheat on your taxes, call your accountant and make a note of it so that the balance can be paid as soon as possible. Failure to do so will inhibit your worship and may even lead to physical illness (1 Corinthians 11:27-30, NRSV).

One final note: from time to time I have been asked by husbands or wives how much of their sins they should confess to their spouse. If for example, a husband has had an on-again, off-again battle with pornography, how much detail should he give in his confession? If a wife had a brief affair with a co-worker, how much detail should be shared? I usually counsel that the wronged party should control the flow of information. The sin should be named: "adultery." Do not try and soft sell the sin—it is what it is. The level of detail should be at the discretion of the wronged party. If unprotected, adulterous sex has gone on, the wronged party should be made aware so that he/she can get a medical check-up. Short of that, the wronged party may decide that explicit details would only make the process of forgiveness more difficult and they may decide that they wish only to know the basics: "When did it start? When did it finish? and Is it truly over in all respects?" In such situations, the help of a pastor or counsellor may be invaluable.

TEN GOOD REASONS TO CONFESS YOUR SINS:

1. The Bible says so. (James 5:16) Do you really need nine more?
2. It may restore life and vibrancy to your worship.
3. It may unlock health and healing in your body.
4. It is way better to confess your sins than to have them revealed.
5. Guilt sucks.
6. Hidden sin leads to dishonesty and deception. Confess and live in the light!
7. If your friend/wife/husband is a Christian and loves with Christian love, sin is not the end of a relationship. "Love keeps no record of wrongs" (1 Corinthians 13:5) and "love endures all things." (1 Corinthians 13:7)

8. Confessing sins to an unbeliever is a great way to start a witnessing conversation. Seriously.
9. It puts sin in its proper perspective. Everything seems bigger in the dark. Confessed sin never seems as serious or as ominous as unconfessed sin.
10. It helps you live at peace with others and that makes Father happy.

PERSONAL STUDY AND REFLECTION:

As Christians, we sometimes mistakenly believe that grace cancels out holiness and that mercy makes justice unnecessary. Such is not the case. Read the story of Zacchaeus in Luke 19:1-10 and then consider the comprehension task below.

Consider the seven statements below. Five of them reflect a fair summary of the Biblical teachings on confession in general and this story in particular. Two of them do neither. See if you can sort them out. The correct answers are in a footnote at the bottom of this page.

1. Once Jesus forgives you, all of your past wrongs are cancelled and it is like they never existed! There is no need to go back and pay for old wrongs best forgotten.
2. Forgiveness is not the same as removal of consequence. If you stole something, God can

forgive you through Christ, but you still need to confess the wrong and pay back what is owed.

3. Refusal to deal with wrongs, either as the wronged party or as the committing party, can actually keep you from receiving forgiveness and salvation.

4. Refusing to confess a past or present sin can actually lead to physical illness.

5. When you go through the difficult process of confession and restoration, you demonstrate to God that you understand the true cost of sin and the true value of forgiveness.

6. You only need to confess to God—only Catholics think you need to confess to other people.

7. You should confess your sins to God and you should confess your sins to any person you have wronged.*

---

* The correct answers are: 2, 3, 4, 5, and 7. Surprised about 3? Read Matthew 6.15, and then reread Luke 19:1-10.

QUESTIONS AND NOTES:

Confess Your Sins
FAQ

The following questions represent the most frequent concerns for new believers starting out in their journey as sin confessors.

1. I heard that if you don't forgive someone who wrongs you, than God can't or won't forgive you of your sins. Is that true?

ANSWER: Yes. Unfortunately, the Bible says that very thing:

> For if you forgive others their trespasses, your heavenly Father will also forgive you; but if you do not forgive others, neither will your Father forgive your trespasses. (Matthew 6:14-15, NRSV)

Theologians debate exactly WHY this is, but no serious student of the Bible debates THAT it is. Some theologians say that this is so because failure to forgive others may reflect an inadequate appreciation of what Christ went through on the cross. They say that this is the thinking behind the Apostle Paul's comment in 1 Corinthians 11:

> Whoever, therefore, eats the bread or drinks the cup of the Lord in an unworthy manner will be

answerable for the body and blood of the Lord. Examine yourselves, and only then eat of the bread and drink of the cup. For all who eat and drink without **discerning the body**, eat and drink judgement against themselves. For this reason many of you are weak and ill, and some have died. But if we judged ourselves, we would not be judged. (1 Corinthians 11:27-30, NRSV)

The word Paul selected, that is translated above as "discerning the body," suggests a bit of word play. Paul is saying two things at once: consider how you are at present within the body of Christ, that is the church. "Are you at peace with all your brothers and sisters? If not, do not take communion." He is also saying, "Consider the body of Jesus. See his wounds and his beaten face. Look at how much he did to remove the weight of your sin and shame. Can you not suffer less to lift your brother's debt?" They are quite likely right that this is what Paul is doing. No doubt the Apostle remembered Jesus saying:

So when you are offering your gift at the altar, if you remember that your brother or sister has something against you, leave your gift there before the altar and go; first be reconciled to your brother or sister, and then come and offer your gift. (Matthew 5:23-24, NRSV)

God does not receive worship of any kind from people who have not granted mercy to others.

2. *How can I forgive someone if they have never even acknowledged the hurt that they did to me?*

ANSWER: This is a very sensitive topic for many. Over the course of our marriage, my wife and I have been privileged to look after a number of high-needs children through a Christian fostering agency. Some of these beautiful children have been horribly sexually and physically abused. At some point in their adult life, they will have to go through the painful process of forgiving the people who hurt them, usually their parents, in order to move forward in health and freedom. There will almost never be an apology or even an acknowledgment of wrong. Can forgiveness really happen in a situation like that? Yes. It is helpful to remember that forgiveness is different than reconciliation. Reconciliation implies working mutually through a set of grievances in order to achieve understanding and shared ground for moving forward. The reconciliation road leads to peace but IT WILL NOT ALWAYS BE POSSIBLE for you to travel that road because it is a road made for two. The Apostle Paul said:

> **If it is possible, so far as it depends on you**, live peaceably with all. (Romans 12:18, NRSV)

Sometimes it won't be possible and sometimes it won't depend on you. Reconciliation is not always possible; but forgiveness is. It is possible to forgive people even before they admit wrong and long before they ask for forgiveness. As Jesus was being nailed to the cross, he said:

> "Father, forgive them; for they do not know what they are doing." (Luke 23:34, NRSV)

Those soldiers had not said sorry nor did they even think they were doing wrong. They had no idea that they were nailing the king of the universe to a wooden cross and yet, Jesus forgave them. That's amazing! It is the Spirit of that Jesus within us that gives us hope of imitating his example. The word forgiveness does not mean "forgetting," it does not mean "reconciling" and it does not mean "trusting again." It means "to let go of." It means that you stop rehearsing the events over and over again in your mind. It means you stop bringing it up in argument to establish precedence. It means it gets wiped off the scorecard and locked in a file marked "not for legal use." It means that when Jesus is calling witnesses at that person's trial, you do not step forward with a stack of grievances. You leave them to the Lord's wisdom and justice—you are out of it. That is what it means to forgive and it can only be done by God's grace and with prayer.

3. Is there value in confessing my sins to a real person?

Answer: Yes. The Bible says:

Therefore **confess your sins to one another**, and pray for one another, so that you may be healed. (James 5:16, NRSV)

That is the real reason behind the recent phenomenon of "accountability partners." I've heard well-meaning Christians get their shorts in a knot about accountability partners saying, "I don't see that in the Bible! It's just so much new age self-helpism." Actually, it is in the Bible—it's confession. The truth is when we threw out the old Catholic Confession booth (which was probably a good thing), we left a void in Christian practice. What do we do with all our dark stuff? Bad things grow in the dark and Christians need a way of pulling their bad things out into the light so that it can shrink and die. Today we call it "accountability," five-hundred years ago we called it "confession," but a rose by any other name is still a rose. Confession is good. If you don't have an accountability partner, get one. I have one. We meet every four to six weeks and ask each other really awkward and embarrassing questions. It's hard to lie to a Christian brother or sister to their face so you end up confessing things you might otherwise not. It's good for the soul and it motivates you to holiness. Whenever I think about sinning now, I will say to myself, "The pain of confessing this to Jon is more than the pleasure this sin offers. Forget it!" That's a good thing.

1000-1100 M
Develop Self-Control

One of the primary ways that Christians are to be different from the people of the world is in the way that we exercise control over our bodies and over our passions. Paul characterizes the unsaved world this way:

> Their end is destruction; their god is the belly; and their glory is in their shame; their minds are set on earthly things. (Philippians 3:19, NRSV)

Eat, drink and be merry, for tomorrow we die! That is the basic moral code of the unsaved world and the only caveat or restriction they recognize is the rather lame "as long as you don't hurt anyone else in the process" bit. How's that working out by the way? The problem with that moral philosophy is that it assumes that people can anticipate the consequences of their actions, which of course, they cannot. Ever heard of the law of unanticipated consequence? It means that there is always an unanticipated consequence! For example, a person might say, "I'm going to drink my self silly tonight. I'm only hurting myself. It's my liver!" However, once the person is good and drunk and they have lost all judgement, it seems like no big deal to drive home. "I'm na exscalen diver!" he slurs. We all know how that story ends. Or what about the overeating of North Americans. Did anyone anticipate that childhood obesity or diabetes would become the paramount health issues of our time? No way. The worst that could happen, we thought, is that little Johnny would be a wee bit tubby. We also failed to anticipate the destruction of the rain forest so that little Johnny could have cheap cheese-burgers, but that's another story. How about our debt-fuelled, credit-driven economy? We fed every desire the advertizers stimulated by taking out lines of credit against the ever-increasing value of our homes. How did that work out? Did anyone see the total and complete collapse of the housing market and the subsequent melt-down of the global economy? The obvious lesson we should learn from this is that we cannot anticipate the consequences of our actions and someone always gets hurt when we make decisions with our bellies, our credit cards or our genitalia. That may sound crude but it is not so different from what the Apostle Paul says, "People who worship their lusts end in destruction."

Christians, on the other hand, are supposed to be different. The Apostle Paul compares the development of self-control in the Christian life to the same practice in athletics,

> Athletes exercise self-control in all things; they do it to receive a perishable garland, but we an imperishable one. So I do not run aimlessly, nor do I box as though beating the air; but I punish my body and enslave it, so that after proclaiming to others I myself should not be disqualified. (1 Corinthians 9:25-27, NRSV)

Self-control is about retraining the body to be content and even excited about living within the boundaries of God's permission. The three areas we struggle to do this in are: sexuality, food and material accumulation. There is ample permission in each of these areas. God is not opposed to sex—he just mandates that it occur between a man and a woman who have made a lifetime commitment to one another, something the Bible refers to as "marriage." Not only does God not have a bad attitude about sex, he wants you to have lots of it, within the boundaries. The Bible actually warns married couples against going more than a few days without sex:

> The husband should give to his wife her conjugal rights, and likewise the wife to her husband. For the wife does not have authority over her own body, but the husband does; likewise the husband does not have authority over his own

body, but the wife does. Do not deprive one another except perhaps by agreement for a set
time, to devote yourselves to prayer, and then
come together again (1 Corinthians 7:3-5,
NRSV)

There is plenty of room to colour within the lines. Likewise,
the Bible does not say that you cannot enjoy food or drink, but
it does condemn gluttony (overeating) and drunkenness (over-
indulgence of wine/drink).

Do not be among winebibbers, or among glut-
tonous eaters of meat; for the drunkard and the
glutton will come to poverty, and drowsiness
will clothe them with rags. (Proverbs 23:20-21,
NRSV)

Perhaps the biggest self-control problem modern Christians
have is in the area of material consumption. The Bible says:

Of course, there is great gain in godliness combined with contentment; for we brought nothing into the world, so that we can take nothing
out of it; but if we have food and clothing, we
will be content with these. But those who want
to be rich fall into temptation and are trapped
by many senseless and harmful desires that
plunge people into ruin and destruction. (1
Timothy 6:6-9, NRSV)

If you are a new Christian, start right away to discipline yourself to live within the permission of God. You are allowed to have sex—even to have lots of it, just make sure it is with your wife or husband. You are allowed to have food and drink, just make sure that only reasonable portions are taken. You are allowed to have material possessions, but you do not need much more than the basics. The pursuit of anything beyond that is a recipe for distraction and ruin. Jesus said:

> Do not store up for yourselves treasures on earth, where moth and rust consume and where thieves break in and steal; but store up for yourselves treasures in heaven, where neither moth nor rust consumes and where thieves do not break in and steal. For where your treasure is, there your heart will be also. (Matthew 6:19-21, NRSV)

Beyond the basics of life, the kingdom of God is our only pursuit. It takes some effort to wean ourselves off of these things, but we are not in this alone. The Bible promises:

> For God did not give us a spirit of cowardice, but rather a spirit of power and of love **and of self-discipline**. (2 Timothy 1:7, NRSV)

God will work with us to rebuild our lives within the walls of his abundant permission. It really is good there, you'll see.

TEN GOOD REASONS YOU SHOULD DEVELOP SELF-CONTROL:

1. The Bible says so. (Romans 13:14) Do you really need nine more?
2. It will detoxify the body of unnatural needs and addictions.
3. It will recalibrate the body for normal needs and contentments.
4. The blessings of God are found within the permission of God.
5. God's ways are wise and his restrictions are for our good. How did that "follow your heart" sexuality work out anyway? God's ways are for our benefit and blessing. Trust and see.
6. If we are self-controlled, we are less likely to hurt other people.
7. If we eat only what we need, have sex only with our lifelong marriage partner and accumulate only the material goods we need to survive, the world will be a better place for all people.
8. Global resources will go much further if 25% of the population stops consuming 80% of the world's food and energy.
9. Since most wars are fought over oil, water or land, self-control would lead to greater peace in the world.

10. Since a great deal of private violence is due to excessive alcohol consumption, sexual deviance and outright greed, self-control would lead to more peace at the personal level.

PERSONAL STUDY AND REFLECTION:

The idea that everyone should pursue happiness and prosperity as they define it, in the vague hopes that we will not hurt each other in the process, has been proven an arrogant delusion. Without reference to the God who created the world and designed all of its laws and precepts, such a plan has no hope of succeeding. Read James 4:1-10 and then consider the comprehension exercise below.

Consider the seven statements below. Five of them represent a correct summary of the passage you just read as well as the general principles we have hit upon in other related Scriptures. Two are quite wrong. See if you can sort them out. The answers are in a footnote on the following page.

1. A great deal of personal and political violence can be traced back to our basic lack of self-control.
2. It is supremely arrogant before God for us to think that we can control the world's resources to supply our needs without placing others at risk.

3. The only way to have peace and contentment is to be humble before God and to follow his leadership.

4. It is unchristian to talk about material self-control. The economies of God's favourite countries would collapse if we eliminated greed-based, credit-fuelled purchasing.

5. It is unrealistic to expect people today to only have sex with their lifelong marriage partners. Because of our need to accumulate huge wads of cash before marrying, we can't get married until our 30's and that is too long to deny our physical urges.

6. A great deal of sexual compromise is due to financial greed. Marriage can get in the way of financial advancement so it is sometimes postponed for too long.

7. It is an act of faith to believe that by following God and trusting in him to make the rules, we will still end up happy and content.*

---

* The correct answers are 1, 2, 3, 6, and 7.

QUESTIONS AND NOTES:

DEVELOP SELF-CONTROL
FAQ

The following questions represent the most frequent concerns for new believers starting out in their journey into self-control.

1. I'm trying to be faithful to my wife (or trying to save myself for marriage) and I use masturbation and pornography to control my urges. Is that ok?

SHORT ANSWER: No. This is a serious issue, and one that has dropped out of Christian teaching over the last several years so it deserves some careful study. Let's start with Matthew 5:27-30. This is one of those Scriptures you read and then just want to praise God for his timelessness and relevance. This passage could have been written yesterday, it so perfectly provides what we need to hear at this time. Let me show you:

> You have heard that it was said, "You shall not commit adultery." But I say to you that every-one who looks at a woman with lust has already committed adultery with her in his heart. If your right eye causes you to sin, tear it out and throw it away; it is better for you to lose one of your members than for your whole body to be

thrown into hell. And if your right hand causes you to sin, cut it off and throw it away; it is better for you to lose one of your members than for your whole body to go into hell. (NRSV)

It's important to understand that Jesus was entering into an existing conversation within Judaism here and he took that conversation in a completely new direction. There was a long and detailed conversation about adultery and sexual purity in Jewish culture in Jesus' day but most of that conversation focused on what punishments should be handed out to women who committed adultery. The punishments were very creative and very specific. They also liked to talk about what exact behaviours constituted adultery. They were sure that if a woman fantasized about another man while having sex with her husband that this constituted adultery and they even concluded that a woman could commit adultery with her right hand by masturbating while thinking of another man, not her husband. So Jesus enters into this rather sordid, mean-spirited debate—something I'm sure his disciples would rather he hadn't done—and he does something utterly amazing. First of all, he directs all of his teaching to men as though they were primarily responsible for establishing sexual purity and then he says, if you even look at a woman with lust in your heart, you have committed adultery with her. **Before it even reaches the right hand, it's a sin**. In a way, he goes further than the Rabbis, but in another way he goes in a completely different direction. It was an amazing teaching.

The foundation of the sexual theology that Jesus introduces here is that purity begins in the mind.

Once again we see that Jesus' concern was for us to live at the very heart of God's design. He didn't spend a lot of time fussing over the outer boundaries—that's what the Pharisees did. Jesus cut through all of that and said, "Forget the outer boundary markers, come here to the heart of the matter. God's desire is for you to be totally content with the mate that God has given you. In body, hand and mind. This is the centre. Live here." The picture that is created is of a crossroads in the mind. If you set your mind on the one road, it will lead you to life and life abundant. If you set your mind on the other road, it will lead to death and frustration. Let's talk first about the road to life.

The road to life, Jesus says, begins with the decision to find pleasure exclusively in the partner God has for you. In the Bible, almost every path begins with a decision we make in our minds. Every narrow road begins with a narrow gate. Before Joshua died he turned to the people that he knew would be facing many choices as they lived in the land God had given them and he said:

> Choose this day whom you will serve, whether the gods your ancestors served in the region beyond the River or the gods of the Amorites in whose land you are living; but as for me and my household, we will serve the Lord. (Joshua 24:15, NRSV)

In the New Testament, again and again it seems we are being encouraged to make the decision to set our minds upon a certain path. Paul says:

> For those who live according to the flesh set their minds on the things of the flesh, but those who live according to the Spirit set their minds on the things of the Spirit. (Romans 8:5, NRSV)

We choose which road we set our minds on and then destiny kind of unfolds. I remember hearing a story when I was a little boy at camp. A young child went for a walk with his grandfather who was trying to explain to the lad about the passions of the body. The grandfather says, "It's like there are two dogs that fight and battle in my soul. The one dog desires me to do good, the other dog desires me to do wrong." "Which dog wins?" asks the young boy. "The one I feed," he replies. The one I feed. What we set the mind on becomes the path we live. Set your minds on things above—determine in your mind to live out the highest path of human sexuality. To focus exclusively on the one God gives you.

Secondly, the road to life leads to an intimate relationship where each partner is fully known and fully celebrated. If we choose in our minds to go down this road we will soon find ourselves in a place we all want to be. We all want to be known and accepted by someone. We don't want one or the other—we don't want to be known but not loved—we call that exposure.

And we don't to be loved but not known—we call that deception. We want both—to be known and accepted, loved and celebrated. There is a picture of that in the Bible. It's in Genesis 2:25:

> And the man and his wife were both naked, and were not ashamed. (NRSV)

This place cannot be reached on the pornography pathway. How can you rest content in your lover's arms when you worry that he is comparing you to some airbrushed silicone hanger he saw on the web? Deceptive fantasy breeds discontent and discontent causes us to hide behind surgery, flattery or lies and it causes us to be unhappy with reality and to despise simple blessings. This human longing to be known and loved lies down one path only.

The road to life ends in satisfaction, contentment and gratitude. This one makes me laugh. You know what's funny? Every study that I've seen where people are asked to rate their sexual satisfaction in life reveals that the most sexually satisfied people on the planet are Christian married couples who have had a stable marriage for ten plus years. When asked that question, Christian women who've been in a healthy marriage for ten years or more consistently score highest. There is some irony here isn't there? We think that God's design will rob us of pleasure so we edit the rules so as to maximize pleasure and what we end up with is deep and abiding dissatisfaction. But when we live out the design, we are blessed. Maybe we should just trust that God knows best? The truth is good sex requires vulnerability, trust and knowledge of one another in order to work properly and maximize pleasure. Do you know that the Hebrew word for "sex" is the same as the word for knowledge? You have to really know someone to give them sexual pleasure and the culture of anonymous self-gratification is at complete odds with that. Having a sexual encounter with a screen image or a fantasy concoction only leads to self-loathing and self-doubt, and it creates a disposition towards consumerism in real life sexual behaviour. We start looking at sex as something we "go get" from someone, instead of something we explore with someone and that's why it doesn't work properly. Having sex God's way is more fun—imagine that?

In the Scriptures, the road to life is always contrasted with the road to death and so it is here. The road to death, Jesus teaches, begins with granting yourself permission to have a breadth of sexual interest. Once again, this journey begins at the cross roads in the mind. You can decide to be completely focused on the mate God gives you or you can give permission to yourself to have a breadth of sexual interest. It all begins with that decision.

The road to death also involves a preoccupation with sexual experimentation. Let me explain what I mean by that. One of the things that researchers tell us about perversion is that it tends to be escalating in nature. It has to be because it doesn't satisfy. It increases the hunger and the appetite and it becomes increasingly difficult to satisfy the urges. A young man or woman may be able to reach a sexual climax by looking at pictures of the opposite sex naked but then after a while those images are no longer stimulating and they need to see couples having sexual intercourse. Soon those images do not satisfy and they need to see group sex or violent sex or homosexual sex. And it escalates. That's why there are so many "fetish" sites on the internet where you can see sexuality that is so far out at the margins because people are on a never-ending quest for the next thing. And far too often people are led to act out in the body what they have fantasized about through the screen—women more often than men studies show—and they can be led into dangerous and even deadly sexual encounters as a result. So what we sometimes call "innocent sexual curiosity" never stays there. It rapidly escalates because it does not satisfy.

The road to death often settles into a ritualism that becomes binding and restricting.

Dr. Mitch Whitman, who studies sexual deviance at Seattle Pacific University says that inevitably pornography and associated masturbation fantasies settle into restrictive and binding ritualized patterns. This may mean that a person feels that they cannot go to sleep unless they masturbate or they get antsy if their wife or husband won't go to bed at a certain time because they need to be on the computer by 11:30 p.m. Habits settle into rituals which steal freedom from the men and women who are subject to them. The helpful side of this is that it is often through these rituals that parents or spouses discover pornography addictions. By changing your own habits as a mom or dad (or a husband or wife) you will sometimes notice an irritation or a strong reaction that implies an inner ritual or compulsion. Be on the lookout for that. Move the computer to a new and more public location and monitor the strength of your spouse's or child's reaction to that. Be nosy and intrusive from time to time and you will often uncover a ritual.

The road to death ends in a state of unmanageability where behaviours are out of control. If you've ever seen the video testimony of Ted Bundy you understand this. Ted Bundy admitted that his addiction to pornography led to compulsive and ritualized behaviour that eventually, he had no control over. Obviously, that is an extreme case but most people who are in the full throws of a pornography addiction will tell you that they want to stop. They hate what they do but their will is overpowered by their compulsion and their behaviour is now out of their control. This is the end of the road. This is slavery, this is hopelessness and this is spiritual death. This destination is the exact opposite of the foolish hope that permitted the first deadly step. Most Christians who permit themselves a dabbling in pornography and masturbation do so in the foolish belief that it will ASSIST in self-control and allow them to avoid adultery or premarital sex. That could not be further from the truth.

2. I recognize how powerful the lure of pornography and masturbation can be for myself, my spouse or my kids. What can I do to safeguard myself or my loved ones from this pit?

ANSWER: There is an old saying that is worth repeating: "Sometimes an ounce of prevention is worth a pound of cure." In the spirit of that, I want to offer you three quick safeguards:

1. Control inputs early. Studies have shown that TV watching that is sexually explicit leads to higher probability of early sexual activity in teenagers and this often first manifests as an experimentation with pornography. Help your kids or your spouse set their minds on things above. Let me just speak to moms and dads for a moment. I want to tell you something that can make a world of difference to you as a parent. Are you ready? Here it comes: YOU ARE IN CHARGE. You are in charge, many parents have forgotten that. It's o.k. if your kids get angry at you or think you are bossy. It's even o.k. if they don't like you. You don't get extra points in heaven for having the happiest kids or for being the most popular parent. God is interested in your child's holiness far more than their happiness. It amazes me how often parents struggle to take control. I had a mother tell me how worried she was about her son's internet use. She came to me all distraught, wringing her hands and wiping her eyes, "My son spends all day locked upstairs in his room on the internet. Whenever I call him down he yells at me to go away. What should I do? I know he's been looking at things he shouldn't be but I just don't know how to get through to him.

Please help me, pastor!" "Mrs Smith," I asked, "do you own a baseball bat?" "A baseball bat? What does that have to do with anything?" "Well," I said, "I suggest that you take that baseball bat up to your son's room and you beat that computer into the ground. Smash it into a thousand pieces. Get a broom and dust up those pieces and throw them into your fireplace and burn them. Problem solved." Her son was 16-years-old! He didn't have a job or a credit card so he had no way to replace that computer. I thought things looked pretty simple but she wasn't so sure. Was there a secret memo that went around the world telling parents that they are no longer in charge? Did I miss that? You are in charge. They can scream and hiss and swear all they like. You are in charge. You decide what shows can be watched, you decide what movies can be watched and you decide whether the computer can be used or not. Control the inputs early and you will have much better results. Obviously if the concern is for yourself or your spouse, a baseball bat will not be the answer but the basic idea is the same. Take control of the T.V. and the internet because they represent opportunity and they represent potential. Nip it in the bud, as they used to say.

2. Be nosy. There was another memo that went around I think that said that people have a high need for privacy. That's not true and it's not Biblical. Excessive concern for privacy is a lie that the enemy has very successfully woven into our culture precisely because most evil things grow in the dark. The Bible says:

Live as children of light—for the fruit of the light is found in all that is good and right and true. Try to find out what is pleasing to the Lord. **Take no part in the unfruitful works of darkness, but instead expose them**. (Ephesians 5:8-11, NRSV)

I'm an adult and I have very little privacy and I want very little privacy. One of our Board members snoops through my giving records to make sure I am tithing. A pastor from Barrie gets a print out of all my internet travel and my secretary reviews all of my VISA receipts. Why? Because privacy stinks and sin grows in the dark. You don't need it and neither do your kids. You should know who they are e-mailing and who they are talking to on the phone and what they are watching on TV and where they go on the internet. They may not like it, but… . who cares? They'll thank you for it when they're thirty. That's the goal of parenting by the way—healthy adults living the life God intended for them. It's not happy teenagers living out all of their adolescent appetites.

I am also not convinced that marriage requires a lot of privacy and I know for sure that bad things happen in a marriage that has too much of it. My wife is free to read my journal, in fact, I encourage her to. She is free to go through my Visa receipts and she is free to read my internet history. She is free to ask me where I am going and to call me to make sure I am where I said I would be. She is also free to veto any potential meeting that makes her feel uncomfortable. My wife knows more about me than she wants to know. A few years ago, I wrote her an ex-cruciatingly detailed letter that outlined every sin I could recall. There were footnotes and Bible references and it was a little bit awkward. I also told her that if there was any sin in there that she wanted the full back story and detail on, she had only to ask. People who feel the need for a lot of privacy generally have something to hide.

3. Model healthy sexuality. Moms and dads, your kids won't like this one any better but believe me, it will pay off. Most parents try and pretend that they are non-sexual beings. "Johnny, your mother and I are going to go write thank you notes for the next three hours in our bedroom with the door locked. Why not surf the internet unsupervised for the eve-ning?" That's not a great strategy! In Jesus' day, the entire family slept in one room. Kids developed a bit of realism around what moms and dads did to make babies. Now, I'm not saying you should invite the kids in for sleepovers on the floor, I'm saying that you should be openly affectionate and sexual in a healthy way with your spouse. Don't hide normal sexuality from chil-dren. Talk about it in an age-appropriate way.

If you are a young adult trying to develop sexual self-control, I suggest cultivating pro-marriage and pro-purity friendships. Research indicates that relationships are the number one indi-cating factor in sexual deviance. If you hang around with people who are colouring outside the lines, you will too. That's a scien-tific and Biblical fact.

Do not be deceived: 'Bad company ruins good morals. (1 Corinthians 15:33, NRSV)

3. I'm already deep into this pit, how do I get out?

ANSWER: Let's talk about a 7 point battle plan for getting out. The first and the last on this list are the most important:

1. Confess to each other. The Bible says:

> Therefore confess your sins to one another, and pray for one another, so that you may be healed. (James 5:16, NRSV)

Again, our obsession with privacy robs us of healing on this. Our pride robs us of it too. There is something very powerful and therapeutic about confessing your struggle to another human being. It drags the sin out of the shadows and into the light and when you pray with another brother or sister on this, powerful things happen. Now I'm not saying that you should walk around confessing this to everyone you meet. I'm saying that if you are in bondage to a sexual sin like pornography, you will likely not experience any growth at all until you take the step to humble yourself and confess your sin to at least one other person. If you are married, that might be your husband or your wife, or it might be a same gendered Christian friend. If you are a young person, it might be your same gendered parent, your youth pastor or an older Christian, same gendered friend. This is the narrow gate on the road back. You can't skip it.

2. Change your thinking. This all begins in the mind. Romans 12:2 says:

> Do not be conformed to this world, but be transformed by the renewing of your minds, so that you may discern what is the will of God— what is good and acceptable and perfect. (NRSV)

There is a way of thinking, a pattern of the mind that is the world's pattern. Unlearn it and learn a new way of thinking— God's way. Study his word and speak to people who know him and you will literally change your mind and learn to think new thoughts.

3. Change your behaviour. You also have to change your behaviours. Remember that the really dangerous middle section of the journey into spiritual death on this is ritualization. When habits are formed that are binding, that's when things get really tough. To get out of that, you have to establish new rituals, new patterns and new behaviours. For example, is the morning shower a time of ritualized behaviour? Then shower at night before bed. Is night time TV a temptation? Then turn the TV off at 9:00 p.m. and take up reading. Is the internet a pitfall? Get a blackberry and send your e-mails from there and get rid of your computer. Or install a program like Covenant Eyes or at the least, move the computer into a public area. Is your credit card an enabler? Cut it. People can live without credit cards you know. If you don't change your behaviour, all you have is good intentions and those lead nowhere.

4. Consider deeper issues. If you have done everything listed above and still you've seen no movement, no loosening of the bondage that you are in, you should consider whether or not there are some deeper issues at play. Have you been abused? Is there a history of sexual deviance in your family? Is there an emotional deficit that expresses itself in compulsive behaviour? Seek professional help on that. Take responsibility for your health and get the help you need to experience break through.

5. Nurture your marriage. This one is so important! Dr. McCarthy in his exhaustive research into marital sexuality and dysfunction found that couples that have sex less than once a month are 75% less satisfied with their marriage and this, in turn increases the likelihood of all forms of sexual deviance. We shouldn't be too shocked by that as Christians, after all, the Bible says the exact same thing:

> The husband should give to his wife her conjugal rights, and likewise the wife to her husband. For the wife does not have authority over her own body, but the husband does; likewise the husband does not have authority over his own body, but the wife does. Do not deprive one another except perhaps by agreement for a set time, to devote yourselves to prayer, and then come together again, so that Satan may not

tempt you because of your lack of self-control.
(1 Corinthians 7:3-5, NRSV)

Dr. McCarthy could have saved himself a lot of trouble by reading the Bible. The Bible says that married couples should have plentiful, regular and generous sex. If you do that, you will be far more able to practise self-control and walk in purity. Very often in adult men and women, pornography addiction is the result of avoidance—couples have unresolved sexual issues that they can't get past so they retreat into fantasy and escapism. That's what gets you into this mess—you get out of it by investing in your marriage and building a healthy, regular and generous sex life with your spouse.

6. Mature your faith. The Bible says:

> Finally, be strong in the Lord and in the strength of his power. Put on the whole armour of God, so that you may be able to stand against the wiles of the devil. (Ephesians 6:10-11, NRSV)

Be strong in the Lord and you will be able to stand. Grow. Expand your carrying capacity for the Holy Spirit and deepen your knowledge of the Holy Scripture and you will grow in your ability to resist the enemy.

7. Cry out to the Lord. Seek liberation from the great liberator. Cry out to him. Sometimes, the Lord delays healing in order to get other work done in a season of vulnerability and humility. Sometimes we pray and we don't immediately get what we ask for, so we quit. God sometimes measures our desire by our persistence. God is also a God of partnership. He often will not do what only he can do until we do what we can do. So pray. Cry out to God until you are healed. The Israelites called out to God for almost four-hundred years before he set them free. Then the Bible says:

> Then the Lord said, 'I have observed the misery of my people who are in Egypt; I have heard their cry on account of their taskmasters. Indeed, I know their sufferings, and I have come down to deliver them from the Egyptians. (Exodus 3:7-8, NRSV)

After four-hundred years of calling out to God, he finally says, "I've seen, I've heard, I know and I will come and deliver." I visualize it like this: it's like there is a bowl in heaven that collects our prayers. God has drawn a line on it near the top. When your prayers fill the bowl and they cross the threshold of that line, he tips the bowl and our prayers fall down on us as a river of anointing and empowerment that lifts us out of our distress. Fill the bowl. Fill it while you do the things God has enabled you to do and in his time, he will deliver you fully.

3. Is it true that Christians shouldn't have any debt? I heard that recently for the first time and am wondering if it's really true.

ANSWER: There is an old saying I recently heard for the first time, "Good morality is good economics." Old sayings tend to make a comeback when they are proved right again through current events. The Bible has an old saying that Christians have become quite adept at ignoring over the last forty years:

> Owe no one anything, except to love one another. (Romans 13:8, NRSV)

Christians used to believe that debt was bad—that it was a sign of discontent, impatience or greed. Debt was what accumulated when you were not content with what your livelihood afforded you or when you could not wait until you had the money in hand or when you simply had to have more than you were entitled to. Debt was for "the heathens," Christians were to be characterized by the opposite of debt: self-giving love. Somewhere along the way we forgot that and Christians became no different than the world with respect to debt.

I grew up in a Christian home and I grew up in the church, yet I don't recall ever being taught that debt was bad. When I got married, my wife and I bought furniture on our credit card, took out a hefty mortgage and leased a car. We've been married for thirteen years now and I can't even say for sure whether we ever did pay for that couch. The credit card debt was rolled into a line of credit that we expanded by putting a porch on the front of our house and buying an air conditioner. Our line of credit has still not been paid off. The couch is old now and free to a good home. I shudder to think how much I have paid for it. How did this happen to me? How did this happen to us? What has it done to the witness of the church?

The statistics tell a story of a church that can no longer impress the world with its generosity, because we can no longer afford to—we owe the credit card companies too much money. Forty percent of church members say they overspend **monthly;** also 40% of church members pay more than $2,000 a year in interest, not including their mortgage.* Forty years ago, before this trend began, Christians were known for giving 10% of their gross incomes to the work of their local churches—we called this the tithe. Over the last forty years—the years of greatest increase in the material prosperity of North America—giving in churches has dropped to an average of 2.5% Giving during the Great Depression was higher by percentage than it was in 2004—at the very peak of North American prosperity. Less than 9% of "born again" Christians tithe, and "born again" Christians lead all giving categories by a wide margin. The church is a shell of what she once was, a shadow of what she should be and capable of far less than the world needs from her. According to the Borgen Project, annual expenditures of just $19 billion between now and 2015 could eliminate global starvation and malnutrition—something the church could do with ease if every North American evangelical really tithed. But at present, that scenario appears very unlikely. Thirty-three percent of North American born-again Christians say it is impossi-

---

* All of these statistics can be found at www.generousgiving.org

ble for them to get ahead in life because of the financial debt they have incurred. The couches we bought on credit, the houses we financed and the cars we coveted now own us and they will not let us do what we ought.

In the summer of 2008, God put a strong call on my heart, "Get my people out of debt." Debt is the world's way, charity is our way. You cannot serve two masters. Either you will hate the one and love the other, or be devoted to the one and despise the other. You cannot serve God and money. The world economy is crumbling under the weight of its own flawed morality. It is time for God's people to pull out. It is time for God's people to owe no one anything, except to love one another.

1100-1200 M
Celebrate Sabbath

've left this one until late in the journey because it's complicated. Salvation is simple but faith is complicated. In the Bible, they talk about "milk" issues and "meat" issues. Milk issues are for baby Christians, meat issues are for the more mature. By this stage in the journey, you are approaching mature
Christianity and you need to meet this head on. (That was not
an intentional pun—it was accidentally funny.) Jesus had an
unusual relationship with the Sabbath. Let's be clear: Jesus was
the Word of God made flesh and he did not, in any way, over
turn or negate the Old Testament. He himself said:

> Do not think that I have come to abolish the law
> or the prophets; I have come not to abolish but

to fulfil. For truly I tell you, until heaven and earth pass away, not one letter, not one stroke of a letter, will pass from the law until all is accomplished. Therefore, whoever breaks one of the least of these commandments, and teaches others to do the same, will be called least in the kingdom of heaven; but whoever does them and teaches them will be called great in the kingdom of heaven. (Matthew 5:17-19, NRSV)

Jesus did not come to break, change or overturn the Ten Commandments which are the heart of the Old Testament torah. Jesus did not break the Sabbath commandment—but he did seem to intentionally mess with what people thought about the Sabbath. In Matthew 12:1-8 it says:

At that time Jesus went through the cornfields on the sabbath; his disciples were hungry, and they began to pluck heads of grain and to eat. When the Pharisees saw it, they said to him, 'Look, your disciples are doing what is not lawful to do on the sabbath.' He said to them, 'Have you not read what David did when he and his companions were hungry? He entered the house of God and ate the bread of the Presence, which it was not lawful for him or his companions to eat, but only for the priests. Or have you not read in the law that on the sabbath the priests in the temple break the sabbath and yet are guiltless? I tell you, something greater than the temple is here. But if you had known what

this means, "I desire mercy and not sacrifice",
you would not have condemned the guiltless.
For **the Son of Man is lord of the sabbath.**'
(NRSV)

The Pharisees had made a bunch of rules about what keeping the Sabbath looked like. Jesus did not say people should break the Sabbath; he said that his authority to define Sabbath superseded theirs. Ultimately, it was this argument with the Pharisees that led to his death. John's Gospel records:

> Therefore the Jews started persecuting Jesus, because he was doing such things on the sabbath. But Jesus answered them, 'My Father is still working, and I also am working.' For this reason the Jews were seeking all the more to kill him, because he was not only breaking the sabbath, but was also calling God his own Father, thereby making himself equal to God. (John 5:16-18, NRSV)

It was the authority to define Sabbath that was being argued over, not the principle itself—a fine distinction lost on many Christians. Jesus did not dispute that there is a sabbath principle woven into the basic fabric of our world. Even non-Christian scientists acknowledge that fields benefit from a sabbath fallow (a year when they are not planted). Biologists will agree that working animals (including humans) cannot work more than six consecutive days without experiencing a significant drop in productivity. The principal of a sabbath rest was not disputed by Jesus.

Neither was the principle of a community pause. The Christians changed the sabbath day from Saturday to Sunday to celebrate the work of Jesus on the cross and his resurrection on the first day of the week. They changed the day, but their use of it appears the same. The author of the Hebrews says:

> And let us consider how to provoke one another to love and good deeds, not neglecting to meet together, as is the habit of some, but encouraging one another, and all the more as you see the Day approaching. (Hebrews 10:24-25, NRSV)

Elsewhere the Scriptures says:

> They devoted themselves to the apostles' teaching and fellowship, to the breaking of bread and the prayers. (Acts 2:42, NRSV)

> On the first day of the week, when we met to break bread… (Acts 20:7, NRSV)

The early church also recognized that not only did a person need one day off per week from his or her normal labours, they also needed to spend much of that time together as a believing community. They needed to learn together, eat together and pray together. This is as true today as it was then—perhaps more so. If you were to ask me why some new believers don't ever make it to Christian maturity and why they start off so well but then disappear, I would say that this issue, more often than not, is to blame. New believers who do not set aside a day to rest from their labours and connect with their believing community soon run out of gas and fall prey to the schemes of the enemy. If you are a new believer, you need to rest. One day a week. Period, This will give you some breathing space and some thinking space. Spend a good chunk of that time in Christian fellowship with your brothers and sisters at church. Go to the Sunday service EVERY WEEK. Invite yourself over to someone's house for lunch. Seriously. Most Christians are infected with the shy disease. They want you to come over for lunch but they are sure you have something better to do. You don't. So let it be known that you can be had for lunch. Let your kids (if you have them) make friends with the kids of your brothers and sisters in Christ—this will solve all sorts of problems down the road! Ask your questions over a reasonable portion of roast beef and potatoes (for reasonable portion, see 1000 –1100 m☺) and watch how veteran husbands treat their wives and vice versa. This time is so valuable; it is impossible to quantify it. Much of what I learned about Christianity as a child, I learned sitting at a table listening to my parents talk to their friends and guests about Jesus and about life. When the plates went away, out came the coffee and the talking went on. Real learning happens in that place. Skip it, and you will miss out on something magical. Whatever you do for work is less important than what happens in that place. Jesus said:

But seek first the kingdom of God and His righteousness, and all these things shall be added to you. (Matthew 6:33, NKJV)

Everything you truly want in life is found in this place—organize every week as though you believe that to be true.

TEN GOOD REASONS YOU SHOULD CELEBRATE SABBATH:

1. The Bible says so. (Exodus 20:8-11) Do you really need nine more?

2. Your body has a natural rhythm of work and rest programmed into it. Six days for work and one for rest. You cannot defy that anymore than you can defy gravity.

3. All work and no play (or praise) makes Johnny a dull (and possibly dead) boy.

4. The best things in life are learned in Christian community. If you are working all day, every day, you will miss out on too much.

5. The kingdom is built by those who show up.

6. Ceasing from our labours reminds us that there is more to life than work and money.

7. Busy people ask too few questions. It takes a solid day of rest to re-calibrate your brain.

8. Pausing from our labours reminds us that we are not as important as we think.

9. Rest allows our priorities to resurface in our brains. Busy people forget that they love the Lord, love their kids, want to grow as a Christian and don't need all of this stupid stuff.

10. Sabbath rest helps us anticipate the joy of the eternal kingdom where we will "rest from our labours." (Revelation 14:13)

PERSONAL STUDY AND REFLECTION:

Read Exodus 20:8-11 and then consider the comprehension task that follows.

Consider the seven statements below. Five of them correctly summarize how we ought to understand this commandment. Two of them are wrong. See if you can sort them out. The correct answers are in a footnote on the following page.

1. The principle of "sabbath" (resting one day in seven) is woven into the natural universe just as surely as the law of gravity.

2. Sabbath is an Old Testament law and is no longer applicable in the New Testament era.

3. Jesus insisted on his authority to define sabbath, but he did not do away with it.

4. The early Christians rejected sabbath as an overly Jewish idea.

5. The early Christians put Christ at the centre of Sabbath. They moved it to Sunday to celebrate his resurrection and they continued to meet for rest, teaching and fellowship.

6. Sabbath is not about how many steps you walk or whether you push buttons on an elevator. It is about resting from your labour and spending time in Christian community.

7. Failure to keep the sabbath is a common reason that new believers fall away.*

---

* The correct answers are 1, 3, 5, 6, and 7.

QUESTIONS AND NOTES:

CELEBRATE SABBATH
FAQ

The following questions represent the most frequent concerns for new believers starting out in their journey into Sabbath-keeping.

1. Isn't Sabbath-keeping a form of legalism? Didn't Jesus do away with the law? Isn't it all grace and freedom now?

SHORT ANSWER: No.

Medium length answer: No and read your Bible. This is a perfect example of what I call "Echo Logic" meaning, Bob says it, then Jo says it, then Terry says it and now that you've heard it three times, it must be true. Repeating a false thing multiple times does not increase its truthfulness. Jesus said:

> Do not think that I have come to abolish the law or the prophets; **I have come not to abolish** but to fulfil. For truly I tell you, until heaven and earth pass away, not one letter, not one stroke of a letter, will pass from the law until all is accomplished. Therefore, whoever breaks one of the least of these commandments, and teaches others to do the same, will be called least in the kingdom of heaven; but whoever does them and

teaches them will be called great in the kingdom
of heaven. (Matthew 5:17-19, NRSV)

Some people even suggest that while Jesus didn't think that
Jesus abolished the law, the Apostle Paul did think so. They will
helpfully quote half of a verse to make this point:

> He (Jesus) has abolished the law with its com-
> mandments and ordinances. (Ephesians 2:15,
> NRSV)

Always be wary of an argument built upon a verse fragment.
The rest of the verse tells us what point Paul is trying to make:

> So that he might create in himself one new hu-
> manity in place of the two, thus making peace,
> and might reconcile both groups to God in one
> body through the cross, thus putting to death
> that hostility through it. (Ephesians 2:15-16,
> NRSV)

The point Paul is making is that the boundary marker of the
law which separated Jews and Gentiles into two people is now
obsolete; we can be one in Christ. He did not mean to imply
that the law was bad. In fact, Paul went to great lengths to avoid
this accusation. He dealt with it head on:

> Why then the law? It was added because of
> transgressions, until the offspring would come

to whom the promise had been made; and it was ordained through angels by a mediator. Now a mediator involves more than one party; but God is one.

Is the law then opposed to the promises of God? Certainly not! For if a law had been given that could make alive, then righteousness would indeed come through the law. But the scripture has imprisoned all things under the power of sin, so that what was promised through faith in Jesus Christ might be given to those who believe.

Now before faith came, we were imprisoned and guarded under the law until faith would be revealed. Therefore the law was our disciplinarian until Christ came, so that we might be justified by faith. But now that faith has come, we are no longer subject to a disciplinarian, for in Christ Jesus you are all children of God through faith. As many of you as were baptized into Christ have clothed yourselves with Christ. There is no longer Jew or Greek, there is no longer slave or free, there is no longer male and female; for all of you are one in Christ Jesus. And if you belong to Christ, then you are Abraham's offspring, heirs according to the promise. (Galatians 3:19-29, NRSV)

Paul says that the law was good. It even helped people get saved because it defined sin and heightened the sense of one's need for salvation and grace. Think of it this way, the law was like an electric fence around the character and design of God. It

269

spelled out how far you could go before you would run up against serious consequences. That is why it is phrased negatively: "Thou shall not commit adultery." In that way, it was very useful. It limited the consequence of human sin by limiting the freedom of people to wander away from God's design. But it was just a stage in the process (a nanny or tutor, Paul says) and was not the beginning or the end. The beginning was promise—the promise to Abraham that was claimed by faith. The end is promise claimed—you guessed it—by faith. The law was an in-between helper. That does not mean that God's character has changed—far from it! Now that we have the promised Holy Spirit within us, we don't **need** the law. The Holy Spirit helps us live at the centre of God's character and design so we are no longer that interested in issues of boundary and outer limit. That is why Jesus always pointed to the centre and drew attention away from the boundary markers:

> **You have heard that it was said** to those of ancient times, "You shall not murder"; and "whoever murders shall be liable to judgement." **But I say to you** that if you are angry with a brother or sister, you will be liable to judgement; and if you insult a brother or sister, you will be liable to the council; and if you say, "You fool", you will be liable to the hell of fire....
>
> **You have heard that it was said**, "You shall not commit adultery." **But I say to you** that everyone who looks at a woman with lust has already committed adultery with her in his heart.

If your right eye causes you to sin, tear it out and throw it away; it is better for you to lose one of your members than for your whole body to be thrown into hell. And if your right hand causes you to sin, cut it off and throw it away; it is better for you to lose one of your members than for your whole body to go into hell.

It was also said, "Whoever divorces his wife, let him give her a certificate of divorce." **But I say to you** that anyone who divorces his wife, except on the ground of unchastity, causes her to commit adultery; and whoever marries a divorced woman commits adultery.

Again, you have heard that it was said to those of ancient times, "You shall not swear falsely, but carry out the vows you have made to the Lord." **But I say to you**, Do not swear at all, either by heaven, for it is the throne of God, or by the earth, for it is his footstool, or by Jerusalem, for it is the city of the great King. And do not swear by your head, for you cannot make one hair white or black. Let your word be "Yes, Yes" or "No, No"; anything more than this comes from the evil one.

You have heard that it was said, "An eye for an eye and a tooth for a tooth." **But I say to you**, Do not resist an evildoer. But if anyone strikes you on the right cheek, turn the other also; and if anyone wants to sue you and take your coat, give your cloak as well; and if anyone forces you to go one mile, go also the second mile. Give to everyone who begs from you, and do not refuse anyone who wants to borrow from you.

You have heard that it was said, "You shall love your neighbour and hate your enemy." **But I say to you**, Love your enemies and pray for those who persecute you, so that you may be children of your Father in heaven; for he makes his sun rise on the evil and on the good, and sends rain on the righteous and on the unrighteous. For if you love those who love you, what reward do you have? Do not even the tax-collectors do the same? And if you greet only your brothers and sisters, what more are you doing than others? Do not even the Gentiles do the same? Be perfect, therefore, as your heavenly Father is perfect. (Matthew 5:21-48, NRSV)

Jesus wasn't kidding when he said that our righteousness would exceed that of the Pharisees. The Pharisees loved to define the outer markers—how many steps could you walk on the Sabbath before it was a sin? Jesus said, "Forget the outer markers. I'll take you to the centre."

Sabbath keeping isn't legalism, it's obedience. (By the way, Sabbath keeping came before the law anyway, but that's a whole other story!) Jesus defined Sabbath, as was his right, but he did not abolish it. It is part of the design of God and it is still at the heart of what it means to be God's child:

Draw near to God, and he will draw near to you.
(James 4:8, NRSV)

2. I want to obey what the Bible teaches about Sabbath but it's so confusing. Give me the straight goods.

ANSWER: Ok. First let me show you what the Bible DOES NOT SAY. In the Babylonian Talmud (a collection of things Rabbis said ABOUT the Bible), there is a list of the sorts of things a person could not do on the Sabbath. Let me show you:

> The generative categories of acts of labour prohibited on the Sabbath are forty less one: he who sows, ploughs, reaps, binds sheaves, threshes, winnows, selects (fit from unfit produce or crops), grinds, sifts, kneads, bakes, he who shears wool, washes it, beats it, dyes it, spins, weaves, makes two loops, weaves two threads, separates two threads, ties, unties, sews two stitches, tears in order to sew two stitches, he who traps a deer, slaughters it, flays it, salts it, cures its hide, scrapes it, and cuts it up, he who writes two letters, erases two letters in order to write two letters, he who builds, tears down, he who puts out a fire, kindles a fire, he who hits with a hammer, he who transports an object from one domain to another—lo these are the forty generative acts of labour less one. (Shabbat 7:2)

Wow! That's a very specific list. Now **that does not come from the Bible**. The Bible says very little about what we can and cannot do on the Sabbath. The Bible says:

> Observe the Sabbath day and keep it holy, as the Lord your God commanded you. For six days you shall labour and do all your work. But the seventh day is a Sabbath to the Lord your God; you shall not do any work—you, or your son or your daughter, or your male or female slave, or your ox or your donkey, or any of your livestock, or the resident alien in your towns, so that your male and female slave may rest as well as you. (Deuteronomy 5:12-14, NRSV)

So the Bible simply says that you should not do your usual labour on the Sabbath. If you are a brick layer, you should not lay bricks. If you are a paint seller, you should not sell paint. If you are a computer salesman, you should not sell computers. That's all it says! It says we should rest from our normal employment and we should not do anything that would cause other people to have to work to support our rest. Slaves, servants and even animals were supposed to get a day off. So when Jesus tells the man to take up his mat and CARRY it (in John 5), he is telling him to break the rules of the Rabbis who explicitly said we were not to carry things from one place to another. When Jesus said, "Go carry that mat, boy, as you head towards the temple," he was sending a message to the establishment that they had it all wrong. "You guys don't get it." he says, "You are all concerned about the wrong things."

The Jewish leaders were all concerned with what sort of activity was prohibited but they missed the discussion about what the Sabbath was originally for. Jesus says more about this in Mark 2 when he says:

> Then he said to them, 'The Sabbath was made for humankind, and not humankind for the Sabbath; so the Son of Man is lord even of the Sabbath. (Mark 2:27-28, NRSV)

This confrontation happened at Jesus' instigation when he had his disciples pick heads of grain on the Sabbath. Technically, this was a violation of the rule against reaping and grinding, but it was not a violation of anything Biblical. These men were not farmers—they were fisherman and tax collectors mostly. Reaping and grinding was not their profession. Jesus uses this incident to teach that the Sabbath was made for man, not the other way around. God gave us the Sabbath because he knew we needed it. It was supposed to be a joy. It was supposed to bring us life.

Jesus makes that point in John 5:21:

> Indeed, just as the Father raises the dead and gives them life, so also the Son gives life to whomsoever he wishes. (NRSV)

Jesus says that the Sabbath is really about extending life to people and ensuring that they can access it. That was the Father's agenda and that is Jesus' agenda and it is so much more important than your list of silly rules. **Jesus says, the purpose of the Sabbath is to allow humanity to seek the things that make for life.** So what are those things? Acts 2:42 demonstrates that the early church knew this answer well. It says:

> They devoted themselves to the apostles' teaching and fellowship, to the breaking of bread and the prayers. (NRSV)

This is how they spent their day together, this is how they sought out REAL LIFE. Teaching and prayer, fellowship and a shared meal. We might summarize by saying,,they understood that two things made for life:

1. The presence of God.

2. The experience of community. The presence of God—teaching from the Word and time spent in prayer. The experience of community—fellowship and a shared meal. That's what really mattered and the Bible calls on us to set aside our employment, our busyness and focus on those things for a day.

We need to hear this today. More than any generation that has ever lived. We need to dial back on the things we do for money. We need this day more than any group of people who have ever lived. We need to make it a priority to be at church once a week—EVERY WEEK—to seek the things that make for life. And we need to be here longer. We do "drive through church" like no other generation that's ever walked the earth. We rush in five minutes late for the service, coming in during the opening song, and we give ourselves five minutes max in the lobby afterward to chat and then BANG! We are out of here. Slow down. Come early. Just like my grandparents' generation put ours to shame in terms of giving, so too, did they in terms of time spent together. They came to church, got here twenty minutes early to pray and prepare. They lingered in the lobby, went downstairs for a church lunch, went home at 3:00 p.m. and came back at 6:00 p.m. for evening service. They spent six hours on a Sunday in community, we spend seventy minutes and we wonder why we do not feel like we are living the abundant life.

Just imagine with me what church would feel like if we did it this way. What if we came to church fifteen minutes early, took our seat and prepared our spirits to worship the Lord? What if we sat under the word for forty-five minutes and spent another thirty to forty minutes in prayer and song, voicing our passions and praise to the LORD? What if we then went downstairs and shared a pot luck meal with one another? What if we all brought something and stayed to clean up? What if we actually KNEW EACH OTHER AND LOVED EACH OTHER? How would church feel? And what if instead of going to Swiss Chalet, and thereby enslaving other people and ensuring that they will never be able to join us, we opened this meal up to single moms from town so that they knew that at least once a week their kids could have a home-made meal? What if we didn't make their meal contingent upon their coming to service, we just fed them because God loved them? What sort of Sabbath would that be?

That's the conversation—it's not about whether you can cut the grass or fuss about in the garden. It's about whether you can stop doing all of the things that distract us and destroy us and whether you can prioritize the time to seek out LIFE. That's the conversation Jesus began with his controversial healings on the Sabbath.

1200-1300 M
Share Your Story

Sometimes you will hear people refer to their "personal relationship with Jesus" and it's important to understand what that means. It means that you can't consider yourself a Christian just because your parents are Christians or you come from a supposedly Christian country. You have to decide for yourself to follow Jesus. There are no innocent bystanders in the Kingdom of God. You chose to be in or you chose to be out. You can't be born into it. A Jewish Rabbi came to Jesus to talk about this very thing. Being a Jew, he assumed he had been "born into" the Kingdom of God by virtue of his having been born Jewish. Jesus told him:

MILE 1

> "Most assuredly, I say to you, unless one is born
> again, he cannot see the kingdom of God."
> Nicodemus said to Him, "How can a man be
> born when he is old? Can he enter a second
> time into his mother's womb and be born?" Je-
> sus answered, "Most assuredly, I say to you,
> unless one is born of water and the Spirit, he
> cannot enter the kingdom of God. (John 3:3-5,.
> NKJV)

You don't chose to be born of water (babies come out
rather wet and unhappy, don't they?), but you have to chose to
be born of the Spirit. Because you make a personal choice, we
refer to it as a "personal relationship." That is definitely true but
it can be misleading. The fact is, there is very little about the
Christian faith other than that initial decision that is "personal."
After that, it gets quite tribal. It is more like a family than anything else. In fact, the Bible refers to the church as the "household of God."

> So then you are no longer strangers and aliens,
> but you are citizens with the saints and also
> **members of the household of God**, (Ephe-
> sians 2:19, NRSV)

I have four kids, so I can assure you that in a large family
there is very little "personal space" or "personal" anything. My
toothbrush is often mysteriously wet, my wallet is often mysteriously empty and my car is often crammed full of booster seats,

wet wipes and "sippy cups." Welcome to family. Your personal faith decision leads pretty abruptly into full-fledged family life. Jesus wants to make sure you make this transition pretty quickly so he commands that you go public with our faith ASAP. In the Gospel of Mark, Jesus heals a man who had been under the power of many demons. The story goes on to say:

> As he was getting into the boat, the man who had been possessed by demons begged him that he might be with him. But Jesus refused, and said to him, '**Go home to your friends, and tell them** how much the Lord has done for you, and what mercy he has shown you.' And he went away and began to proclaim in the Decapolis how much Jesus had done for him; and everyone was amazed. (Mark 5:18-20, NRSV)

This guy had only been saved for a brief period and Jesus commands him to go on a speaking tour and give his testimony to everyone he knew. His "personal salvation" became front page news.

Living our faith publicly and speaking our faith audibly is not really an optional component of Christianity. The Scriptures say:

> For one believes with the heart and so is justified, and **one confesses with the mouth and so is saved**. (Romans 10:10, NRSV)

MILE 1

Jesus takes this pretty serious, even saying:

> Everyone therefore who acknowledges me be-
> fore others, I also will acknowledge before my
> Father in heaven; but whoever denies me before
> others, I also will deny before my Father in
> heaven. (Matthew 10:32-33, NRSV)

Private Christianity is apparently not an option. If you are a
new Christian, you need to tell your story and make your confession. The best place to start is at your baptism. Shortly after
you make your personal faith decision, ask your church for an
opportunity to make a public baptismal confession. In our
church, before we dunk the new believer under the water, we
give them the microphone so that they can tell the church the
story of how they came to know Christ as their Lord and Saviour. This is one of the most exciting things in the life of the
church! Nothing fires the heart like the testimony of baby Christians!

The next place you should begin sharing your story is with
your friends and family members. They know you better than
anyone and they will be the most impacted by what you have to
say. You don't have to create a "spiel" or a five minute presenta-
tion with flip charts and graphs. Just tell the story of how you
came to call Christ Lord and Saviour. It could be as simple as:
"Mom, you've watched me make a lot of bad decisions over the
last ten years. I was so arrogant to think that I could predict the
consequences of my actions and it was just plain insane of me to

think that I could re-write the moral code of the universe to suit my appetites and desires. I made a huge mess and hurt a lot of people. I came to the conclusion last week that it would be stupid of me to try and untangle this mess on my own and try again—I'd probably make just as big a mess my next try at it. So, I decided to turn the control of my life over to Jesus Christ. I believe that with him at the wheel, my life is going to turn around. I've asked him to forgive all my sins and past mistakes. The two of us are going to work together to make amends with all the people I've hurt and to forge a new path going forward. I thought you'd want to know." Maybe something as simple as that even intimidates you. I know of a man who was so shy that he couldn't talk to anybody about anything! When he accepted Christ as his Lord and Saviour, he wanted to tell people but he didn't have the words. His name was Jim. So he made a pin that said in big red letters: J.I.M. and he wore it everyday. People would say, "What's with the pin Jim? We all know your name." He would reply, "It's not my name. It stands for Jesus Is Mine - J.I.M. I made Jesus my Lord and I wanted people to know." That's all he could get out but it was pretty effective, believe me. Your story doesn't have to be perfect, it just has to be true and it has to be public.

MILE 1

TEN GOOD REASONS YOU
SHOULD SHARE YOUR STORY:

1. The Bible says so. (Romans 10:10) Do you really need nine more?

2. Decisions made in secret are soon forgotten. Taking your decision public will cement the reality of it in your mind.

3. The same reason people get married: Warm sentiments in the back of a car are not nearly as binding as public statements made before friends and family.

4. There are probably a lot of people who will find Jesus through the same door you did. Sharing your story may give them the help they need.

5. How can people believe the Gospel if they never hear it? Most people don't go to church, so their only chance is if you tell them.

6. It will make evangelism less scary. Everything is scary if you haven't done it. Go on the same roller coaster sixty-seven times and it isn't so scary. The more you tell your story, the easier it gets.

7. It will lighten your fears about persecution. I've told my testimony more times than I can remember and I've never been punched in the face (at least not for telling my story. I've been punched in the face for

other unrelated reasons. I have an older brother, after all.)

8. It will ease the burden on your pastor. Too many of us think that it is our pastor's job to lead our friends to Christ. Wrong. It's your job. Your friends know you and like you. They probably think your pastor is weird.

9. It will let God know that you are not ashamed of him. Would you like it if your kids pretended not to know you when you dropped them off at school?

10. Too many people believe that no one can change. Tell them the story of how God is changing you. The world needs fewer pessimists.

PERSONAL STUDY AND REFLECTION:

Let's read the story of that man that Jesus set free from demons and commissioned to be a roving storyteller. It's found in Mark 5:1-21. Read that now, and then consider the comprehension task that follows.

Consider the seven statements below. Five of them accurately summarize the teaching of the passage you just read. Two do not. See if you can sort them out. The correct answers are in a footnote on the following page.

1. You have to go to Bible School or Seminary before you are allowed to tell anyone the Gospel.
2. Every saved person should tell their story.
3. The demon-possessed guy had been a Christian for about ten minutes (or thereabouts) when he was commissioned by Jesus to tell his story.
4. Jesus correctly assumed that people who knew the demon-possessed man would be very impacted by the change they observed in his behaviour.
5. Jesus probably went around and visited with all of the people this rookie talked to to make sure he told the story correctly.
6. Actually, it appears that Jesus moved on to another territory, assuming that the young man had the Decapolis pretty much covered.
7. The Gospel spreads best when everyone simply tells the story of what God is doing in their lives.*

---

* The correct answers are 2, 3, 4, 6, and 7.

QUESTIONS AND NOTES:

SHARE YOUR STORY
FAQ

The following questions represent the most frequent concerns for new believers starting out in their journey into story sharing.

1. My testimony isn't very interesting so I don't feel like me "telling my story" will lead many people to Christ. Plus, I am really afraid of public speaking. Is their still a role for me in this?

ANSWER: A lot of people ask this question in one form or another. I think it is because we use the phrase "personal evangelism" so much to describe Gospel sharing. The word "personal" makes it seem like this is something you have to do by yourself and the word "evangelism" makes it seem like a story you have to tell on stage, with a microphone and an outrageously gelled hairstyle, preferably while turning "Jesus" into a three-syllable word. Not so. The truth is, our shared life together, lived visibly before the world, is in itself a pretty compelling story. Let me show you what I mean.

Rodney Stark is a secular sociologist who wrote a book called The Rise Of Christianity, not to commend Christian virtue, but to try and answer a question that has mystified pagan observers for over one thousand seven hundred years: how did a little tribe of Christians, numbering no more than three thousand people in the year AD 60 grow to become the majority religion in the Roman Empire, numbering more than thirty million people in less than two hundred and fifty years? Think about that for a moment. In the time of the Apostle Paul, there were just over 3000 Christians, the historians estimate. None of the churches he wrote to had more than hundred people in them, except perhaps the church in Rome. Two hundred and fifty years later there were at least thirty million Christians. How did that happen? Even scholars who don't love Jesus wrestle with this as one of the most amazing miracles in history. Do you know what the near consensus answer is? The reason for this growth according to historians is the ethic of humble service within the early Christian community.

Christians were famous for providing basic nursing to their own sick and elderly, something pagans did not do. Most pagans in the Greco-Romans system had no concept of life after death and so they rarely would have contact with sick people, fearing to catch whatever they had. They left their old and infirm to die in isolation. The Christians not only cared for their own poor but would also go into the homes of the sick and dying pagans and nurse them. There were two great plagues in the Roman Empire that decimated the population. The first was during the reign of Marcus Aurelius, made famous to modern people through the movie Gladiator. During that plague 30% of the pagan population died. The Christian death rate was less than 10%. Why? Well, you and I might talk about the Holy Spirit and we might quote Psalm 91. But the historians will tell you it was because basic nursing cuts down mortality rates by two-thirds. There was another plague fifty years after that and again 30% of the pagan population perished and again good Christian men and women, with no thought of their own lives, changed the sheets, emptied the chamber pots and spooned broth to their sick pagan neighbours and yet still their mortality rate was less than 10%. This became pretty convincing evidence of the superiority of our God and of our faith. It resulted in a massive conversion of pagans to Christianity. Pagans wanted to be part of a society where the rich cared for the poor and where the healthy nursed the sick. They wanted to worship a God who had power over disease and whose servants acted like they believed it. Evangelism became a pretty easy task at that point.

My point is that this was the way God intended evangelism to work. He wanted the world to look at the STORY of the CHURCH and see the Gospel miracle played out as though on stage. This is how the Bible said it would happen. Look very carefully at Ephesians 3:8-10:

> Although I am the very least of all the saints, this grace was given to me to bring to the Gentiles the news of the boundless riches of Christ, and to make everyone see what is the plan of the mystery hidden for ages in God who created all things; **so that through the church** the wisdom of God in its rich variety might now be made known. (NRSV)

Isn't that incredible? Paul says, "I've been charged to do this evangelism thing, so I am focused on making the church the visible demonstration of that miraculous story." Wow! What does that do to the modern day heresy of the Jesus and Me movement? "I have my personal relationship with Jesus Christ. I am at home watching religious television right now, doing my devotions in my Daily Bread pamphlet. I don't need to go to church because that is just so much religious legalism. I'm not into religion. I'm having a relationship with Jesus Christ." HERESY!! The mystery of God is not made known through people having a personal relationship with Jesus Christ. It is made known through the CHURCH!!! Now, maybe you think there is a Greek "get out of jail free card" here, but there isn't. The word Paul used is *ecclesia* which in normal Greek usage means, and I'm quoting directly from the dictionary here, "a gathering of citizens called out from their homes." The Christians adopted the word and it came to mean, and again I'm quoting directly, "an assembly of Christians gathered for worship in a religious meeting." Did you hear that? Gathered people at a Christian religious meeting—SUNDAY CHURCH that is, is the vehicle THROUGH WHICH GOD IS REVEALING THE MYSTERY OF HIS RECREATIVE GRACE. How about that? Let that settle on you. Do you understand what that means? It means that CHURCH IS THE MESSAGE. You are a part of that. I am a part of that. It means that WE ARE THE MESSAGE. That is the story.

That feels like new information, doesn't it? It shouldn't, the Bible says this again and again. We read passages like 2 Corinthians 5:20 which say:

> So we are ambassadors for Christ, since God is making his appeal through us. (NRSV)

But we have an automatic filter in our brains which translates all "us" verses into "me" verses. So, in our disgustingly individualistic Western culture, we read that as, "God is making his appeal through ME." But it doesn't say "ME," it says "US." Let me tell you a little secret: "THERE IS NO PERSONAL EVANGELISM." It doesn't exist. Now, that's hard for me to hear because I took a course in Bible school called "Personal Evangelism." It taught me how to use the Evangelism Explosion (EE) curriculum so that I could assault people in cafeterias and bus stations, pretending to be taking a religious survey. I used it many times to harass countless numbers of Chicago pedestrians with no fruit whatsoever. Isn't it funny how God doesn't bless what he never told us to do? Now, I'm not saying we shouldn't share the Gospel, I'm saying **we shouldn't do it as a solo sport**. This is new information; I know, it feels new even though it isn't, so let me slow down and unpack some implications.

First of all, what this means is that when we get the church right, the cause of the Gospel flourishes. Do you see that? See if this is true. God is revealing the mystery of the Gospel through the church, using the church as an object lesson and an agency

for his grace. We immediately start to see the connection between the quality of our church community and the progress of
our Gospel message. What a shame it is that the secular scholars
have had to remind us what lay behind the startling progress of
the Gospel in the first two hundred and fifty years of our exis-
tence. Jesus told us never to forget:

> By this everyone will know that you are my dis-
> ciples, if you have love for one another. (John
> 13:35, NRSV)

When we understand, in the light of incarnation theology,
that **we are the message**, we start taking the quality of our
community very seriously, because it is our Gospel proclamation.

Of course, the opposite is equally true; when we get church
wrong, the cause of the Gospel is greatly hindered. Do you
know one thing I did learn by religiously assaulting people back
in Bible School? I learned why people don't want to be Christians. One of the EE questions is essentially, "Why don't you go
to church?" The most common answer I heard was "because
Christians are jerks." Then they'd either tell me a story about
some preacher that had fallen morally, some Sunday School
teacher they had who had treated them poorly or they would
speak more historically and talk about the Crusades or the fact
that the southern slave holders were almost all some form of
Christian. At first, this confused me because I wanted to talk
about Jesus and they wanted to talk about Christians. The EE

instructors would tell us, "Steer the conversation back to Jesus. Don't get sucked into talking about Christians." But you know what? The only Jesus these people know is the one they saw in so-called believers. That is the problem. WE ARE THE BODY OF CHRIST. We are the only version of Jesus most people have ever seen and so when we get church wrong, the cause of the Gospel is greatly hindered.

That is why a good church will take church discipline very seriously. A good church understands that if we don't do the work and deal with our garbage, then the lost are not going to embrace Jesus. So, they suck it up and we deal with sin. Believe me, most pastors don't want to do it; I don't want to do it. I don't enjoy calling people and asking if I can meet with them to discuss their gossip or their adultery or their drunkenness. Those meetings tend to go horribly bad and I would much rather meet with happy people to discuss their latest dream or revelation or blessing. Those are fun. Discipline meetings are not fun but they have to happen. We have to stamp out sins—all sins—but especially those that shame the name of Jesus.

The long and the short of this is that, even if you are not great at "stage evangelism," you have an important role to play in telling the Gospel story. You can help us make our story GREAT, INSPIRING, REVELATORY and COMPELLING. Commit to making your church a story about the miracle of the Gospel. That is evangelism at its finest.

2. Ok, so my primary and best contribution to this Gospel story piece is helping to build a compelling community. Does that get me off the hook for witnessing to my friends and co-workers?

ANSWER: No. The Bible says:

> Always be prepared to give an answer to everyone who asks you to give the reason for the hope that you have. But do this with gentleness and respect. (1 Peter 3:15, NIV)

If you live a compelling Christian life as part of a compelling Christian community, you will inevitably be asked to explain yourself. This is the best witnessing opportunity you are likely to get, so make good and careful use of it.

My wife and I were involved with Christian fostering, mostly to high-needs kids for about nine years. We got into it because my wife had been a Jr. Kindergarten teacher and a nanny and she had a significant passion for children's work. We got into it because she wanted to stay home with our children and we needed to make a little bit of money. This was a way to do that. There are a lot of ways to make a little bit of money, but we figured if she could do something that was with children and that blessed the Kingdom, then so much the better. So, we hooked up with a Christian agency and started looking after children in our home. A few years in, we were entrusted with a little native girl who had been severely sexually abused and suffered from numerous handicaps. She lived in our home for three years until she was moved to a specialized medical facility. We did our best to love and care for her and we laboured in love for her. Over time, our home became a place of healing and restoration for her and she left our home far healthier than when she had come. But what we learned by accident was how compelling and intriguing Gospel images are to our culture. We were shocked by how many people would ask us the same question, "Why would a middle-class, white family with beautiful children of their own take a disabled, native child into their home?" No one could understand this and they asked us that question time and time again. We found ourselves, completely by accident, having Gospel conversations with everyone from our Real Estate agent, our soccer parents, our neighbours and even our own relatives. But being asked a question is no good if you don't have an answer. So we came up with one. We started answering that question by saying, "Sally (not her real name) is a child of God. She is wonderful and interestingly made. We believe that it is our great privilege to have her in our home." As you can imagine, this started some conversations, many of which went on into full-blown evangelistic dialogues. The point is, use what is interesting or compelling about your spiritual life (if there isn't anything, start DOING something interesting and compelling as an outflow of your spiritual life) to craft a beginning point for a Gospel story. This will become your "natural opening" for numerous effective Gospel encounters.

3. Isn't telling "my story" kind of arrogant? Doesn't it draw attention to me instead of Jesus?

ANSWER: Not if you do it right. The Apostle Paul understood this dynamic and frequently used his own story to tell THE STORY. He had no problem telling his followers:

> Therefore I urge you to imitate me. (1 Corinthians 4:16, NIV)

That sounds kind of arrogant in our ears but Paul understood that everyone follows Jesus through the example and leadership of someone else. Everyone's Jesus is incarnated. You have to see something lived in a human life before you can imitate it. The trick is telling your story in a way that safeguards God's glory. Paul knew how to do that too:

> But by the grace of God I am what I am, and his grace towards me has not been in vain. On the contrary, I worked harder than any of them— though it was not I, but the grace of God that is with me. (1 Corinthians 15:10, NRSV)

There is an art form to telling a story of God's work in your life such that he gets the glory rather than you. It's more than just throwing in the odd "by God's grace," though that is important. It begins with the humility to recognize that everything that is done through you begins with a grace gift of God. But it doesn't mean that you have to pretend that you weren't there. God uses people and we are more than Holy Spirit hand puppets. Practise telling stories in a way that God gets the glory, but doesn't falsely imply that you were an unwilling participant. Sometimes the order of the story will make that point. When Nehemiah was telling the story of a great victory over a superior enemy so that future generations could be encouraged by his example, he understood this skill. He said:

> So we rebuilt the wall, and all the wall was joined together to half its height; for the people had a mind to work. But when Sanballat and Tobiah and the Arabs and the Ammonites and the Ashdodites heard that the repairing of the walls of Jerusalem was going forward and the gaps were beginning to be closed, they were very angry, and all plotted together to come and fight against Jerusalem and to cause confusion in it. **So we prayed to our God, and set a guard** as a protection against them day and night. (Nehemiah 4:6-9, NRSV)

We prayed to our God AND set a guard. That's a skilfully told story. It is clear that Nehemiah wanted the emphasis on the power and grace of God but he also wants the people to learn that we have a role to play too. True it is a secondary role, but it still matters. Give God the glory in your story telling, but also do not rob people of your example. It is a tricky road to find, so approach it carefully and prayerfully.

1300-1400 M
Edit Your Associations

I have good news and bad news. The good news is that you have made a lot of progress if you have made it this far. The truth is, a lot of people spend their whole lives on the access ramp of the Christian life. They meet Christ at the Narrow Gate and they pitch a tent and march around it day after day like the Jewish army at Jericho. They live and die within a few hundred metres of the Narrow Gate. But beyond the Narrow Gate, there is the Narrow Way. The call of Jesus is not "meet me", "love me" or even "accept me." The call of Jesus is "follow me." So, the good news is you've come a long way. The bad news is that this next piece is really tough. Not only is it tough, it is also counter-intuitive. It sounds like it shouldn't be true—it sounds like the opposite of true. Jesus said, "love your enemies" (Matthew

5:44) and the Bible says, "love is the fulfilment of the law." (Romans 13:10) How then can it be true that as new believers, we have to edit our associations and put some distance between ourselves and some of the people we used to call friends?

First of all, we need to get the facts straight. Jesus did not say, "Be friends with everyone." He said, "Love your enemies." When you put those statements side by side you immediately spot the difference. To love your enemies actually means to love people you are NOT friends with. The Apostle Paul did not say, "Be best buds with bad influences." He said "associate with the lowly." (Romans 12:16) The Bible says that Jesus was "a friend of sinners." It does not say that his companions were fools. The Bible is clear that there are some people we should not be friends with. The Apostle Paul says:

> Do not be deceived: 'Bad company ruins good morals.' (1 Corinthians 15:33, NRSV)

As Christians we are always trying to figure out how to be a good influence on the world without being negatively influenced ourselves. Jesus knew how hard this balance would be to strike, so he prayed:

> I am not asking you to take them out of the world, but I ask you to protect them from the evil one. They do not belong to the world, just as I do not belong to the world. Sanctify them in

the truth; your word is truth. (John 17:15-17, NRSV)

Jesus knew that we would not feel completely comfortable in the world once we had been sanctified (set apart) by his truth. He prayed that we would figure out a way to be "in the world but not OF the world." That is a tricky thing. We want to love the people in our neighbourhoods and reach out to them with the Gospel, but we do not want to be so cozy with the world that our own character is compromised. The Bible warns:

> Do you not know that friendship with the world is enmity with God? Therefore whoever wishes to be a friend of the world becomes an enemy of God. (James 4:4, NRSV)

As a new believer, you need to engage this tricky calling. In practical terms, there will always be people you need to sever ties with once you become a Christian. There may be a group of guys that you used to visit the strip club with or a group of girls you used to gather with who did nothing but gossip. You will likely discover that there is no way to continue being close friends with those people without being dragged into activity that is not honouring to God. You don't have to blacklist those people, but you will likely have to let them know that you can't hang out the way you used to.

I had to do this with my hockey friends when I made a commitment to the Lordship of Christ in my own life. Hockey is well-known for its "beer and brawl" leagues. If you have not made it to the NHL by a certain age, competitive hockey tends to degenerate into beer and brawl fests populated by angry wannabes who are trying to hold onto their fading professional dreams for as long as possible. That may seem to be a gross generalization but it happened to be very true of the group of guys I was playing with at the time. My commitment to the Lord meant that I needed to cut ties with that crew. Our whole social context seemed to revolve around discussing our fights and/or sexual conquests over enormous quantities of post-game beer. I saw no way to redeem or reform this and needed to simply remove myself from it. It was a hindrance to me in following Christ. The Scriptures call on us to:

> Throw off everything that hinders and the sin that so easily entangles, and let us run with perseverance the race marked out for us. (Hebrews 12:1, NIV)

Some new believers overestimate their own immunity to sin and temptation and forget that God has more than just us on the payroll. They risk being drawn back into the same sins they have been saved out of by bravely marching back into the devil's den. There is a time for holy cowardice in the Christian journey. Paul tells a young man that he is mentoring:

> Flee also youthful lusts; but pursue righteousness, faith, love, peace with those who call on

the Lord out of a pure heart. (2 Timothy 2:22, NKJV)

Flee. Run away! And join instead with those who call on the Lord out of a pure heart. The Bible is absolutely clear that whether you grow in righteousness or fall back into sin has a great deal to do with how you edit your associations.

> Whoever walks with the wise becomes wise, but the companion of fools suffers harm. (Proverbs 13:20, NRSV)

As a new believer talk to your mentor (you asked for one back at the 700-800m mark remember?) about your friendships and associations. Do you work at a bar or restaurant where everyone abuses alcohol and drugs? Get a new job. Do you have certain friends that only get together to drink themselves into a stupor? Get some new friends. Are you part of any clubs (The Masons, The Shriners, etc.) that are not compatible with Christianity? Leave them. Use the wisdom and maturity of your mentor to help you with this because the Bible does not say that you should sever all ties with the unsaved world. That would take you out of the game completely! You can mess this up by editing too harshly just as surely as you can mess this up by not editing at all. This requires wisdom. We should keep many/most of our previous associations because they are the people we are most likely to win for Christ. The Bible says in Matthew 9 that when a tax collector named Matthew (the author of the Gospel of Matthew) accepted Christ, he immediately invited all of his business colleagues to a dinner where he introduced them to Jesus. Had Matthew edited ALL of his associations, he would have missed out on a fantastic opportunity to share the Gospel. We must use wisdom and discretion when we edit our associations, but we must do it none the less.

TEN GOOD REASONS YOU
SHOULD EDIT YOUR ASSOCIATIONS:

1. The Bible says so. (1 Corinthians 15:33) Do you really need nine more?
2. Your associations may have been the reason for some of the mess you just got saved out of.
3. God has lots of people on the team. You are not the answer to every problem and God may have another way to get the Gospel to certain people you know.
4. Early on in the Christian life we really need to be surrounded with wise people who can help us grow.
5. When you stick a white glove in mud, the glove gets muddy; the mud does not get "glovey."
6. Until you have your feet solidly on the shore, you are just one more drowning man. Drowning men make poor lifeguards.

7. Iron sharpens iron (Proverbs 27:17) and wise friends will help you grow much quicker.

8. Jesus prayed for your ability to balance being in the world without being of it. You can trust in that prayer to help you sort through this.

9. Our friends influence our families. There are certain "friends" that can lead our kids and loved ones in very dangerous directions.

10. The Bible says, "A little bit of yeast spoils the whole batch of dough." (1 Corinthians 5:6) Jesus used the analogy of yeast both ways: to remind us to be people of influence and to remind us to beware the influences we expose ourselves to.

PERSONAL STUDY AND REFLECTION:

Read the passages below and then consider the comprehension task that follows.

- 2 Corinthians 6:14-18
- 1 Corinthians 5:11

Consider the seven statements below. Five of them correctly summarize the passages you just read. Two of them are wrong. See if you can sort them out. The correct answers are in a footnote on the following page.

1. While we can and should be *friendly* with all people, we really should not be too closely connected with anyone who is not a believer.
2. Christians should be friends with everyone! Jesus was a friend of sinners after all.
3. Christians should love everyone, and should count sinners among their friends—but there is a limit to how closely we should be associated with some of those sinners. Jesus didn't open a carpentry shop with sinners; he talked to them about the Gospel.
4. The most dangerous people of all to be too connected with are people who say they are Christians but who disregard the clear teachings of Christ. You should have nothing to do with these people.
5. Because God is joined to us through Christ, whatever we join ourselves to has implications for God. Therefore, we should be very careful about our intimate associations.
6. A brave Christian goes looking for friends in all the deepest pockets of darkness. If Jesus were on the earth today, he would be playing poker at the casino and making friends with the strippers.

7. A new Christian will need to work with his/her mentor to ensure that his/her associations do not lead to harm and spiritual ruin.*

---

* The correct answers are 1, 3, 4, 5, and 7.

QUESTIONS AND NOTES:

EDIT YOUR ASSOCIATIONS

FAQ

The following questions represent the most frequent concerns for new believers starting out in their journey into association editing.

1. My husband and I used to do a lot of crazy/sinful things before I became a Christian. Now he thinks I'm no fun and I feel myself getting dragged back into my old ways. Should I "edit out" my husband?

ANSWER: You might be surprised how often this question comes up (I got asked it again last week) and you might be surprised how long this question has been coming up. The Apostle Paul dealt with this very issue in one of his churches.

> To the married I give this command—not I but the Lord—that the wife should not separate from her husband (but if she does separate, let her remain unmarried or else be reconciled to her husband), and that the husband should not divorce his wife.
>
> To the rest I say—I and not the Lord—that if any believer has a wife who is an unbeliever,

and she consents to live with him, he should not divorce her. And if any woman has a husband who is an unbeliever, and he consents to live with her, she should not divorce him. For the unbelieving husband is made holy through his wife, and the unbelieving wife is made holy through her husband. Otherwise, your children would be unclean, but as it is, they are holy. But if the unbelieving partner separates, let it be so; in such a case the brother or sister is not bound. It is to peace that God has called you. Wife, for all you know, you might save your husband. Husband, for all you know, you might save your wife. (1 Corinthians 7:10-16, NRSV)

Don't get hung up on the phrase, "I not the Lord" as Paul is simply indicating that he has no direct quote from Jesus to offer in response to their question but he does "have the Spirit" so there is no difference in authority. It is a helpful reminder that sometimes we have to use our brains in partnership with the Holy Spirit to answer questions that are not covered in the teachings of Jesus. The point Paul is making, however, is that the believer should never initiate the divorce. If the unbelieving partner finds the faith of his/her spouse absolutely unpalatable and initiates a divorce, then the believer is free and able to re-marry. But, if it is at all possible to maintain the marriage, it should be done. So, how do you stay in a marriage without losing your faith?

Let me preface this by saying, "I not the Lord." Jesus didn't address this so we have to use our Holy Spirit wisdom here and apply other Biblical principles to this concern. The first thing I would say is do not cause offense needlessly. Many wives and husbands irritate their unsaved spouses unnecessarily. They become inhibited sexually, they stop laughing, they frown at everything—none of those things are necessary (or even advisable) for a Christian and therefore, can be safely abandoned. The second thing I would counsel is to avoid ruining your testimony in order to share the Gospel. Many wives nag their husbands right out of the kingdom, often while trying to win them to Christ. I know this is politically incorrect to say, but it has been my experience. Of course, there are MANY sins that seem to particularly afflict husbands, but nagging seems to be a wife-thing at times and it is not helpful to the cause of the Gospel. The Bible says:

> Wives, in the same way, accept the authority of your husbands, so that, even if some of them do not obey the word, they may be won over without a word by their wives' conduct, when they see the purity and reverence of your lives. (1 Peter 3:1-2, NRSV)

It is CONDUCT and life change that will win the spouse, not nagging and finger waving. Continue in joy; live fully and generously within the Lord's permission for your marriage (i.e., have lots of wonderful, creative and generous sex—see 1 Corinthians 7:3-5) and do not pester over issues that you do not need to pester over. Remember that as Christians, we judge each other, NOT THE PEOPLE OF THE WORLD. The Bible says that very thing:

> For what have I to do with judging those out-
> side? Is it not those who are inside that you are
> to judge? God will judge those outside. (1 Co-
> rinthians 5:12-13, NRSV)

As a believer, you are NOT TO JUDGE AND PESTER your unbelieving spouse about the things he/she likes to do. They are free to live outside of God's design. God did not build an electric fence around the tree of the knowledge of good and evil and neither should you. You can refuse to participate in something and still be pleasant about their freedom to partake. Live your life by God's design and show your spouse the value and beauty of that way and invite him or her to join you. Try that strategy and see if there is improvement.

2. My family members (parents, brothers, sisters, etc.) are not be-lievers and my Christian commitments often conflict with family gatherings. Also, the activities at those gatherings are not always appropriate for me as a new believer, what should I do?

ANSWER: The truth is that Christianity has always been divisive. You may not have heard that before, but it is. Jesus said:

Do not think that I have come to bring peace to the earth; I have not come to bring peace, but a sword. For I have come to set a man against his father, and a daughter against her mother, and a daughter-in-law against her mother-in-law; and one's foes will be members of one's own household. (Matthew 10:34-36, NRSV)

Jesus wasn't saying that he wanted people to be disconnected from family. He was just saying that he knew it would happen and he knew that division was an unavoidable consequence of his life and ministry. He also knew that people would have to choose. He made his choice:

The crowd came together again, so that they could not even eat. When his family heard it, they went out to restrain him, for people were saying, 'He has gone out of his mind.' And the scribes who came down from Jerusalem said, 'He has Beelzebul, and by the ruler of the demons he casts out demons.' And he called them to him, and spoke to them in parables, 'How can Satan cast out Satan? If a kingdom is divided against itself, that kingdom cannot stand. And if a house is divided against itself, that house will not be able to stand. And if Satan has risen up against himself and is divided, he cannot stand, but his end has come. But no one can enter a strong man's house and plunder his property without first tying up the strong man; then indeed the house can be plundered.

313

'Truly I tell you, people will be forgiven for their sins and whatever blasphemies they utter; but whoever blasphemes against the Holy Spirit can never have forgiveness, but is guilty of an eternal sin'—for they had said, 'He has an unclean spirit.'

Then his mother and his brothers came; and standing outside, they sent to him and called him. A crowd was sitting around him; and they said to him, 'Your mother and your brothers and sisters are outside, asking for you.' And **he replied, 'Who are my mother and my brothers?'** And looking at those who sat around him, he said, 'Here are my mother and my brothers! **Whoever does the will of God is my brother and sister and mother.'** (Mark 3:20-35, NRSV)

Jesus knew that his ministry and his teaching would divide families—it divided his. That is one of the reasons that the church absolutely HAS TO WORK, for many people, it will be the only means of support and fellowship after they have been kicked out of their earthly families. Jesus said that anyone who turned back from following him because of the personal cost would be counted as unworthy of the kingdom of God:

Whoever loves father or mother more than me is not worthy of me; and whoever loves son or daughter more than me is not worthy of me. (Matthew 10:37, NRSV)

He stated the same thing positively later in the same Gospel:

> Jesus said to them, 'Truly I tell you, at the renewal of all things, when the Son of Man is seated on the throne of his glory, you who have followed me will also sit on twelve thrones, judging the twelve tribes of Israel. And everyone who has left houses or brothers or sisters or father or mother or children or fields, for my name's sake, will receive a hundredfold, and will inherit eternal life. (Matthew 19:28-29, NRSV)

In most places in the world, new Christians pay a heavy price for conversion. I do some mission work in India and in that country, becoming a Christian is expensive. It costs you all of the government subsidies that are caste based, it costs you job opportunities and it almost always costs you your family. The same is true in much of Africa. A pastor friend of mine is from Nigeria and when he became a Christian, his Muslim family put a death warrant out for him, held a funeral for him and took back all of his land and inheritance. His wife left him and he had to flee to Canada with nothing. For most of us, it simply means skipping the odd reunion and dropping down a peg or two on mom's affection list. You'll live.

1400-1500 M
Explore Your Gifts

Some would argue that we should have talked about this BEFORE we talked about learning to serve (500-600m), but my experience has been that the discipline of service usually precedes a believer's discovery of their giftedness. In fact, it is usually through the practice and discipline of service that one's giftedness comes to light. A spiritual gift is not some mysterious "divine virus" implanted by the Holy Spirit. A spiritual gift is an ability God gives you to use and a ministry God promises to bless in your life. The Bible promises that EVERY believer has a spiritual gift:

> To each is given the manifestation of the Spirit
> for the common good. (1 Corinthians 12:7,
> NRSV)

Paul's point is pretty clear: every saved person is given some manifestation of the Holy Spirit. There is no such thing as a saved person without a spiritual gift. A saved person may not know what their gift is, but they can be sure that they have one. If you have confessed Christ as Saviour and you follow him as Lord, then you have a gift. If you don't know what it is, ask someone who knows you, chances are they know what it is. If that doesn't work, try and take a spiritual gift test. They are not infallible but they are useful in highlighting where God is particularly using and blessing you. Every saved person has some manifestation of the Holy Spirit.

The Bible also says that the spiritual gifts are given to build up the church. 1 Corinthians declares:

> Since you are eager for spiritual gifts, strive to
> excel in them **for building up the church**. (1
> Corinthians 14:12, NRSV)

"For the common good" and "for building up the church"— Paul is very clear on this: the gifts are given for the good of the church. They are not given for our entertainment, nor are they given to confirm our status. Sometimes we cry out for gifts not because our church is lacking something, we cry out for a gift because we are insecure in our faith. "O Lord, if I could just have the gift of healing, then I would be sure that I was saved and sure that you love me and sure that you have some special purpose for me." But the gifts aren't given to make us feel special or to confirm our faith, they are given to build up the church.

At points in the past, some Christians have felt the need to make grand statements about which gifts are suited to each different season in the history of the church. This is a fairly silly thing to do since the Bible is clear that gifts are given:

> Just as the Spirit chooses. (1 Corinthians 12:11, NRSV)

The Holy Spirit is passionate about seeing your church equipped to prevail in its calling, so we can pretty much anticipate that he will send whatever gifts he thinks are necessary to get the job done. He will decide, not us.

Once you know what your gift is, it's important to remember that everything you've learned thus far about living in Christian tribe is still true. Just because everyone has a gift and everyone has a role, does not mean that every voice is equal and that there is no leadership or command centre in the kingdom of God (700-800m). Paul wants to be very clear on that. He says in 1 Corinthians 12:27:

> Now you are the body of Christ and individually members of it. And God has appointed in the church first apostles, second prophets, third teachers; then deeds of power, then gifts of heal-

ing, forms of assistance, forms of leadership, various kinds of tongues.

There is a central command centre in the Body of Christ, just like there is a central nervous system in a physical body. Imagine a body where every piece of the body had a personal vision statement. The eye wanted to look at mountains, the ear wanted to hear a symphony and the left leg wanted to go for a jog, while the right leg wanted to do deep knee bends. We call that a seizure in real life, don't we? That's not good. Those folks end up in some form of medical restraint and are given a horse tranquillizer. A body can't function without some sort of unified command centre—so it is in the Body of Christ. The Bible says:

> Obey your leaders and submit to them, for they
> are keeping watch over your souls and will give
> an account. Let them do this with joy and not
> with sighing—for that would be harmful to you.
> (Hebrews 13:17, NRSV)

Gifts are not the end of leadership in the church. If you have the gift of prophesy, the Bible has a word on that:

> Let two or three prophets speak, and let the
> others weigh what is said. (1 Corinthians 14:29,
> NRSV)

Now, what "others" might be useful in weighing a prophet's words? People with the gift of knowledge, who are well-trained in the Scriptures? I would think so. Who else? The over-seeing pastor or elders who know the needs of the church and are in tune with the issues God is addressing at the time? I would think so. If they know the problem and a prophet receives a word that might be the answer, it makes sense that they would be useful in crafting an interpretation of the prophetic word. If a person who is flowing in the prophetic came to me and said, "The Lord gave me a dream last night that we should sell the building and start meeting in homes," I would not take that and immediately contact a Real Estate agent. I would first search the Scriptures. Did I miss something? Is it wrong for us to have buildings? No, not that I can see. Then I would take it to the Board and ask them to pray about it. If none of them felt a strong confirmation that this was to be explored, we would simply ignore it. Gifts operate under and in partnership with the command centre that functions within the church. Gifts submit to Scripture and they also submit to leadership.

TEN GOOD REASONS YOU SHOULD EXPLORE YOUR GIFTS:

1. The Bible says so. (1 Corinthians 14:1) Do you really need nine more?
2. It is always more profitable and enjoyable to serve within your area of giftedness than to serve merely out of duty and a sense of obligation.

3. It humbles you to realize that you have a gift, or some gifts, but do not have ALL the gifts. It reminds you that you need to be connected in tribe.
4. When we know our gifts, we get a glimpse into what God dreams for the church.
5. It is an incredible experience when God's ability superimposes itself over our weakness.
6. The fact that you were given a gift means that there is a church out there that is deficient in something. Until you make the match, the kingdom suffers.
7. Gifts are often the key to discovering calling. Why would God gift you at something if he didn't intend for you to use it?
8. Gifts in a box are no good to anyone. Open it, use it, sharpen it and refine it for the glory of God!
9. Gifts allow each of us to participate in the Divine Purpose. This is why you were created—this is your purpose, to work alongside of Father in his enterprise.
10. Gifts bless the church and the church is God's girlfriend. When you release good into the church, God is pleased. Pleasing God is good.

MILE 1

PERSONAL STUDY AND REFLECTION:

If you are brand new to Christianity, you will probably profit from reading 1 Corinthians 12, 13 and 14. That's a big chunk of Scripture, but it's worth it. For the purposes of this exercise though, focus in on 1 Corinthians 12:1-31 and then consider the comprehension task that follows.

Consider the seven statements below. Five of them accurately summarize the teaching of the passage you just read. Two do not. See if you can sort them out. The correct answers are in a footnote on the following page.

1. Every saved person has a spiritual gift.
2. The spiritual gifts are given as the Spirit chooses.
3. Some spiritual gifts were only given out in Bible days but are no longer permitted at this time.
4. Spiritual gifts are given to build up the church.
5. The gifts are given variously; some have a certain gift, others have another. This causes us to need each other and work as a team.
6. Every real believer has the gift of tongues. This proves that they are really saved.
7. There is no such thing as a "proof gift" that you have to have to prove you are a Christian. (Are all eyes in the body? No. Do all speak in tongues? No.)*

---

* The correct answers are: 1, 2, 4, 5, and 7.

QUESTIONS AND NOTES:

EXPLORE YOUR GIFTS
FAQ

The following questions represent the most frequent concerns for new believers starting out in their journey into spiritual gifts.

1. I heard that some spiritual gifts "expire," is that true? Are there some gifts mentioned in the Bible that were only useful in the first century of the church's life?

ANSWER: One of the silly things that we do sometimes as Christians is elevate our own experience to the level of doctrine. Such and such a thing happened to me, therefore, it's true, or such and such a thing has not happened to me, therefore, it is false. Let's say together some very important words: MY EXPERIENCE IS NOT AUTHORITATIVE. What is authoritative? The Word of God. But back in the late 20th century a small group of Christians noticed that their particular community had not experienced certain spiritual gifts in a long time. They concluded that because they didn't have it—it didn't exist and they created a theological idea called "cessationism." That's a fancy word for "gifts that expire." They began to teach that certain gifts, like healing, tongues and miracles were only given out to the first generation of the church—the twelve disciples and the special apostles. These "sign gifts," as they referred to them, were only needed until the Bible was written. After which time, God had nothing of importance to say. Now, it should be noted that this teaching had a very brief life. It appeared, as I mentioned, in the late 19th century and has almost entirely faded out in our time. Martin Luther knew nothing of this idea, John Calvin had never heard of it and Wesley and Finney would have found themselves in deep water if they'd known of this because these sign gifts seemed to follow them wherever they went. The cessationists have only one passage to draw support from and they take it horribly out of context. The passage is from 1 Corinthians 13—a passage that we refer to as what? The Love Chapter. It is a chapter about the high value of love—the one universal Spirit manifestation. Paul has been teaching in 1 Corinthians 12 on the various gifts that people receive and he goes on to say, in essence, "though we may have gifts that differ, the one spirit manifestation we all share is LOVE. Love is present in every true believer." That is the context. Here is the section they rip out of its context:

> Love never ends. But as for prophecies, they will come to an end; as for tongues, they will cease; as for knowledge, it will come to an end. For we know only in part, and we prophesy only in part; but when the complete comes, the partial will come to an end. (1 Corinthians 13:8-10, NRSV)

As for tongues, they will cease!!!! That's where they get the term "cessationism"—to cease. Tongues will cease. And they have decided that tongues have ceased—they ceased along with the other sign gifts after the Bible was written by the Apostles. However, there are more problems with that statement than there are words in it. First of all, the Bible was not written exclusively by Apostles. The books of the New Testament are: "Matthew, MARK—oops!" We got two books in and we have a problem. Mark was not an apostle, nor a disciple. Well, there goes that theory. By the way, the third book is? Luke. Same problem. There is also the gargantuan mistake of taking the phrase "when the perfect comes" to refer to the Bible. Did the church get perfect when they finally had the Bible in a nice black leather cover? No. When does the Bible say we will get perfect? 1 John 3:2-3 provides the answer:

> Beloved, we are God's children now; what we will be has not yet been revealed. What we do know is this: when he is revealed, we will be like him, for we will see him as he is. And all who have this hope in him purify themselves, just as he is pure. (NRSV)

When do we get perfect church? When Jesus comes back because we will be caught up to meet him in the air and, in the twinkling of an eye, we will be changed. So, the perfect hasn't come and the gifts remain for what? The building up of the church. The cessationists are not consistent in this misuse of

Scripture anyway. You'll never hear a cessationist argue that the gift of knowledge has ceased, they like that one. They only get excited about the gift of tongues ceasing. The truth is, this passage has nothing to do with setting a time table for cessationism. The point of the passage is to show that gifts are various and temporary, but love is forever. When we are in the eternal kingdom with Jesus, we won't need tongues because we will know each other fully and we will speak to God face to face. We won't need knowledge because all that is hidden will be revealed. But we will still enjoy what? Love. Love is eternal; gifts are situational and temporary. All gifts are temporary by the way, not just tongues. We won't need teachers or evangelists after the second coming either, will we? The prophet Jeremiah, speaking of that day, says:

> No longer shall they teach one another, or say to each other, 'Know the Lord', for they shall all know me, from the least of them to the greatest, says the Lord (Jeremiah 31:34, NRSV)

But you'll never hear a cessationist say that the gift of teaching is gone from the church or that we don't need the gift of evangelism now that we have the Bible. The bottom line is the idea that we can slap an arbitrary expiry date on the gifts we are uncomfortable with is completely ridiculous and unsupportable. There are very few serious theologians left on the planet who will attempt to do so. It was an idea that had a brief hay day in the 70s, 80s and 90s, but is thankfully fading back into total obscurity. The Spirit gives gifts AS HE CHOOSES, not as we allow.

2. Did the Spiritual gifts mostly disappear after the first generation or did they continue on?

ANSWER: Good question. You will sometimes hear that (see above), but that is not the case. One generation after the "New Testament era," Justin Martyr writes:

> Daily some are becoming disciples in the Name of Christ… who are also receiving gifts, each as he is worth. These are illuminated through the name of this Christ. For one receives the spirit of understanding, another of counsel, another of strength, another of healing, another of foreknowledge, another of teaching and another of fear of God. (Justin Martyr c.160)

This was not "apostolic residue," but rather a continuing phenomenon. Writing several generations removed from the New Testament era and speaking of the Holy Spirit, Novatian declares:

> This is He who places prophets in the church, instructs teachers, directs tongues, gives powers and healing, does wonderful works, offers discrimination of spirits, affords powers of gov-

ernment, suggests counsels, and orders and arranges whatever other gifts there are of the charismata. (Novatian c. 235)

Therefore, from the beginning and carrying well on into Christian history, there was the expectation that the Holy Spirit would empower his church with whatever gifts were **deemed necessary** to meet the ministry challenges of the day. The confusion of today resides in the debate as to whether the Holy Spirit has significantly narrowed his gift list. Were certain gifts only given before the New Testament documents were completed? Did they then become unnecessary? Were other gifts given to lend momentum to the early church but should now be considered unneeded and perhaps even dangerously distracting? These are the questions that make us hesitant to celebrate the generosity of the Holy Spirit and that often leave us languishing in the powerlessness of the church.

3. I'm a new believer and the church I go to seems a little bit afraid of spiritual gifts. Why is that?

ANSWER: I come from a very conservative, evangelical background where it was taught that tongues was of the devil and prophecy happened only in the Old Testament. So, I have wrestled my way through this issue. I think that there is a lot less theology to this than most let on. The bulk of the argument is fear-based and a lot of that fear has some rational basis to it. The truth is spiritual churches can be messy. It's true. It's not only true, experientially, it's true Biblically. Look at 1 Corinthians 1:

> I give thanks to my God always for you because of the grace of God that has been given you in Christ Jesus, for in every way you have been enriched in him, in speech and knowledge of every kind—just as the testimony of Christ has been strengthened among you—so that you are not lacking in any spiritual gift as you wait for the revealing of our Lord Jesus Christ. (1 Corinthians 1:4-7, NRSV)

Paul is gushing over this church in a way he doesn't gush over any other church in the New Testament. "You have been so blessed! You have received a HUGE portion of grace and gifting. You have EVERY spiritual gift in operation in your church. How wonderful for you!" Wouldn't it be nice to have EVERY spiritual gift operating within our church? That would be wonderful! Or would it? As the letter goes on, you find out that this very spirit-filled church was also extremely messy. There was sexual immorality, their services were disruptive, weird and even offensive to newcomers and it was a bit of a gong show. Paul had to work harder with this church than with any other church he founded to get them on the path of truth. But you know what is interesting? He never once said, "I wish that you were a little less spiritual. I wish that certain gifts would stop functioning so that we could clean this up." He never said that. He just kept pushing them towards truth. Nowhere is this better illustrated than with the gift of tongues. The gift of tongues appears to have broken out like a rash in Corinth. It's interesting because Paul doesn't speak about it at all with some of his other churches but it had been given out in spades at Corinth. The gift was so prevalent that it was becoming disruptive in the services. Every few seconds a person was bursting out in tongues and interrupting things and it was out of hand. So, we expect for Paul to pray, "Oh Lord, please withdraw or at least stop sending the gift of tongues—we have been over-blessed in this area." No, instead he says this:

> Now I would like all of you to speak in tongues, but even more to prophesy. (1 Corinthians 14:5, NRSV)

He doesn't say, "we need less tongues." He says, "we need more prophesy." A little more truth and this thing will settle out nicely. You see, to bring a messy church into balance, you don't SUBTRACT SPIRIT, you ADD TRUTH. For some churches, messy will be a stop on the road towards true worship, but don't let fear make you turn back and retreat from Spirit. Press through into truth and then on into balance.

Part of the fear is also the fact that Spirit-led churches are very mobile. The Spirit MOVES! In fact, in the Old Testament the common manifestations of the Spirit were as cloud and fire and when the Spirit showed up it was usually time for the Israelites to MOVE!

MILE 1

The Lord went in front of them in a pillar of cloud by day, to lead them along the way, and in a pillar of fire by night, to give them light, so that they might travel by day and by night.

Neither the pillar of cloud by day nor the pillar of fire by night left its place in front of the people. (Exodus 13:21-22, NRSV)

The Spirit of the Lord was IN FRONT of the people, leading them along the way. It never left the FRONT of the people. You see, that's the trouble with the Holy Spirit—he doesn't settle down in the centre of the people. He is always moving towards the front. He is always stirring us forward and the people of God have always preferred to sit.

The Spirit of God wanted to lead the people into the Promised Land, but the people wanted to go back to Egypt. "We had it fine there! Sure we were slaves, but we had lots of food, we've lived there for so long, all of our friends are there, let's just go back!" But the Spirit didn't want to go back, he wanted to go forward. Let me ask you a scary question: what happens to those who refuse to go forward? They die in the desert. That's not good. Hebrews 3:7-11 says:

Therefore, as the Holy Spirit says,
'Today, if you hear his voice, do not harden your hearts as in the rebellion, as on the day of testing in the wilderness, where your ancestors put me to the test, though they had seen my works for forty years.

> Therefore I was angry with that generation, and I said, "They always go astray in their hearts, and they have not known my ways." As in my anger I swore, "They will not enter my rest." (NRSV)

Who says that? The Holy Spirit. The Holy Spirit really doesn't like it when he says, "Forward march!" and we whine, "Can't we just stay here?" Those people die in the desert while the Spirit-led people enter the promise land.

It is also true that at times, the Holy Spirit can be overpowering. I personally identify with this one more than the other two. I like moving and I understand the necessity of mess on the way to balance, but I sometimes fear the overpowering presence of the Lord. Sometimes I fear it, but I also know that Biblically speaking, it is to be expected. Look at Isaiah 6:1-5:

> In the year that King Uzziah died, I saw the Lord sitting on a throne, high and lifted up, and the train of His robe filled the temple. Above it stood seraphim; each one had six wings: with two he covered his face, with two he covered his feet, and with two he flew. And one cried to another and said: "Holy, holy, holy is the Lord of hosts; the whole earth is full of His glory!" And the posts of the door were shaken by the voice of him who cried out, and the house was filled with smoke. Then I said: **"Woe is me, for I am undone!** Because I am a man of unclean lips, and I dwell in the midst of a people of unclean

lips; for my eyes have seen the King, the Lord of hosts." (NKJV)

The Hebrew word translated "undone" means "disintegrated." "Oh no! God showed up in the temple and everything started to shake and I FLEW APART and was disintegrated." The Spirit of God can be overpowering. We miss that sometimes when we read the Bible so we are not prepared for it when it happens. Even though the experience above CHANGED ISAIAH FOREVER, even though his encounter purified him and prepared him for a powerful prophetic ministry, we would just as soon pass on the whole procedure. The people of Moses' day felt the same way.

> When all the people witnessed the thunder and lightning, the sound of the trumpet, and the mountain smoking, they were afraid and trembled and stood at a distance, and said to Moses, 'You speak to us, and we will listen; but do not let God speak to us, or we will die.' (Exodus 20:18-19, NRSV)

Moses tried to convince them to draw near, but they wouldn't listen. So verse 21 tells us:

> Then the people stood at a distance, while Moses drew near to the thick darkness where God was. (NRSV)

The sad truth is that a lot of us are afraid of the presence of the Lord and would prefer if the Spirit kept his distance. When the Spirit of God shows up, there is shaking and refining and confrontation and deliverance and transformation and— AHHHHH! That's just a little too much. Let's hire a pastor who will meet with God and then he can come and just tell us what God says. Don't be afraid. The Spirit is overwhelming, but the Spirit is good.

As true as all of that is, if you are a new believer, I urge you to caution in sharing this enthusiasm with your pastor. The Holy Spirit can be terrifying for pastors, I know because I am one. When he shows up in power and fresh gifts, it feels like he has taken control of the church (which he has) and that takes some getting used to. Share your perspective humbly and then pray into it. Wait, be kind and patient; be prayerful and watch as the Spirit blesses that. Many a church has been reinvigorated by the patient, faithful prayers of humble people.

4. My church has recently started moving in the presence and gifts of the Holy Spirit. Do you have any advice for us?

ANSWER: Stay in the truth. Nowhere in the Bible does it suggest that LESS TRUTH is the way to MORE SPIRIT. In fact, the Bible says:

> Let what you heard from the beginning **abide** in you. If what you heard from the beginning abides in you, then you will abide in the Son and in the Father. (1 John 2:24, NRSV)

Abide—REMAIN—in the ancient truth and you will abide in God. The Old Testament says it this way:

> Listen to me, you that pursue righteousness, you that seek the Lord. Look to the rock from which you were hewn, and to the quarry from which you were dug. (Isaiah 51:1, NRSV)

Look to the rock from which you were hewn—the original source and foundation. We are not to be abiding in some truth of our own construction, nor in a half truth, nor in an emasculated, truncated truth born of fear and forgetfulness. No. We must abide in his truth rather than our own. The timeless, life-giving truth of God. Abide there. If you've left it, go back and find it. Dig it up and sit on it. You don't have to leave the truth to go and find the Spirit. You don't have to jump off the one leg to stand on the other. Some of us are afraid of that, aren't we? We're afraid that if our church goes off in search of the Spirit, it will involve leaving the truth behind, but that's ridiculous. What does the Bible say? It calls on us to take up:

> The sword of the Spirit, which is the word of God. (Ephesians 6:17, NRSV)

The Sword of the Spirit IS the Word of God. You don't have to leave the truth of the Word to find the power of the Spirit. They are connected, the power of the one is the power of the other. It's a two-edged SWORD. UNCHANGING YET ALIVE. Spirit and Truth. You can stay in the truth, even as you seek out the Spirit.

Let me share one other thought directly from Scripture, 1 Peter 2:5 says:

> Let yourselves be built into a **spiritual house**, to be a holy priesthood, to offer spiritual sacrifices acceptable to God through Jesus Christ. (1 Peter 2:5, NRSV)

We usually focus on the call to allow ourselves to be built into a house from the status of living stones. We see this primarily as a call to move from individualism to tribalism and it is that. But, we also need to hear this other call, "Let yourselves be built into a SPIRITUAL house." Let your church become a house where God lives. Don't shut the windows because things get messed up when he blows through. Let your church be a house INDWELT OF GOD'S SPIRIT. Don't try and swim on the surface of the Spirit, sink in.

When Isaiah sank into the presence of the Spirit, it was overwhelming and terrifying, but it didn't kill him. It purified him and prepared him to be sent into ministry. To answer the question above, I quoted from the story in Exodus about the people's fear of the presence of God. I left one verse unquoted in that story which you should see now. The people had said, "Don't allow God to speak to us—he'll kill us!" Moses tried to convince them otherwise but they wouldn't listen and they stayed away. This is what Moses had said to them:

> Moses said to the people, 'Do not be afraid; for God has come only to test you and to put the fear of him upon you so that you do not sin.' (Exodus 20:20, NRSV)

The Spirit of God hasn't come to kill you! He's come to test you and to purify you, so that you do not sin. He's come to make you holy, so that he can use you as a kingdom of priests and a holy nation. I don't think the Holy Spirit will wreck your church, I really don't. I think that if you "test everything" but "forbid nothing," you will be o.k. I have more faith in the power of the Holy Spirit and the Word of God to guide you than I do in the power of the enemy to deceive you.

1500-1600 M
Consolidate Allegiance

Sometimes Christians talk as though the Gospel is this super-uniting idea that will make one big happy family out of all the peoples of the earth. I'm not sure Jesus knew about that. He said:

> Do you think that I have come to bring peace to the earth? No, I tell you, but rather division! From now on, five in one household will be divided, three against two and two against three; they will be divided:
>> father against son
>> and son against father,
>> mother against daughter
>> and daughter against mother,

> mother-in-law against her daughter-in-law
> and daughter-in-law against mother-in-law.'
> (Luke 12:51-53, NRSV)

That doesn't sound like the right setting for a round of Kumbaya. Jesus predicted that the Gospel message would cut through our world like a hot knife through butter, leaving every living person on one side of the other. What side are you on? A lot of people think they can live on both sides. Can't you be a Christian and still be well-thought-of by the world? Can't you enjoy the things of God AND the things of the world? The Apostle John thought not.

> Do not love the world or the things in the world. The love of the Father is not in those who love the world; for all that is in the world— the desire of the flesh, the desire of the eyes, the pride in riches—comes not from the Father but from the world. And the world and its desire are passing away, but those who do the will of God live for ever. (1 John 2:15-17, NRSV)

Jesus didn't think so either, in fact, he predicted:

> Because you do not belong to the world, but I have chosen you out of the world—therefore the world hates you. Remember the word that I said to you, "Servants are not greater than their master." If they persecuted me, they will perse-

cute you; if they kept my word, they will keep yours also. (John 15:19 20, NRSV)

The truth is if you want to be a Christian, you have to pick a side. Friendship with the world is enmity (conflict) with God. I didn't make that up, though I wish I had, it's from the Bible:

> Do you not know that friendship with the world is enmity with God? Therefore whoever wishes to be a friend of the world becomes an enemy of God. (James 4:4, NRSV)

The Bible says that the way of the world - all of its lusts and all of its ignorance and all of its pride—is PASSING AWAY. Why align yourself with something that is halfway dead? There are two worlds: a dying world and an eternal world. One is decaying unto ultimate death and one is being born and will live forever. Choose wisely! As you grow in your faith, you need to consolidate your allegiance. Everyday you wake up, you need to think about ways that you can move more completely into God's camp and extricate yourself more fully from the ways and values of death. We do that in two primary ways. The first is by thinking differently:

> Do not be conformed to this world, but be transformed by the renewing of your minds, so that you may discern what is the will of God— what is good and acceptable and perfect. (Romans 12:2, NRSV)

Stop thinking like this world! Who cares what Oprah thinks? Oprah is the High Priestess of this dying world, so unless you want to decay and die, learn to ignore her counsel. When talking with new believers, they will often say, "I know the Bible says such and such, but don't you think that is a bit extreme? I mean, I heard Oprah say…" Unless Oprah is prepared to die on a cross and rise from the dead to secure your salvation, you need to care less what she thinks and more what Jesus thinks. Jesus said:

> Why do you call me "Lord, Lord", and do not
> do what I tell you? (Luke 6:46, NRSV)

You can't ask Jesus for salvation and Oprah for advice. You get both from the same source or nothing from the same source. Learn to think like the King of the New World, not the Queen of the Old World.

The other way we consolidate our allegiance is by investing differently. Jesus said this:

> Do not store up for yourselves treasures on
> earth, where moth and rust consume and where
> thieves break in and steal; but store up for your-
> selves treasures in heaven, where neither moth
> nor rust consumes and where thieves do not
> break in and steal. For where your treasure is,
> there your heart will be also. (Matthew 6:19-21,
> NRSV)

People invest where they live. If you live in this world, then you will invest in its stuff. If you are a citizen of the coming world, you will make your deposits there. As you grow into faith, you should grow less interested and less invested in stuff. In fact, Jesus said:

> Take care! Be on your guard against all kinds of greed; for one's life does not consist in the abundance of possessions. (Luke 12:15, NRSV)

O.k., so a Christian should not have an ABUNDANCE of possessions. How many should we have?

> **Sell your possessions**, and give alms. Make purses for yourselves that do not wear out, an unfailing treasure in heaven, where no thief comes near and no moth destroys. For where your treasure is, there your heart will be also. (Luke 12:33-34, NRSV)

Sell your possessions? Was Jesus a communist? That must be taken out of context. Look at Luke 14:33:

> So therefore, none of you can become my disciple if you do not **give up all your possessions**. (NRSV)

When you are not exactly sure what Jesus is getting at, it's helpful to look at all the verses you can find where he addresses

343

a subject and then let them interpret each other. To do that, we
need to see one more. In Luke 19, we see this:

> Zacchaeus stood there and said to the Lord,
> 'Look, **half of my possessions, Lord, I will
> give to the poor**; and if I have defrauded any-
> one of anything, I will pay back four times as
> much.' Then Jesus said to him, 'Today salvation
> has come to this house, because he too is a son
> of Abraham. For the Son of Man came to seek
> out and to save the lost..' (Luke 19:8-10,
> NRSV)

Jesus doesn't appear to think that owning anything at all is a
sin. He seems rather to think that possessions are far less necessary than we think and are usually an impediment (stumbling
block) to real faith. It appears Jesus would say, "The fewer possessions you have, the better off you are." The more of your stuff
you give away, the more you communicate to God that you are
living entirely for the eternal kingdom. God tends to meet that
kind of faith with amazing provision and that makes it a great
way to live! Christians, if they hold any possessions, should hold
them loosely and warily.

TEN GOOD REASONS YOU SHOULD CONSOLIDATE ALLEGIANCE:

1. The Bible says so. (Deuteronomy 30:19-20) Do you really need nine more?
2. Light shines better if it looks less like dark.
3. Salt works better if it tastes less like meat.
4. When the star player shows up for the closing seconds of the fourth quarter to strike his enemy with a death blow, it is good to have on a brightly coloured jersey indicating that you are on his team. (Revelation 19:11ff.)
5. The blessings of God flow more powerfully the deeper you move into the kingdom.
6. Dead stuff stinks.
7. Who wants to be on the losing team?
8. Accumulating material stuff is silly because when you die it stays here.
9. Thinking like Oprah puts a pretty low ceiling on your intellectual development.
10. When you are filled with the mind of Christ, you will be fit for the dominion that was meant to be yours. (Genesis 1:26-27)

Mile 1

Personal Study and Reflection:

Read 1 John 2:15-17 and 2 Corinthians 5:17-20 and then consider the comprehension task that follows.

Consider the seven statements below. Circle the ones you think are correct and put an "x" beside those you think are false. The correct answers are in a footnote on the following page.

1. God created the whole world and he loves what he created. However, this present world is currently under the dominion of the devil and is therefore opposed to God. How can a Christian love what is opposed to God?

2. Jesus came to the world to show that God loves and accepts the world. Christians should be in the world as loving and accepting people.

3. Jesus came into the world to bring a crisis of decision. Some will retreat further into the darkness and curse of the world, while others will move towards life and light. Those who choose the light will be part of the remaking of all things.

4. The value system of this world is dead. It is collapsing under its own ignorance and darkness. Trying to reach out to something dead is just stupid.

5. Like an ambassador from China maintains his traditional Chinese dress and mannerisms, so we as

ambassadors of the kingdom should look far more like Jesus than we do in the mission field.

6. Our primary loyalty and orientation is towards the kingdom of God—not our host country.

7. The Gospel is divisive in nature. Any attempt to soften it usually leads to the distortion of it.*

---

* 2 is false. The rest are correct. Jesus came to love the world, but he did not 'accept' it. He came to remake it and redeem it.

Questions and Notes:

CONSOLIDATE ALLEGIANCE
FAQ

The following questions represent the most frequent concerns for new believers starting out in their journey into consolidated allegiance.

1. I'm struggling to reconcile the "'salt and light" thing with the "come out from them" thing. Are there places in the world that I should simply not try and go?

ANSWER: Fabulous question!! I am asked this fairly often by young people selecting a career. One of the disturbing trends out there in "Christian" culture is the suggestion that God wants to redeem every aspect of this fallen world. That sounds like a true statement, but is it? God desires all people to be saved, I gladly grant that, but is God trying to redeem the casino industry or is he trying to shut it down? This is an important distinction because some well-meaning Christians will advise a young believer to go out and try and become a fashion model or advertizing agent or movie star because all of those industries need "to be redeemed." Really? Is that realistic? Is that Biblical? Luckily, this very issue is addressed in Scripture. The Apostle Paul had a church that was going through this very thing. Some of them wondered whether there were aspects of fallen culture they could go back into as "covert agents" for Jesus and Paul warned them that, in some cases, this is very unwise:

> For what partnership is there between righteousness and lawlessness? Or what fellowship is there between light and darkness? What agreement does Christ have with Beliar? Or what does a believer share with an unbeliever? What agreement has the temple of God with idols? For we are the temple of the living God; as God said,
>
> "I will live in them and walk among them, and I will be their God, and they shall be my people. **Therefore come out from them, and be separate from them**, says the Lord, and touch nothing unclean; then I will welcome you, and I will be your father, and you shall be my sons and daughters, says the Lord Almighty." (2 Corinthians 6:14-18, NRSV)

There are certain things that are so unclean, so thoroughly WRONG that we cannot be apart of them for any reason, not even to redeem them. This requires wisdom and counsel but we have to do it. I'm not saying you should live in a cave and eat canned food for the rest of your life, but there are A FEW THINGS in culture that we should have nothing to do with— and we certainly should not send our young people out like lambs to the slaughter into those places. The fashion industry is probably a good example. An industry dedicated to creating greed and discontent is not an industry where a Christian will function well. The same could be said of large advertising firms. My sister worked at the top of the food chain in advertising, making commercials for some of the biggest players in the game: McDonalds, Coke, Miller Beer, etc. (She even worked for the WWF for a while, not the animal people, the wrestler people.) She will tell you that advertising is based on generating discontent. You have to make a person feel like their life has no purpose or value, unless they purchase your product. She told me once, "How else can you sell products that everyone knows are bad for them? Image, deception and discontent are the name of the game." That doesn't sound like a redeemable industry.

The Christian journey sometimes calls for strategic cowardice. Paul counselled a young man once:

> Flee also youthful lusts. (2 Timothy 2:22, NKJV)

I wish we offered similar wisdom to young people choosing careers today. In the majority of cases, we should go into the world as salt and light, however, in a minority of cases, there are places, industries and contexts we should not have anything to do with. Know the difference and act accordingly.

2. Is Christianity "anti-stuff"? Some Christians seem to think that the more stuff you have, the more God loves you, but then other Christians think it's a sin to have a lot of nice things. Which is it?

ANSWER: Christianity is not "anti-stuff" and it is definitely not true that having stuff is proof that God loves you and is blessing your life. The church needs some education on the matter of "stuff" because we are way out of wack on this one. Economists tell us that if we were to extend the average, middle-class, North American lifestyle to every person alive today, it would take the resources of six to eight planet earths. Did you hear that? If we were to build houses the size of our houses for every family alive today, if we were to let them use as much water as we use, if we were to let them have as much steel for their SUVs as we use and if we were to let them have as much gas as we have in our cars, then it would take the resources of more than six planet earths. What that means is that it can't be done. We hold, and we have consumed already, much of what the world would need to build a better life for itself. It can't be done. Our lifestyle, the middle-class lifestyle, is so extravagant, so luxurious that it cannot be extended to the rest of the planet because there simply is not enough food, water, steel and gas to go around. We are the richest people to ever walk the planet earth. Did you know that the average middle-class North American has a higher standard of living than any king that walked the earth prior to 1900? By all of the criteria that the UN uses to assess standard of living such as: access to clean water, food intake, leisure time, availability of transport, access to quality health care, child mortality rates, life expectancy, etc, most of the people reading this book in North America are wealthier than any king that ever walked the face of the earth until 1900. Now, here is why that is cause for concern; Jesus said to the rich young man:

> How hard it is for those who have wealth to enter the kingdom of God! Indeed, it is easier for a camel to go through the eye of a needle than for someone who is rich to enter the kingdom of God. (Luke 18:24-25, NRSV)

When Jesus said that, there was not a single person on earth as rich as you and me. Two generations ago, in my grandfather's day, the gap was not so large between the rich and the poor, between us and them. My grandfather owned a grocery store in Orillia on Front Street. He went out of business because he was too kind-hearted. Poor families would come in and claim to be buying cat food for their cats, but he knew they didn't have any cats. He knew they would be feeding it to their kids, so he would give them cans of tuna instead. He would let people buy groceries on credit knowing that they would never pay. His was not a rich generation. But they were givers. The people who study giving trends tell us that Christians gave more by percentage in the Great Depression than they do today. So, how is it that as we have become wealthier, as we have become the richest and fattest generation in human history, that we give less than ever before in the history of the church? Somewhere along the way we got out of wack on "stuff." We give as though we were poor and yet the world has never seen such wealth as ours. We are the ones who throw in mites while day after day thirty thousand children die of starvation and preventable diseases. We are too poor in character to be the church this world needs. It's time to be more invested in the kingdom of God and less invested in the fading treasures of this dying world. Does that mean you can't own a car? Of course not. But why do you need two? Why do you need three? Why are they so big and why do they need to be so nice? You can own a car if you need to and you can own a house. Food, shelter, clothing, even transportation are necessary things in most places and Jesus used all of those things, though he appears to have possessed few of them. But we have a lot more than that, don't we? We need to have less.

Let me tell you a story. The other day I was invited to a banquet. I got there early and, along with a few friends, we made our way into the locked banquet room. The food was laid out for us on the table and we just couldn't help ourselves, so we ran up to the buffet table to get an early start. There was so much food and it was so tantalising that one plate just didn't seem to be enough. So we each filled as many plates as we could carry and went back to our table. But since the other guests were still milling about outside the room, we went back and filled up more plates until we each had a stack of about 8 plates in front of us. Then another group of guests arrived and seeing the amount of food we had taken and realizing that now there may not be enough to go around, they ran to the table and filled up a plate and also an extra plate. Finally, the last group of guests arrived and when they went to the table, there wasn't any food at all. They looked over at my table but I was too busy eating to notice. They became angry and started muttering amongst themselves. One of them came over and began shouting that we had ruined the banquet and had stolen their food. My friends were indignant. They had done nothing illegal—"to the early bird goes the worm," they said. The late comers began muttering in a language I did not understand and they began making threatening gestures. One became so angry that he threw a pitcher of water at our table and it splashed everywhere, ruining some of our food. Our table held a hasty conference and it was decided that action was required. One of the men at the table had a gun and he pulled the gun and pointed it at the late comers and warned them to stay away. They began to grumble some more and things looked like they might be getting out of hand. We decided that a pre-emptive strike was in order and we grabbed one of the grumblers by the collar, at gun point, took him outside and beat him senseless. We left his body there in the hallway as a warning to others. It was quite a day. After the meal, I gave my testimony but no one responded. Oh well, all you can do is sow the seeds.

That story, of course, is true in one way and not true in another. I hope you know which is which. A fellow I know is a high-level Christian leader and he gets invited to sit at the table when famous Christians in the United States gather to conference. He was at such a conference just recently. The men around that table would be people you know, each and every one of them. They preach on TV and pastor the largest churches on this continent. They began to talk about the dangerous and desperate state of world affairs. The Muslims are very upset with us and are growing in power and seem quite committed to striking at us. The Chinese are angry because we are imposing standards on them as they industrialize that we will not impose on ourselves. Everyone seems so angry at us. Finally, when discussing what the Christian lobby would say to Washington about the potential of a pre-emptive strike against Iran, one leader stood up and looked the group in the eye and he said, "Gentlemen, we've reached the time in history when it is either them or us."

I think it is odd that the response of Christian leaders to the anger of the world's poor is to build bigger walls and bigger guns to protect our stolen loot. Maybe that is not the way of Christ. Maybe it is time to share our food with the hungry. To open up our mansions to the homeless poor. To share our resources, to repent of our selfishness and thievery and to model the humility and downward mobility of Jesus. Maybe it's too late in the game for such "simplistic" approaches. Maybe the hatred of the world for us fatties is too deep and too entrenched to stop what is coming. Maybe that's true. But maybe there is still time for a few people to bravely show the way of Christ, to bravely live lightly-invested in this world and heavily-invested in the world to come. Lord, may it be so.

3. I feel bad for wanting so much worldly stuff, but I do! I want the newest cell phone, gadget and it drives me crazy when my friends have something I don't. How can I stop "wanting"?

ANSWER: First of all, let me say that I know how you feel and that this one is really tough for all of us. We live in a culture that specializes in manufacturing the feeling of discontent.

A few years ago, Francis Fukuyama made a big splash on the academic scene when he released his book, "The End of History and The Last Man." It was a number one best-seller and won a pile of awards. As the title suggests, it was a very controversial book. The End of History! What did he mean by that? Did he mean that there would be no more significant events or happenings? Did he mean that the end of the world was upon us? No. You see Francis Fukuyama said that history is moved along by the emergence and triumph of great ideas, and according to Fukuyama, we had discovered the last great idea. Do you know what he said was the last great idea? Democratic capitalism. That's right! You see according to his book, the whole reason we won World War Two was not because we had better generals or better soldiers, it was because we could produce more stuff. Our democratic capitalist factories made more stuff than their national socialist factories. He goes on to say that the reason that the Soviet Empire fell apart was not because people preferred our ideology to Karl Marx's ideology, it was because people preferred our stuff to the stuff they could get over there. Fukuyama has interviews with many of the first people across the fallen Berlin Wall in his book and do you know what the first thing they wanted to do in West Berlin was? Go shopping! You see our clothing stores had better clothing than their stores. Our car dealers had BMWs and Mercedes and those were cooler than what you could get over there. Fukuyama contends that what defeated Communism was not ideology, it was materialism. In fact, he contends that the whole reason that the USA and Britain forced the Soviet Union into a nuclear arms race was not so that we could drop bombs on them, but so that we could bankrupt them. We knew that our economies were better than theirs and that our factories could out produce theirs because our system is the best system for producing stuff.

And so Fukuyama says, we have reached the end of history because no idea will ever emerge that will topple democratic capitalism. There is no system out there that will ever defeat democratic capitalism because democratic capitalism stands firm on the most fundamental characteristics of humankind: greed and covetousness.

Think about it. How does capitalism work? When the economy starts going soft, what does the government do to make it work again? (Tax cuts) And what are you supposed to do with that tax cut? Buy stuff! If we all buy more stuff, then the economy will turn around. The problem with Democratic Capitalism is that after a while we all have all the stuff we need. So what do the companies do then? They hire advertisers to make you buy stuff you don't need. Why is it so hard to buy Christmas presents for people now a days? Because it's hard to shop for people who already have everything they need. If I were to look at your Christmas list from this past year, I'm sure I wouldn't see: "Dear Santa, please send me the warm socks I need to survive the coming winter." Right? So what do we get for each other? Singing trout and Tickle Me Elmo. Our whole system depends on the ability of advertisers to convince you that you need, that you must HAVE these items.

The problem though is that after we buy all these things on our credit cards, we have to work longer hours to pay it all off. That's why the percentage of double income families has skyrocketed over the past ten years and the average work week implies more hours than ever before. That's why our houses are 15% bigger than they were ten years ago. Did you know that? The average new home is 15% larger than ten years ago. Which is funny because family size is smaller. So there are fewer people living in bigger houses. Why? Because we need more storage space for all our stuff.

We need to change our desires because they are literally destroying our culture. But can that be done? The Scriptures say yes:

> Take delight in the Lord, and he will give you
> the desires of your heart. (Psalm 37:4, NRSV)

We read that sometimes and we think it means that if we really delight in the Lord, he will give us whatever we want. It doesn't mean that, but that's what we want it to mean. What it actually means is that if we delight in the Lord, if we want only what is his purpose, only what is His will, only what is His pleasure, in return he will put into your heart new desires that will lead us in paths of life. He will download new feelings and new desires such that you will do the will of God, not because you HAVE to, but because you WANT to. And isn't that the highest goal of the spiritual life? To do the right thing out of a desire to do the right thing. I mean really, how impressive is it if I grit my teeth and speak words of love to you, not because I want to, but because I have to and I force myself to do right? Is it not much better to do it because I want to, because I am the sort of person who wants to speak those words to you? Can't you just hear David, the writer of this Psalm, saying, "Change my heart O God!" Change my heart! Make me more than a man who DOES right; make me a man who LOVES right! And isn't that why David is described as a man after God's own heart?

I would never lift up my own experiences to the level of Scripture. You should believe or not believe what you read in this book based on your evaluation of God's Word, not on your trust in me. Don't trust me—study these things on your own—test the Spirit as the Word says. But let me tell you anyway that I have experienced this to be true in my own life. There was a desire in me that I wished for years to be rid of. At times, I exercised self-control over this desire and at other times it mastered me. I tried to defeat it and lost as often as I won. The desire, the feeling was evil in and of itself, but it also occasionally produced actions that were evil. Over time, I gained a level of mastery over the actions but the desire was still present in me. But I can tell you that the Lord can change the desire of your heart because, as I gave myself more and more to God's purposes and to God's glory and to God's will for my life, I found that he gave me in return a new set of desires to replace the old. And now, I do not "have mastery" over a sinful feeling, I have a new feeling such that what once I desired, now tastes like ash and death in my mouth. God can and will change the desires of your heart.

4. Is this why the church is so powerless and so irrelevant today? Is it because we have been shaped by the lusts of the world instead of being shaped by the desires of the Spirit?

ANSWER: Let me answer this by asking what impact would the church have if we figured out how to be less invested in the world and more invested in the kingdom of God? Think about that. I mean what would actually happen if we experienced the transformational power of Jesus Christ, not just in our minds, not just at the theological and confessional level, but what if our very desires were transformed and we HUNGERED and THIRSTED for the things of God? What would that look like? What would happen? Well for starters, given that our whole culture is based upon greed-based purchasing and the economy is driven by debt-empowered covetousness, if a whole bunch of us started being content with what we have, we would get noticed. It's possible that the whole system would grind to a halt. If 30%

of North Americans stopped purchasing things they don't need, we would need to find a new basis for our culture and that may not be a fun process. What else would happen? God asked this question once in Isaiah 55:2-9. He said to his people:

> Why do you spend your money for that which is
>   not bread,
> and your labour for that which does not satisfy?
> Listen carefully to me, and eat what is good,
> and delight yourselves in rich food.
> Incline your ear, and come to me;
> listen, so that you may live.
> I will make with you an everlasting covenant,
> my steadfast, sure love for David.
> See, I made him a witness to the peoples,
> a leader and commander for the peoples.
> See, you shall call nations that you do not know,
> and nations that do not know you shall run to
>   you,
> because of the Lord your God, the Holy One of
>   Israel,
> for he has glorified you.
>
> Seek the Lord while he may be found,
> call upon him while he is near;
> let the wicked forsake their way,
> and the unrighteous their thoughts;
> let them return to the Lord, that he may have
>   mercy on them,
> and to our God, for he will abundantly pardon.
> For my thoughts are not your thoughts,

nor are your ways my ways, says the Lord.
For as the heavens are higher than the earth,
so are my ways higher than your ways
and my thoughts than your thoughts.
(NRSV)

The promise of God in this passage is that if we his people can be content with God and God alone, then the nations will flock to us and they will learn that what we have in him truly satisfies. Because the things they desire, obtain and then consume do not satisfy, they always want more! But if the thing we pursue truly satisfies us, they will come and we won't be able to keep them away and he will pardon them and teach them his ways. When that happens, we won't need church growth conferences either. If God's people can become TOTALLY satisfied with the presence of God and totally FIXATED on the kingdom of God, the world will change. You watch and see.

But seek first the kingdom of God and His righteousness, and all these things shall be added to you. (Matthew 6:33, NKJV)

EPILOGUE
Multiply Your Experience

We began this journey by recalling that Jesus did not say, "Submit to me," "Choose me," or "Praise me"—the fundamental call that started this whole thing was "Follow me." The decision to follow Jesus is the beginning of everything! It leads to submission, it leads to new choices, it leads to worship but it begins with following. Jesus told us where this would end too. He said:

> Follow Me, and **I will make you fishers of men**. (Matthew 4:19, NKJV)

Follow me and then lead others. As Christians, we talk way
too much and way too early about leadership. There are conferences, books, CDs and resources, but the truth is the best followers make the best leaders. We really need conferences on
"followership" and books on "followership" because when we
figure out how to follow Jesus, we will know everything we need
to teach others. If we start talking about leadership too early, we
are just the blind leading the blind. That is why the Scriptures
say that a leader in the church:

> Must not be a recent convert, or he may be
> puffed up with conceit and fall into the con-
> demnation of the devil. (1 Timothy 3:6, NRSV)

The Christian life is a process of learning and then teaching,
following and then leading, soaking up and then passing on. The
Apostle Paul said to a young man he had been mentoring:

> You then, my child, be strong in the grace that is
> in Christ Jesus; and what you have heard from
> me through many witnesses entrust to faithful
> people who will be able to teach others as well.
> (2 Timothy 2:1-2, NRSV)

The early part of your Christian journey has been domi-
nated by learning. You never stop learning, but at some point
you discover that you now know enough to begin teaching and

leading some others. You can take what you have been taught and pass it on to others.

This entire mentoring curriculum was designed to be completed in about nine months—about the time it takes for a human baby to be prepared for its introduction to the world. If you have been meeting twice a week with your mentor to discuss this material, then you are at least nine months into your spiritual journey. Are you ready to begin leading others? Ask your mentor. If he/she points out a few things you need to work on, receive that in humility and go work on those things. If he/she gives you the green light, connect with your pastor and let him know that you are ready to begin leading another. This does not mean that you stop meeting with your mentor. I have been a pastor for sixteen years and I still meet with a mentor. For the rest of my life, I anticipate having a person over me and several people under me—that's how the kingdom is designed. Jesus himself was under the Father's authority:

> Jesus said to them, 'Very truly, I tell you, the Son can do nothing on his own, but only what he sees the Father doing; for whatever the Father does, the Son does likewise. (John 5:19, NRSV)

Jesus followed the Father and then he called on his disciples to follow him. After three years of learning, he turned to them and said:

MILE 1

> Go therefore and make disciples of all nations,
> baptising them in the name of the Father and of
> the Son and of the Holy Spirit, and teaching
> them to obey everything that I have com-
> manded you. (Matthew 28:19-20, NRSV)

Teach people what I taught you. This is the Christian Way: learn, teach. Follow, lead. Are you ready for the Way? This is the end of the access ramp, but it is just the beginning of an incredible life—the elevated highway of our God. This is the trail—you made it! You still learn, you still serve, you still worship, you still give—all of the things you began on the access ramp carry on, but now (this thing is new): you are a disciple maker. You are part of the largest movement in human history. You have completed the journey from "Gate" to "Way." Well done. Now get in the game.

TEN GOOD REASONS YOU SHOULD MULTIPLY YOUR EXPERIENCE:

1. The Bible says so. (Matthew 28:19-20) Do you really need nine more?
2. You've come this far, why would you want to bail now?
3. God will use your unique experiences to forge a trail to health and salvation for someone else.

4. The kingdom of God is built person by person, soul by soul.
5. Jesus said he would help us by sending his Spirit, so we need not fear. (John 14:18-26)
6. The sooner we get this thing done, the sooner we can party up in glory! Pitch in because many hands make light work.
7. You are the only Bible many people will ever read. That's a cheesy line, but it's still true.
8. The Gospel is incarnated in human stories. You are now a Gospel story. Pour that out into someone else.
9. There is nothing wrong with saying, "Follow me, as I follow Jesus." The Apostle Paul said it all the time. (1 Corinthians 4:16)
10. People follow people—they don't follow ideas.

PERSONAL STUDY AND REFLECTION:

Read 2 Timothy - all of it. You are a big boy or girl now and can handle a big chunk of text. Timothy was a young man that Paul mentored. The Apostle referred to him as his "son in the faith." Scholars believe these are the last words written by Paul. He was executed a few days or even hours later. These are the things he wanted to say to his protégé. There is no comprehension task at the end. You are now a teacher and I believe that you will make good use of what you just read. Blessings to you on the way.

The Mile 1 Journey

Necessity is the mother of invention. In 2008 the Lord began showing up in our church in new and powerful ways. We had an explosion of new/old gifts, a deep movement of repentance and humility and an outbreak of evangelistic harvest. We had nearly 200 people come to know Jesus Christ as Saviour and Lord in a 24 month period. When we started realizing that something unusual was going on we began to game plan how to follow up with all of these new converts, as well as those we knew were soon to be coming. I sent a trusted former elder to some Christian book stores to find me the best follow up material on the market. A few weeks later we met and he expressed some confusion and frustration. Between the two of us we discovered that there are lots of books on how to get saved, a MOUNTAIN of books on why the church is no longer cool (super helpful I'm sure) and many books on specialized Christian topics, most of which are about why the church is no longer cool. Books for new believers were in short supply.

When you can't buy something, you have to make it, so that is what we did. Mile 1 was created in the disciple making laboratory. It has been tested and refined and edited more times than I care to remember. Over the course of the eighteen months that we have been using it here we have been able to get about half of our new converts into the program. What we have observed is that those who immediately get into a structured follow up program with a Mile 1 mentor or small group have a significantly higher "keep rate" than those that do not. As a pastor, that says a lot to me about the necessity of this program, or something similar that you create in house. This is the game my friends; Jesus said in no uncertain terms:

> I appointed you to go and bear fruit, fruit that
> will last (John 15:16. NRSV)

Weekend converts are not the goal. Long lasting fruit, that multiplies the seed and itself bears fruit a hundred fold—that is the goal and that is the journey and Mile 1 is just that; it is Mile 1.

For more Mile 1 resources or to order additional, discounted copies of this book visit my website at beaconcitypublishing.com.